ACKNOWLEDGEMENTS

Several people have freely and generously given their time and expertise to the production of this book. Some have read part or all of the manuscript and suggested improvements, as well as making corrections (however, any errors which remain are my responsibility). Others have generally supported and inspired me through the long process of writing and re-writing. In particular, I would like to thank Peter Cox, Richard Farhall, Dr Tim Key, Dr Michael Klaper, Dr Chris Langley, Professor Tom Sanders, Colin Spencer, Dr Margaret Thorogood and the Vegan Society.

This new edition of *Vegan Nutrition* is dedicated to fellow vegans around the world. Their choice of a compassionate lifestyle is helping to heal a damaged planet, and create a fairer world for all its inhabitants.

VEGAN
NUTRITION

THE
Vegan
SOCIETY

Gill Langley, MA PhD MIBiol

First published December 1988

Second edition published August 1995

© G R Langley

ISBN 0 907337 18 X

Design by Taylor McKenzie, 30 Britton Street, London

Publication Manager: Richard Farhall

Printed on recycled paper by Litho Techniques (Kenley) Ltd,
46–50 Godstone Road, Whyteleafe, Surrey

Published by the Vegan Society, Donald Watson House,
7 Battle Road, St Leonards-on-Sea, East Sussex TN37 7AA, United Kingdom
Tel. 01424 427393

CONTENTS

FOREWORD

The number of vegans has increased substantially since *Vegan Nutrition* was first published in 1988, and veganism is ever more widely understood and respected. Scientific research on vegan nutrition has also grown during these seven years, and this new edition of the book is a much weightier volume than the first. Gill Langley systematically reviews the results of all published research, with coverage including the nutritional adequacy of vegan diets and their effects on indices of health. Both the advantages and the potential shortcomings of vegan diets are carefully considered, and the reader rapidly gains an accurate picture of what is known today.

Research on vegan nutrition and on the health of vegans is very important. Veganism seems to be particularly prone to misconceptions and prejudice; some non-vegans have the opinion that vegans are generally under-nourished, whereas some uncritical vegans believe that their diets are natural and somehow guaranteed to be healthy and nutritionally adequate. Scientific research shows that both these views are false: sensible vegan diets provide ample amounts of all the essential nutrients, but established dietary guidelines must be followed to ensure sound nutrition. Less information is available concerning the long-term health of vegans: on average vegans are thinner and have lower blood cholesterol concentrations than non-vegans, and they probably suffer less from coronary heart disease and large bowel cancer, but further research on these and other diseases is required.

The world is changing rapidly as we approach the end of the twentieth century. The growth in veganism is exciting, as it offers improvements in the treatment of animals and solutions to some of the environmental problems facing us. Amongst this excitement it is essential that we can make choices on the basis of sound evidence. *Vegan Nutrition* will play a key role by making this evidence available in the field of nutrition. It will be an invaluable reference for vegans, potential vegans and health professionals. I hope that it will also encourage nutritionists to conduct further studies, since information on the long-term health of vegans is still scanty. I am sure that it will be widely read.

Timothy Key, BVM&S, MSc, DPhil, Imperial Cancer Research Fund
Cancer Epidemiology Unit, University of Oxford.
January 1995

INTRODUCTION

We were few in number and widely dispersed, and all of us were heavily involved in our own careers . . . The War was ending, food rationing was at its most severe and was to continue for another seven years. There were few health-food shops, and even these had little to offer in protein foods suitable for vegans. The vegetarians had been successful in obtaining an additional cheese ration in lieu of meat, but all my approaches to the Ministry of Food to obtain some comparable concessions for vegans failed . . . There were no vegan recipe books, and vitamin B_{12} had not yet been discovered.

Vegan Society founder Donald Watson — creator of the word 'vegan' — reflecting on the formation of the Society in 1944[7]

When the first edition of *Vegan Nutrition* was published in 1988, some 1.5 million British people were vegetarians, and the number was rising. The results of a 1995 survey show that vegetarians make up 4.5% of the adult British population — a doubling of numbers since 1984[1]. Some of these 2.6 million or so people go further than omitting meat, poultry and fish from their diets, and eliminate all animal products. These complete vegetarians — known as vegans — rely solely on the plant kingdom for their nourishment, and the 1995 survey indicated there were approximately 170,000 adult vegans in Britain.

The reasons for becoming vegan are numerous, and include ethical concern for the rights and welfare of animals; and of people in the Third World, much of whose grain and soya harvests is exported to feed farm animals in Western countries. Awareness of environmental degradation can be another prompt to adopting a vegan diet, as people see habitats increasingly disturbed by the grain monoculture necessary to feed farm animals; by pollution from fertilizers and farm slurry, which contaminate our waterways; by the replacement of habitat-rich hedgerows with stock-proof wire fencing; and by clearance of rainforests and other natural woodlands to create short-term grazing, which can lead to erosion and desertification. Some people turn to veganism in the interests of maintaining or restoring good health, and yet others for religious or aesthetic reasons.

WHO SHOULD READ VEGAN NUTRITION?

Many vegans are well informed on general nutrition but would like more detailed knowledge, either for their own interest or to answer the questions about their diets that vegans are inevitably asked.

Veganism is growing, but a clear understanding of it still eludes many, perhaps most notably the media whose treatment of the subject is often as poorly informed as it is dismissive. Magazine and newspaper journalists, driven by imminent deadlines, frequently repeat ancient myths without checking their facts and predict dire health consequences even for vegetarians, let alone vegans! Vegetarians and others who may be attracted to veganism in principle can be concerned, understandably in the face of the propaganda from the meat and dairy lobbies, about the ability of a plant-based diet to sustain good health. Vegan parents, like omnivore parents, often welcome advice on the dietary needs of their children.

On the other hand, health professionals such as nutritionists, dietitians, health visitors, community health workers and general practitioners sometimes find themselves at a loss to advise on various aspects of vegan nutrition. Much information available in standard reference works is out of date — indeed, fifty years after the word 'vegan' was coined several well-known medical dictionaries still advise their readers to mispronounce it! (the correct pronunciation is *vee*-gan, not vee-jan or vay-gan).

A survey of members of the California Dietetic Association conducted a few years ago revealed that their knowledge of vegetarianism in general was surprisingly low. They recognized that there are economic and health benefits in being vegetarian, but in simulated counselling sessions they often did not support people's dietary choice and tried to persuade children and pregnant and breast-feeding women to eat meat.

A 1988 report in the *Journal of the Royal Society of Medicine*[2] revealed the lack of nutrition education in medical schools. A questionnaire revealed that only half the house physicians at medical schools had been taught about simple nutritional matters, and several doctors expressed a wish to learn more. Interestingly, another report in the journal in 1992 showed that the situation had not much improved[3]. More than a hundred medical students answered an examination question on what dietary advice they would give to patients suffering from diabetes, high plasma cholesterol, high blood pressure and other diet-related conditions. Although

98% of the students passed their exams, 82% failed the nutrition question! And a survey of GPs in Ireland revealed that 96% thought nutrition was important in preventing ill health, but 49% were unhappy with their own level of knowledge and 85% were interested in further nutrition education[4].

While we can't expect every doctor or dietitian to be an expert on veganism, we can hope that they will have access to a reliable and readable reference work on the subject. *Vegan Nutrition* can precisely fill this niche. In addition, it will be of assistance to hospital and other dietitians with the responsibility for providing nutritionally balanced meals for vegans in their care.

WHY A NEW BOOK?

Things have moved on since *Vegan Nutrition* was first published. Nutritional knowledge has expanded and become more complex. Many of the nationally recommended amounts of various nutrients have been replaced by new recommendations. The vitamin and mineral contents of some foods have been revised, yielding sometimes surprisingly different values. Links between nutrition and health are better understood, and new ideas are developing. Since 1988 there have been many more investigations into the nutritional adequacy of vegan diets, as well as studies of the health of vegans.

The demand to know about vegan nutrition has continued, and this entirely new book covers all these issues, providing sound, readable information for every type of reader. By consulting hundreds of original research papers, which are fully referenced at the end of the chapters, I've been able to summarize the most up-to-date information, in layperson's terms. Additionally, a new chapter about vegan mothers and children draws together advice and information of special relevance to families.

The chapters dealing with food groups and nutrients start with brief nutritional notes for non-experts, followed by a summary of the recommended intakes of each nutrient. Then, studies of vegans and what they reveal about different aspects of vegan nutrition are reviewed. A new feature, **Key Points**, has been introduced to highlight the main issues. A number of tables and figures provide extra information, and each chapter ends with a clear summary. For quick and easy reference, each chapter has a detailed contents list, and there is an extensive index.

OFFICIALLY RECOMMENDED INTAKES

Vegan Nutrition includes officially recommended daily amounts for foods, energy and nutrients where these have been published. However, it's important to realize that nutrition is still an inexact science and that the recommendations are only informed estimates. They have wide inbuilt safety margins, and are calculated for a generalized population so that they will over-estimate or under-estimate the needs of many individuals.

In 1991 the UK changed and extended its system of recommending daily nutrient intakes[5]. The well-known Recommended Daily Amounts were replaced with Dietary Reference Values (DRVs), a term which encompasses a set of recommended values, as follows:

* **The Estimated Average Requirements** (EARs), provided for energy, protein, vitamins and minerals, are average requirements as estimated from studies of the population. Being an average implies that half the population may need more than this amount of a nutrient, while half may need less.

* **The Reference Nutrient Intakes** (RNIs) are larger amounts, calculated to provide enough or more than enough protein, minerals and vitamins for 97% of the population. Thus the RNI for a nutrient exceeds most people's actual needs.

* **The Lower Reference Nutrient Intakes** (LRNIs) are amounts thought to be sufficient only for the minority of people in a population who may have low needs for protein, and some minerals and vitamins. The LRNI therefore underestimates the needs of most people.

In devising the new system, the Department of Health's Panel hoped that it "would reduce the chance of misunderstanding the true nature of its figures as estimates of reference values and not as recommendations for intakes by individuals or groups". So, for any individual or group of individuals, if their consumption of a nutrient falls above or below the RNI this does not, on its own, tell us whether they are receiving adequate amounts for their personal needs.

If someone's daily intake of a nutrient drops for a while below their own individual requirements, a deficiency need not follow — our bodies can often cope with a temporary shortage. A deficiency is characterized by adverse symptoms, so a lower than recommended consumption or a lower than average blood level of a nutrient, does not necessarily mean a deficiency if a person remains in good health and has no adverse symptoms.

On the other hand, the line between sufficiency and deficiency can be very fine.

In 1994 the UK government's Committee on the Medical Aspects of Food Policy (COMA) published a report on nutrition and heart disease[6]. It was something of a milestone in translating numerical recommendations for food groups and nutrients into simple, easy-to-understand advice on how to make healthy food choices. Practical suggestions included reducing consumption of whole cow's milk, butter and cheese; eating 50% more fruit, bread, potatoes and other vegetables; and eating less fat, sugar, cakes, bisuits, soft drinks and confectionery. Like many other recent official reports, the proposals would bring the 'average' diet considerably closer to a vegan pattern of consumption.

MORE THAN FACTS AND FIGURES

Because this book discusses scientific studies it may seem as though vegans have been reduced to a mass of facts and figures. Behind the statistics lies a diversity of people — there are few 'typical vegans' and no single typical vegan diet. Many of the original pioneers of veganism in the late 1930s and 1940s are now over 70 years old. There are teenagers and young adults who have been vegans from birth, but also senior citizens who have only recently changed to veganism. There are animal rightists, macrobiotics and Rastafarians. Buddhists, Jains, Bahais and some Christians may be vegans because of their religious beliefs, and many people adopt veganism for health reasons.

Amidst all this diversity, some general trends have been identified. Vegans tend to be committed to their dietary principles, and try to draw the attention of others to the advantages of their lifestyle. Perhaps because of their numerical minority, vegans are more likely than vegetarians to join organizations where they can link up with like-minded people. There are more vegan women than men; and vegans are more health-conscious than the general population, many using predominantly whole foods. Many vegans drink alcohol, but less than average, and only a small proportion smoke. They often take a holistic approach to health, seeing the importance of emotional and spiritual aspects as well as physical factors, and alternative, rather than drug-based, medicine often appeals to them. The professional and managerial classes and graduates are better represented among vegans than in the general population.

THE VEGAN SOCIETY

Since its foundation in 1944, and ahead of orthodox nutritional advice by several decades, the Vegan Society has advocated a diet which emphasizes fresh, unrefined and minimally processed plant foods, low in fats and refined sugars, high in carbohydrates and fibre. Today the Society continues to advise and educate, not only on the nutritional implications of veganism, but on its relevance to the well-being of animals and the environment.

Vegan Nutrition clearly shows that vegan diets, with the judicial use of fortified products, provide all the essential nutrients for health and fitness at any age. For vegans, for those aspiring to veganism, and for those whose task is to advise on dietary matters, *Vegan Nutrition* is a unique and indispensable information source.

Gill Langley, MA PhD MIBiol,
Hitchin, Hertfordshire.
March 1995

REFERENCES

1 *The Realeat Survey, 1984–1995* (1995). Conducted by Social Surveys (Gallup Poll) Ltd.

2 Judd, P.A. (1988). Teaching nutrition to medical students. *J. Roy. Soc. Med.* 81:176–178.

3 Parker, D., Emmett, P.M. & Heaton, K.W. (1992). Final year medical students' knowledge of practical nutrition. *J. Roy. Soc. Med.* 85:338.

4 Mallon, B.L. & Kennedy, N.P. (1995). A survey of nutrition interest among general practitioners. *Proc. Nutr. Soc.* In press.

5 Department of Health (1991). *Dietary Reference Values for Food Energy and Nutrients for the United Kingdom.* Reports on Health & Social Subjects no. 41. London: HMSO.

6 *Committee on Medical Aspects of Food Policy (1994). Nutritional Aspects of Cardio-vascular Disease.* Reports on Health & Social Subjects no. 46. London: HMSO.

7 Watson, D. (1988). Out of the past. *The Vegan* IV(2):10–11.

GUIDELINES ON VEGAN DIETS

The Vegan Society has always pioneered sound, ethically-based nutrition, and continues to do so. The Society advocates choosing a wide variety of foods from the following food groups:

- **Whole grains and grain products** — eg. wheat, millet, barley, rice, rye, oats, maize; wholemeal breads and pastas
- **Pulses and products made from them** — eg. peas, beans, lentils; tofu (soya bean curd)
- **Fresh vegetables**, including green leafy vegetables and salads
- **Fresh and dried fruits**
- **Nuts**
- **Seeds** — eg. sunflower, sesame and pumpkin

Vegetables should be cooked as lightly as possible, and the cooking water (which contains minerals and vitamins) used in soups and stocks. Salads and raw vegetables are particularly good sources of vitamins and minerals. Seeds are better digested and hence more nutritious if they are ground or milled, in the form of spreads such as tahini (sesame seed spread). Dried fruits are good sources of some minerals. A plant-based diet is rich in natural sugars, and added sugar should be kept to a minimum, although black molasses is an excellent source of calcium and iron.

A dietary supply of vitamin B_{12} can be ensured by the use of fortified foods such as yeast extracts and nutritional yeast; and some soya milks, savoury soya protein foods, margarines and breakfast cereals. Vitamin D is easily obtained from the action of daylight, especially in summer and autumn, on the skin.

After weaning, parents of vegan infants should provide energy-dense foods, such as suitably-prepared grains, pulses and dried fruits, as well as fresh fruits and vegetables. However, low-Calorie, high-fibre foods such as leafy vegetables and fresh fruits can fill small stomachs too quickly, and shouldn't be over-used at first. Low-salt yeast extracts and fortified soya milks provide essential vitamin B_{12}, as well as other important nutrients.

ABBREVIATIONS AND GLOSSARY

AA Arachidonic acid — a long-chain polyunsaturated fatty acid

BMA British Medical Association

BMI Body Mass Index, which is calculated as body weight (in kilograms) divided by height^2 (in metres)

Calorie(s) Kilocalorie(s), a unit of measurement of food energy. This has been used in preference to the kilojoule (kJ) or megajoule (MJ) to assist the layperson (1MJ = 1 million joules or 239 Calories; 1 Calorie = 4.18kJ)

cm centimetre(s)

COMA Committee on Medical Aspects of Food Policy (UK)

DHA Docosahexaenoic acid — a long-chain polyunsaturated fatty acid

EAR(s) Estimated Average Requirement(s) (UK) — of a nutrient in the diet. An estimate of the average needs of a group of people. About half may need more, and half may need less

EPA Eicosapentaenoic acid — a long-chain polyunsaturated fatty acid

FAO Food and Agriculture Organization

g gram(s). 1 ounce = 28.4 grams; 100g = 3.5 ounces

HDL(s) High-density lipoprotein(s) — carries cholesterol around the body

HMSO Her Majesty's Stationery Office (UK)

kg kilogram(s). 1kg = one thousand grams or 10^3 grams

l litre(s)

lb(s) pound(s) weight (avoirdupois)

LDL(s) Low-density lipoprotein(s) — carries cholesterol around the body in the bloodstream. Thought to be the form of cholesterol which blocks the arteries

LRNI(s) Lower Reference Nutrient Intake(s) (UK). A daily amount of protein, a vitamin or a mineral that is enough, or more than enough, for only the few people who have low needs

MAFF Ministry of Agriculture, Fisheries and Foods (UK)

mg milligram(s). 1mg is one-thousandth of a gram, or 10^{-3} gram

ml millilitre(s). 1ml is one-thousandth of a litre, or 10^{-3} litre

mm millimetre(s). 1mm is one-thousandth of a metre, or 10^{-3} metre

MMA	methylmalonic acid — a metabolite of vitamin B_{12}
mmol	**millimole(s).** 1 mmol is one-thousandth of the molecular weight of a substance, in grams
mo	**month(s)**
NACNE	**National Advisory Committee on Nutrition Education** (UK)
NAS	**National Academy of Sciences** (USA)
ng	**nanogram(s).** 1ng is one-thousand-millionth of a gram, or 10^{-9} gram
OPCS	**Office of Population Censuses and Surveys** (UK)
oz	**ounce(s).** 1oz = 28.4 grams
pg	**picogram(s).** 1pg is one-million-millionth of a gram
pg/ml	**picogram(s) per millilitre**
pmol	**picomole(s).** 1pmol is one-million-millionth of the molecular weight of a substance, in grams
P/S ratio	ratio of polyunsaturated fats to saturated fats in the diet
PUFA(s)	**polyunsaturated fatty acid(s)**
RDA(s)	**Recommended Dietary Allowance(s)** (USA) — of a nutrient in the diet
RNI(s)	**Reference Nutrient Intake(s)** (UK). A daily amount of protein, a vitamin or a mineral that is enough, or more than enough, for about 97% of people. The RNI is similar to the Recommended Daily Amount used previously in the UK
Tbsp	**tablespoonful(s)**
tsp	**teaspoonful(s)**
UK	**United Kingdom**
US(A)	**United States (of America)**
VLDL(s)	**Very low-density lipoprotein(s)** — carries triglycerides around the body
WHO	**World Health Organization**
yr	**year(s)**
%	**per cent**
µg	**microgram(s).** 1µg is one-millionth of a gram or 10^{-6} gram
<	less than
>	more than

TABLES, FIGURES AND KEY POINTS

PROTEIN
AND ENERGY

. . . soy protein has been shown to be nutritionally equivalent in protein value to proteins of animal origin and, thus, can serve as the sole source of protein intake if desired.

The American Dietetic Association position statement
on vegetarian diets, 1993[9]

Proteins are large molecules made from smaller units called amino acids, which are strung together like beads in a necklace. After eating, proteins are digested in the stomach and small intestine where the 'beads' — the component amino acids — are released, and then absorbed into the bloodstream. Our bodies make the proteins they need for maintaining tissues and for sustaining growth from the amino acids released by digestion — re-stringing the 'beads' in a different order. Amino acids are also used by our bodies to make hormones and other physiologically active substances.

There are twenty amino acids commonly found in both plant and animal proteins. Plants can synthesize all the amino acids they need from simple inorganic substances such as carbon, nitrogen, sulphur and water. Humans and other animals cannot, and we have only a limited ability to convert one amino acid into another. For adults there are generally considered to be eight indispensable amino acids which must be present in the food we eat, and these are isoleucine, leucine, lysine, methionine, phenylalanine, threonine, tryptophan and valine. Infants also need food sources of histidine, and possibly taurine.

PROTEIN REQUIREMENTS

Experts are still not entirely sure how much protein we need, and estimates have been revised often in recent years. The national and international organizations which advise on nutrient requirements suggest standards which are calculated to meet or exceed the requirements of practically everyone in the population. They explicitly take into account individual variation, and so these levels have a wide inbuilt safety margin. The World Health Organization's 1985 recommendations[1] still form the basis of most national proposals for protein intake.

In 1991[30] the UK's Department of Health introduced new terms of reference for nutrient intakes. It recommends a series of Reference Nutrient

Intakes (RNIs) for protein, depending on gender and age, derived from the WHO figures (*see Table 1.1, below*). The RNI is estimated to be enough or more than enough for about 97% of people in a group, and the 1991 UK recommendations for children are a half to a third lower than the 1979 recommendations they replaced. The US Recommended Dietary Allowances introduced in 1989[28] are 0.8g of protein per kilogram of body weight a day for most adults which, at about 58g and 50g for men and women respectively, are similar to the UK values.

TABLE 1.1

UK REFERENCE NUTRIENT INTAKES FOR PROTEIN

Age group	RNI for protein, grams/day	
Infants and children		
0–12 months	12.5–14.9	
1–3 years	14.5	
4–10 years	19.7–28.3	
11–14 years	42.1 (boys)	41.2 (girls)
15–18 years	55.2 (boys)	45.0 (girls)
Men		
19–50 years	55.5	
50+ years	53.3	
Women		
19–50 years	45.0	
50+ years	46.5	
Pregnancy*	+6	
Breast feeding*		
0–6 months	+11	
6+ months	+8	

From *Dietary Reference Values for Food Energy and Nutrients for the United Kingdom, 1991*[30].

* To be added to normal daily intake.

These recommendations are based on the complete digestibility of milk or egg protein. Protein from plant sources may be slightly less digestible, and the UK's Department of Health recommends that vegetarians and vegans multiply the above figures by a factor of 1.1.

Another common way of looking at protein intake is to express it in the form of Calories provided by protein as a percentage of the total Calories consumed each day, ie:

$$\frac{\text{Number of Calories eaten as protein}}{\text{Total number of Calories eaten}} \times 100\% = \text{Protein intake (as \% of energy intake)}$$

The World Health Organization suggests that eating 10% of our daily energy intake as protein will provide an adequate amount. The UK's current recommendation for protein intake[30], converted to a percentage of energy, works out at approximately 9%. The protein intake of omnivore populations in the Western world is between 10% and 15%, being 15% in the UK.

The foods which commonly provide most protein in a vegan diet are the pulses (peas, beans, lentils, soya products); grains and grain products (wheat, oats, rice, barley, buckwheat, millet, pasta, bread); nuts (brazils, hazels, almonds) and seeds (sunflower, pumpkin, sesame). The average protein level in pulses, at 26% of their energy (Calorie) content, is greater than that of meat. Soya beans and firm tofu are particularly protein-rich at about 40% and 43% respectively. Protein comprises 7%–17% of the energy content of grains, and 8%–17% of nuts and seeds. Bread and potatoes supply 10% of their Calories as protein. Since all these foods are also 'energy dense', it is easy to see why as long as energy requirements are met, **plant foods can easily supply the recommended amounts of protein.** Table 1.2 (*page 6*) shows the protein content of some plant foods.

PROTEIN QUALITY — PEOPLE AREN'T RATS

Nutritionists once believed that all plant proteins are of a poorer quality than all animal proteins, because the amino acids are present in less than ideal proportions. In the early years of research into protein quality this belief derived from experiments with laboratory rats, when it became clear that amino acid supplementation of a plant source of protein improved its biological value to the point where it would support the growth of weanling rats.

A major problem with the rat growth tests is that rats and humans have different nutritional requirements, and consequently the tests over-estimated the value of some animal proteins while under-estimating the value of some vegetable proteins[3]. In 1991, after decades of using it, the World Health Organization formally abandoned the rat growth test on the

Table 1.2

PORTIONS OF SOME PLANT FOODS PROVIDING *10g* OF PROTEIN

Foods	Weight of food providing 10g protein
NUTS (shelled) Peanuts	39g (1.4oz)
Almonds	47g (1.7oz)
Pistachios	50g (1.8oz)
Cashews	57g (2.0oz)
Brazils	71g (2.5oz)
Hazels	71g (2.5oz)
PULSES Soya flour	24g (0.9oz)
Soya beans, dried & boiled	71g (2.5oz)
Whole lentils, dried & boiled	114g (4.0oz)
Chickpeas, dried & boiled	119g (4.2oz)
Kidney beans, dried & boiled	119g (4.2oz)
Tofu, steamed	124g (4.4oz)
Peas, boiled	159g (5.6oz)
GRAINS Wholemeal flour	79g (2.8oz)
Whole barley, before cooking	95g (3.4oz)
Wholemeal bread	109g (3.8oz)
Rye flour, 100%	122g (4.3oz)
Wholemeal spaghetti, boiled	213g (7.5oz)
Brown rice, boiled	385g (13.5oz)
SEEDS (shelled) Pumpkin seeds	41g (1.4oz)
Sunflower seeds	51g (1.8oz)
Sesame seeds	55g (1.9oz)
OTHERS Apricots, dried	250g (8.8oz)
Potatoes, baked incl. skins	256g (9oz)
Spinach, boiled	454g (16oz)

For each food type, *the foods containing the most protein are at the top of each list.*

Values taken from Holland *et al*, 1991[25] & 1992[43], and Tan *et al*, 1985[26].

British Reference Nutrient Intake for adults: 45–55.5 grams of protein[30].

grounds that it is inadequate as a method of assessing the value of proteins to the human body[37].

The proteins in each type of food have their own characteristic patterns of amino acids, being richer in some and limited in others. For many years the chemical 'quality' of a protein, reflecting its amino acid pattern, was by custom measured against the protein in a hen's egg, which counted as 100%.

By this method, in each protein the amino acid furthest below the standard reference is known as the limiting amino acid — which is not necessarily the one present in the lowest absolute *amounts*, but in the lowest *proportion* compared to that found in hen's egg protein. In most grains and seeds, for example, the limiting amino acid is lysine, while in most pulses it is methionine. Tryptophan is the limiting amino acid in corn (maize), and in beef it is methionine. Although each food has a limiting amino acid, most foods have all amino acids in adequate amounts for human health.

The WHO's 1985 report[1] formulated new amino acid scoring patterns. These were based on estimated *human* needs at different ages, rather than by comparison with foods judged to be of high value, like hen's egg. In 1991 the WHO confirmed the new method of scoring the value of protein, which takes into account the amino acid pattern and the digestibility of the protein[37]. Digestibility may be affected by the structure of the protein itself, as well as by other factors such as the amount of fibre, tannins or phytates in the food. Thus protein from plant sources may be slightly less digestible, and some authorities consequently suggest that 10% more plant proteins may be needed. The UK's Department of Health[30] recommends that people eating plant-based diets should multiply the RNIs in **Table 1.1** by a factor of 1.1 to obtain the recommended intake.

PROTEIN COMBINING UNNECESSARY

Misleading research on rats also led to the theory of protein combining[4]. The idea was that complementary protein foods with different limiting amino acids, such as beans and grains, should be eaten at each meal in order to enhance amino acid availability. Even vegetarians are sometimes advised to combine vegetable proteins with dairy foods. This advice is now very out of date.

Protein combining may reduce the amount of protein required to keep the body in positive protein balance[5], but several human studies have indicated that this is neither necessary nor even always the case. For example, over a 60-day period seven human volunteers were fed diets in which the protein was derived solely either from beans, corn and refined wheat; beans, rice and refined wheat; or a combination of the plant foods with the addition of cow's milk[6]. All subjects remained in positive nitrogen balance (a measure of the adequacy of dietary protein), and there were no significant differences in nitrogen balance between the subjects eating only plant foods, and those whose diet was supplemented with milk.

Another study looked at the nutritive value of a plant-based diet in which wheat provided 76% of the protein[7]. The aim was to determine whether this regime could be improved by adding other sources of plant protein — such as pinto beans, rice and peanut butter. The diets were entirely vegan, contained 46g of protein, and were fed to 12 young men over a 60-day period during which they continued with their normal daily activities. All the volunteers remained in positive nitrogen balance; and replacing 20% of the wheat protein with beans, rice or peanut butter did not improve the levels of indispensable amino acids in their bloodstream.

Even more startling perhaps were the findings of a 59-day investigation with six male subjects who consumed diets in which virtually the sole source of protein was rice[8]. At two protein levels (36g and 48g per day), the diets comprised either rice as the sole source of protein, or replacement of 15%–30% of the rice protein with chicken. The partial replacement of rice with chicken protein did not significantly affect the nitrogen balance of the volunteers (in contrast to earlier experiments with rats which showed that a rice diet did not sustain normal growth). In this human study, even on the low-protein diet, rice as the sole source provided between 1.5 and 4.5 times the WHO recommended amounts of all indispensable amino acids. On the higher-protein diet, rice alone provided between 2–6 times the indispensable amino acid levels suggested by the WHO, and all subjects were in positive nitrogen balance.

The American Dietetic Association's 1993 policy statement on vegetarian diets[9] confirms that, because amino acids obtained from food can combine with amino acids made in the body, it is not necessary for vegans or vegetarians to combine protein foods at each meal. Plentiful amounts of amino acids will be obtained if a mixture of different foods is eaten each day. Moreover the Association stated that "soy protein has been shown to be nutritionally equivalent in protein value to proteins of animal origin and, thus, can serve as the sole source of protein intake if desired".

Better ways of assessing the quality of a protein have been devised, based on estimated human needs rather than on the results of tests on rats. Even foods with a 'poorer' amino acid pattern generally contain more than enough for human requirements. Several human studies show clearly that diets based solely on plant foods easily supply the recommended amounts of all the indispensable amino acids, and protein combining at each meal is not necessary. In particular, soya protein is equivalent in biological value to animal protein.

STUDIES OF ADULT VEGANS

Although expert nutritionists now agree that vegan diets supply adequate, good quality protein, the first question every vegan (and nearly every vegetarian) is asked is, do you get enough protein? Several studies have provided the answer.

In 1967 Frey Ellis and Pamela Mumford[10] reviewed a number of studies from the 1950s and '60s and found that vegans took between 10%–11% of their daily energy intake in the form of protein, compared with 11%–15% in the case of vegetarians. In 1966 Hardinge and colleagues[11] calculated that vegan men and women achieved the recommended intakes of all indispensable amino acids, and that the pattern of their amino acid intake quite closely resembled that of the protein in human milk, while that of vegetarians and omnivores (with a generous intake of animal proteins) was more similar to the amino acid pattern of cow's milk.

In 1981, Abdulla and colleagues[12] measured protein intakes in six healthy Swedish middle-aged vegans. Protein comprised 10% of total energy, compared with 12% for Swedish omnivores of similar age. Although energy consumption in this vegan community was low, their intake of all indispensable amino acids was, at the minimum, almost double the recommendations of the US proposals, and more than double the WHO recommendations.

The protein intake of 22 British vegans was compared with age- and sex-matched omnivores, and found to be slightly lower but well in excess of official recommendations[13]. Andrew Lockie and colleagues[14] found that the average protein intake of 10 vegans was somewhat lower than that of omnivores and vegetarians, but still met UK recommendations. The same was true of a survey published in 1987[15] comparing 11 vegans with 11 omnivores, and an analysis of 18 vegans reported in

1986[16]. The Oxford Vegetarian Study[32,38] analysed the diets of 52 vegans and found their average protein consumption to be 11.8% of total energy, compared with 12.3% for lacto-ovo-vegetarians, 12.9% for fish-eaters and 15% for meat-eaters.

A 1993 comparison of protein consumption by three dietary groups confirmed earlier studies: the vegans ate an average 11.3% of their total energy as protein, while the intake of lacto-ovo-vegetarians was 12.3%, and that of fish-eaters was 13.4 %[31]. Expressed as grams of protein eaten each day, the intakes of the 38 vegan subjects (47g for women, 65g for men) exceeded the UK Reference Nutrient Intake. Grains contributed 30%–40% of the vegans' protein intake, soya bean products 10%, and vegetables 7%–10%. **Table 1.3** summarizes data on protein intakes by adult vegans.

TABLE 1.3

AVERAGE DAILY PROTEIN INTAKES OF VEGANS, VEGETARIANS & OMNIVORES

Publication	Protein intake as % of total energy intake		
	Vegans	**Vegetarians**	**Omnivores**
Ellis & Mumford, 1967[10]	10	12	
(results from two studies)	11		
Abdulla et al, 1981[12]	10		12
Roshanai & Sanders, 1984[13]	11.4		13.8
Lockie et al, 1985[14]	11.4	14.1	14.1
Rana & Sanders, 1986[16]	9.7		12
Sanders & Key, 1987[15]	11.3		15.3
Laidlaw et al, 1988[34] (men only)	11.3		
Thorogood et al, 1990[38]	11.8	12.3	15
Draper et al, 1993[31]	11.3	12.3	
Approximate mean intake	10.9%	12.7%	13.7%

UK recommends a protein intake of 9%.
WHO recommends a protein intake of 10%.
Average British intake: 15%.

Some people may need a dietary source of the amino acid taurine, even though normally the body can make it from other amino acids. Taurine deficiency may be a factor in a number of disorders including cardiovascular disease. A 1986 study[16] suggested that vegans are able to synthesize adequate amounts of taurine from other amino acids in their food, since taurine levels in the bloodstream and breast milk of vegan subjects was adequate — even though taurine is not present in plant foods. However, a more rigorous investigation indicated that levels of taurine in the bloodstream of 11 American vegan men were 20% lower than those of omnivore control subjects[34]. Vegans excreted only one-third of the taurine found in the urine of omnivores, an adaptation for conserving the amino acid. More studies would be needed to clarify the position, but there have been no reports of taurine deficiency in vegans.

Carnitine is a naturally-occurring substance necessary for the metabolism of fats, and is found mainly in meats and dairy products. Vegetables and fruits contain less than 1% of the carnitine levels found in meat, and cereal products contains less than 5%. Carnitine is not an essential nutrient because it can be made in the body from the amino acid lysine, but low bloodstream levels of carnitine have occasionally been found in people whose diets contained little carnitine.

Since it is believed that there is relatively little carnitine in a plant-based diet, Kenneth Lombard and colleagues compared levels in the bloodstream and urine of adults and children of three dietary groups in the USA[27]. Compared with omnivores, "strict vegetarians" (probably vegans) and lacto-ovo-vegetarians had somewhat lower levels of carnitine in their bloodstream, although within the normal range. The vegans excreted considerably less carnitine in their urine. Among the children, the vegans and lacto-ovo-vegetarians showed more marked lowering of carnitine levels in the blood, but the study did not show any risk of deficiency. Only one report[33] has been published documenting carnitine deficiency in the infant of a vegan mother, who fed the child a highly restricted and atypical diet of almond milk.

PROTEIN AND HEALTH RISKS

Excessive protein consumption may be associated with health risks. **Kidney function** can be compromised by too much protein in older people and in patients with kidney disease; also, a high protein intake may adversely affect calcium balance and contribute to **mineral loss from** bone (*see* **Calcium**, *in* **Minerals**). The Office of Population Censuses and Surveys' 1990 report[29] of British adults showed that average protein intakes are higher than recommended, being 84g a day for men and 64g for women. The UK Department of Health report[30] suggests that the safe upper limit of protein consumption is double the amounts shown in **Table 1.1**. Some people, especially those involved in very intense physical activity or who take protein supplements, are likely to be exceeding this maximum safe level.

Different types of dietary protein may have differing effects on cholesterol and fats in the bloodstream. When men with high blood cholesterol ate a meal in which the protein was from soya beans, their insulin and glucagon responses were much less extreme than when the protein source was casein, from milk[35]. The greater hormonal responses with casein suggest that this milk protein leads to higher levels of cholesterol and fats in the blood. These, in turn, are risk factors for **coronary heart disease**.

A survey of 620 women in Singapore revealed that, among pre-menopausal women, those who regularly ate soya protein and soya products in general had about half the normal risk of developing **breast cancer**[39]. In contrast, the consumption of red meat and animal protein was linked with an increased risk of breast cancer in pre-menopausal women.

Diets rich in meat protein lead to more uric acid in the urine, and a general increase in urine acidity. Because of the acidity, the uric acid does not easily dissolve and can form into **kidney stones**[42].

Studies show that vegan diets provide the amounts of protein recommended by the World Health Organization and by the UK's Department of Health. On the other hand, many omnivores eat more protein than guidelines recommend, and this may have disadvantages for their health.

ENERGY REQUIREMENTS

An individual's energy requirement depends on many factors, including age, gender, body weight and physical activity. Since it is impossible to generalize, national and international guidelines usually provide recommendations for different groups within the population.

In 1991 the UK's Department of Health published new Estimated Average Requirements (EARs) for energy intake from food. The EAR is the average energy intake for each group of people. For example, for a man of average weight and average physical activity (ie. light working occupation, inactive leisure time) the Estimated Average Requirement for dietary energy is 2,550 Calories. For women, the comparable figure is 1,920 Calories. For adults whose physical activity level is very high, these figures rise to 3,872 Calories for men and 3,011 Calories for women. EARs have also been established for infants and children (*see Table 1.4*).

TABLE 1.4

UK ESTIMATED AVERAGE REQUIREMENTS FOR ENERGY (CALORIES)

Age group		EARs in Calories/day
	Females	Males
Infants and children		
0–12 months*	515–865	545–920
1–3 years	1,165	1,230
4–14 years*	1,545–1,845	1,715–2,220
Adults		
15–18 years	2,110	2,755
19–75+ years**	1,940–1,810	2,550–2,100
Pregnancy*** (last trimester)	+ 200	
Breast feeding***	+ 240–570	

From *Dietary Reference Values for Food Energy and Nutrients for the United Kingdom, 1991*[30]. The values for adults are for typically sedentary people.

* The child's energy needs *rise up* through the range with increasing age.

** The adult's energy needs *decrease down* through the range with increasing age.

*** To be added to normal intake.

The Office of Population Censuses and Surveys[29] found the average energy consumption of British people, including alcohol, to be 1,680 Calories for women and 2,450 Calories for men (average value 2,065).

The men's intake is close to the Department of Health guidelines while the women's intake is much lower than recommended, yet 53% of all men and 41% of all women in Britain are overweight or obese.

The energy intakes of groups of vegans, vegetarians and omnivores, as measured in several studies, are summarized in **Table 1.5**. The results suggest that the average energy intake of vegans, at 2,138 Calories, is similar to that of vegetarians (2,178 Calories) and omnivores (2,220 Calories), and falls between the national average of 2,065 Calories and the UK recommendation of 2,235 Calories.

TABLE 1.5

AVERAGE DAILY ENERGY INTAKES OF VEGANS, VEGETARIANS AND OMNIVORES

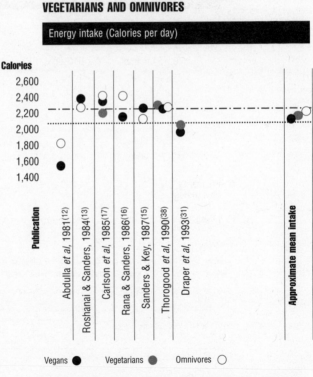

Energy intake (Calories per day)

Vegans ●   Vegetarians ●   Omnivores ○

— · — UK Department of Health recommendations (for men and women): 2,235 Calories

········· Average British intake (men and women): 2,065 Calories

Studies indicate that the energy intake of vegans is close to the average for British adults, and similar to UK recommendations. However, most vegans (and vegetarians) are lighter in weight than average omnivores. This may reflect particular features of their diets, or indicate that they take more physical activity — or both.

PROTEIN AND ENERGY NEEDS OF CHILDREN

This subject is dealt with more extensively in **Vegan Mothers and Children**. Here, only a summary of the main points is presented.

Children's over-riding nutritional need is for energy rather than protein *per se*. Short-term studies with malnourished infants who had been rehabilitated, showed that nitrogen balance was similar whether the protein source was cow's milk, cottonseed and rice, soya beans, rice, soya beans and peanuts, soya beans and rice, cottonseed and peanuts, or cottonseed alone[18]. In crossover studies lasting 2–3 months on each diet, babies fed rice and cottonseed, or rice and peanuts, as protein sources grew as well as infants fed wheat supplemented with lysine. All babies gained weight satisfactorily and at equivalent rates, although two infants fed rice alone did not grow as well as those fed cow's milk.

As long as children's energy needs are being met they will thrive on a diet in which protein is available from a mixture of plant foods.

STUDIES OF VEGAN CHILDREN

An American investigation of 48 children from a vegan community called The Farm, in Tennessee, was published in 1980[19]. Parents completed a three-day diet diary for their children, whose ages were 2–5 years, and each child was measured and weighed.

Energy intake for both sexes in all age groups except one exceeded the US RDAs, and all groups exceeded the equivalent UK recommendation. Protein consumption in all groups was higher than the current US and UK recommended intakes. Average amino acid intakes by the American vegan children were higher than those reported by the US National Academy of Sciences. In some age groups the children were below the national average for height and weight, but all groups except one met or exceeded reference values for triceps skinfold thickness. In interpreting these results it should be borne in mind that hereditary factors were not taken into account. A larger, follow-up study[40] of children at The Farm confirmed that their growth was close to the norm.

A different group of American vegan children was studied by Ken Resnicow and colleagues[41]. Aged between 5 and 17 years, eight of the nine children's weights and heights were in the normal range (one girl was noticeably shorter and heavier than average).

In 1981 a study of 23 British vegan children, aged 1–4.5 years old, was published[20]. The mean protein intake of the vegan children was 109% of the UK recommendations at that time, and more than double the 1991 recommendations. The average energy consumption in each age group was slightly below 1979 and 1991 recommendations, but except for two individuals was within the normal range found in British children. The children were lighter in weight than average, but all were within the normal range for weight and height, with the exception of two children whose parents were of short stature.

A follow-up survey of the children, aged 5.8–12.8 years, was published in 1992[36]. They continued to grow and develop normally, being very slightly shorter and considerably leaner than average and enjoying good health. Their protein consumption was average, at 12.4% of total Calories consumed. Their energy intake was 95% of the Estimated Average Requirement set by the UK Department of Health — almost identical to that of most British children.

Infants and children reared on a varied vegan diet obtain adequate protein and energy, and are healthy and grow normally. Although they tend to be of lighter build than omnivore children they are within the normal ranges for height and weight. Regular consumption of suitably-prepared high-energy foods, such as grains, pulses and nuts, will ensure a satisfactory intake of protein and energy.

PROBLEMS IN INFANCY — OTHER DIETS

Medical reports of vegan infants suffering from protein and energy deficiencies are extremely rare, and case studies must be interpreted with caution, as they are atypical. When such cases are scrutinized it becomes clear that usually the infants have not been weaned onto a varied and balanced vegan diet as advocated by the Vegan Society, but onto poorly planned fruitarian or macrobiotic regimes.

In other instances, parents have not consciously adopted a vegan diet for themselves and their children, but rather have eliminated certain foods from their infants' diets on a piecemeal basis and without seeking advice.

Two cases of malnutrition (kwashiorkor) in infants in Cleveland, USA, were reported in 1975[22]. Although the infants' diets, as described, contained no animal products, the parents were not vegans or vegetarians, but had restricted their children's diets because they believed that foods such as cow's milk were causing health problems. Four cases of malnutrition in infants raised on unorthodox diets were reported in 1979[21]. In none of these cases were the parents providing a varied and balanced vegan diet, but were following more restrictive fruitarian or macrobiotic principles. A child in Chicago, USA, was fed a diet which did not contain enough Calories and protein[23]. With advice, the child was returned to health successfully on a *vegan* diet.

PROBLEMS WITH VEGAN INFANTS

Two reports of protein and/or energy deficiencies in infants raised on vegan diets illustrate the need for energy-dense foods to be included in the diets of very young children. Summaries are presented here, with fuller details available in **Vegan Mothers and Children**.

Protein-Calorie malnutrition was reported[24] in 25 vegan infants, mainly in the 3–12 month age group, in a community of black Hebrew Americans living in Israel. The main problem was over-dilution of home-made plant milk; also the remaining foods were insufficiently energy-dense. Forty-seven infants under the age of 3 years from the community were well, although those aged between 4 and 18 months were small for their age. Catch-up growth meant that children older than 18 months were within the normal range for height and weight.

The second instance involved a Swiss infant of a vegan mother and lacto-vegetarian father[33]. After being breast-fed for 2.5 months, the child was fed largely on an extract of almonds in water, prepared by the mother. By the age of 7.5 months he was failing to thrive, with muscular weakness and other symptoms caused by nutrient deficiencies, including a lack of Calories.

There have been only two recent reports of protein and/or Calorie malnutrition in infants reared by vegan parents on a vegan diet, and these were due to over-dilution or inadequate variety of weaning foods. Other published cases of protein and energy deficiency in infants given alternative diets involved restrictive macrobiotic or fruitarian regimes, or dietary limitations imposed by non-vegan parents for perceived health reasons.

PROTEIN AND ENERGY — SUMMARY

A varied wholefood vegan diet contains adequate levels of energy and protein to sustain good health in all age groups, as evidenced by studies of vegans across the world. National and international recommendations for protein intake can be easily met on a vegan diet. The main protein-rich plant foods — pulses, nuts, grains and seeds — are energy-dense, and their use ensures that appropriate levels of nitrogen and indispensable amino acids are available. Potatoes and other vegetables also provide useful amounts of protein.

Vegans eat the recommended amounts of protein and energy, unlike most omnivores who consume too much protein, which can have health disadvantages. And, from a wider health perspective, it is significant that animal protein is often associated with saturated fat, while plant protein is usually associated with fibre.

There is no need to worry about combining proteins in each meal. A varied vegan menu, with foods from two or more plant groups each day, will provide adequate protein.

Well-planned vegan diets sustain good health and normal development in vegan infants and children. After weaning, infants must have an adequate intake of dietary energy. Vegan parents can ensure this by using suitably-prepared pulses, grains, nuts and seeds, with smaller amounts of bulky, less energy-dense fruits and vegetables. Cases of protein and energy deficiency in vegan infants are exceedingly rare.

REFERENCES

1 Food and Agriculture Organization/World Health Organization/United Nations University (1985). Energy and protein requirements. *WHO Technical Report Series* 724. Geneva: WHO.

2 National Advisory Committee on Nutrition Education (1983). *Proposals for Nutritional Guidelines for Health Education in Britain*. London: Health Education Council.

3 Millward, D.J., Newsholme, E.A., Pellett, P.L. & Uauy, R. (1992). *Amino acid scoring in health and disease*. In: Protein-Energy Interactions — Proceedings of a workshop held by the International Dietary Energy Consultancy Group. Switzerland: IDECG

4 Lappé, F.M. (1976). *Diet for a Small Planet*. New York: Ballantine Books.

5 Kofrányi, E., Jekat, F. & Müller-Wecker, H. (1970). The minimum protein require-ments of humans, tested with mixtures of whole egg plus potatoes and maize plus beans. *Z. Physiol. Chem.* 351:1485–1493.

6 Clark, H. E., Malzer, J.L., Onderka, H.M., Howe, J.M. & Moon, W. (1973). Nitrogen balances of adult human subjects fed combinations of wheat, beans, corn, milk, and rice. *Am. J. Clin. Nutr.* 26:702–706.

7 Edwards, C.H., Booker, L.K., Rumph, C.H., Wright, W.G. & Ganapathy, S.N. (1971). Utilization of wheat by adult man: nitrogen metabolism, plasma amino acids and lipids. *Am. J. Clin. Nutr.* 24:181–193.

8 Lee, C., Howe, J.M., Carlson, K. & Clark, H.E. (1971). Nitrogen retention of young men fed rice with or without supple-mentary chicken. *Am. J. Clin. Nutr.* 24:318–323.

9 Havala, S. & Dwyer, J. (1993). Position of the American Dietetic Association: veg-etarian diets. *J. Am. Diet. Assn.* 93:1317–1319.

10 Ellis, F.R. & Mumford, P. (1967). The nutritional status of vegans and vegetarians. *Proc. Nutr. Soc.* 26:205–212.

11 Hardinge, M.G., Crooks, H. & Stare, F.J. (1966). Nutritional studies of vegetari-ans. V. Proteins and essential amino acids. *J. Am. Diet. Assn.* 48:25–28.

12 Abdulla, M., Andersson, I., Asp, N-G., Berthelsen, K., Birkhed, D., Dencker, I., Johansson, C-G., Jägerstad, M., Kolar, K., Nair, B.M., Nilsson-Ehle, P., Nordén, Å., Rassner, S., Åkesson, B. & Öckerman, P-A. (1981). Nutrient intake and health status of vegans. Chemical analyses of diets using the duplicate portion sampling technique. *Am. J. Clin. Nutr.* 34:2464–2477.

13 Roshanai, F. & Sanders, T.A.B. (1984). Assessment of fatty acid intakes in vegans and omnivores. *Hum. Nutr.: Appl. Nutr.* 38A:345–354.

14 Lockie, A.H., Carlson, E., Kipps, M. & Thomson, J. (1985). Comparison of four types of diet using clinical, laboratory and psychological studies. *J. Roy. Coll. Gen. Pract.* 35:333–336.

15 Sanders, T.A.B. & Key, T.J.A. (1987). Blood pressure, plasma renin activity and aldosterone concentrations in vegans and omnivore controls. *Hum. Nutr.: Appl. Nutr.* 41A:204–211.

16 Rana, S.K. & Sanders, T.A.B. (1986). Taurine concentrations in the diet, plasma, urine and breast milk of vegans compared with omnivores. *Br. J. Nutr.* 56:17–27.

17 Carlson, E., Kipps, M., Lockie, A. & Thomson, J. (1985). A comparative evalua-tion of vegan, vegetarian and omnivore diets. *J. Plant Foods* 6:89–100.

18 Knapp, J., Barness, L.A., Hill, L.L., Kaye, R., Blattner, R.J. & Sloan, J.M. (1973). Growth and nitrogen balance in infants fed cereal proteins. *Am. J. Clin. Nutr.* 26:586–590.

19 Fulton, J.R., Hutton, C.W. & Stitt, K.R. (1980). Preschool vegetarian children. *J. Am. Diet. Assn.* 76:360–365.

20 Sanders, T.A.B. & Purves, R. (1981). An anthropometric and dietary assessment of the nutritional status of vegan pre-school children. *J. Hum. Nutr.* 35:349–357.

21 Roberts, I.F., West, R.J., Ogilvie, D. & Dillon, M.J. (1979). Malnutrition in infants receiving cult diets: a form of child abuse. *Br. Med. J.* 1:296–298.

22 Lozoff, B. & Fanaroff, A.A. (1975). Kwashiorkor in Cleveland. *Am. J. Dis. Child.* 129:710–711.

23 Berkelhamer, J.E., Thorp, F.K. & Cobbs, S. (1975). Kwashiorkor in Chicago. *Am. J.*

Dis. Child. 129:1240.

24 Shinwell, E.D. & Gorodischer, R. (1982). Totally vegetarian diets and infant nutrition. *Pediatrics* 70:582–586.

25 Holland, B., Welch, A.A., Unwin, I.D., Buss, D.H., Paul, A.A. & Southgate, D.A.T. (1991). *McCance and Widdowson's The Composition of Foods*. 5th edition. Royal Society of Chemistry and Ministry of Agriculture, Fisheries and Foods.

26 Tan, S.P., Wenlock, R.W. & Buss, D.H. (1985). *Immigrant Foods*. 2nd Supplement to *McCance & Widdowson's The Composition of Foods*. London: HMSO.

27 Lombard, K.A., Olson, A.L., Nelson, S.E. & Rebouche, C.J. (1989). Carnitine status of lactoovovegetarians and strict vegetarian adults and children. *Am. J. Clin. Nutr.* 50:301–306.

28 National Research Council (1989). *Recommended Dietary Allowances*. 10th edition. Washington DC: NAS.

29 Gregory, J., Foster, K., Tyler, H. & Wiseman, M. (1990). *The Dietary and Nutritional Survey of British Adults*. London: HMSO.

30 Department of Health (1991). *Dietary Reference Values for Food Energy and Nutrients for the United Kingdom*. Reports on Health & Social Subjects no. 41. London: HMSO.

31 Draper, A., Lewis, J., Malhotra, N. & Wheeler, E. (1993). The energy and nutrient intakes of different types of vegetarian: a case for supplements? *Br. J. Nutr.* 69:3–19.

32 Key, T.J.A., Roe, L., Thorogood, M., Moore, J.W., Clark, G.M.G. & Wang, D.Y. (1990). Testosterone, sex hormone-binding globulin, calculated free testosterone, and oestradiol in male vegans and omnivores. *Br. J. Nutr.* 64:111–119.

33 Kanaka, C., Schütz, B. & Zuppinger, K.A. (1992). Risks of alternative nutrition in infancy: a case report of severe iodine and carnitine deficiency. *Eur. J. Pediatr.*

151:786–788.

34 Laidlaw, S.A., Schultz, T.D., Cecchino, J.T. & Kopple, J.D. (1988). Plasma and urine taurine levels in vegans. *Am. J. Clin. Nutr.* 47:660–663.

35 Sanchez, A., Hubbard, R.W., Loder, C. & Sabate, J. (1988). Plasma insulin and glucagon response to dietary protein in men. *Am. J. Clin. Nutr.* 48:922.

36 Sanders, T.A.B. & Manning, J. (1992). The growth and development of vegan children. *J. Hum. Nutr. Diet.* 5:11–21.

37 Food and Agriculture Organization/World Health Organization (1991). *Protein quality evaluation in human diets*. Report of a joint FAO/WHO Expert Consultation. FAO Food and Nutrition Paper 51. Rome: FAO.

38 Thorogood, M., Roe, L., McPherson, K. & Mann, J. (1990). Dietary intake and plasma lipid levels: lessons from a study of the diet of health conscious groups. *Br. Med. J.* 300:1297–1301.

39 Lee, H.P., Gourley, L., Duffy, S.W., Estève, J., Lee, J. & Day, N.E. (1991). Dietary effects on breast cancer risk in Singapore. *Lancet* 337:1197–1200.

40 O'Connell, J., Dibley, M., Sierra, J., Wallace, B., Marks, J. & Yip, R. (1989). Growth of vegetarian children: the Farm study. *Pediatrics* 84:475–481.

41 Resnicow, K., Barone, J., Engle, A., Miller, S., Haley, N.J., Fleming, D. & Wynder, E. (1991). Diet and serum lipids in vegan vegetarians: a model for risk reduction. *J. Am. Diet. Assn.* 91:447–453.

42 Breslau, N.A., Brinkley, L., Hill, K.D. & Pak, C.Y.C. (1988). Relationship of animal-protein rich diet to kidney stone formation. *J. Clin. End.* 66:140–146.

43 Holland, B., Unwin, I.D. & Buss, D.H. (1992). *Fruit and Nuts*. 2nd supplement to *McCance and Widdowson's The Composition of Foods*. 5th edition. Royal Society of Chemistry and MAFF.

CARBOHYDRATES

A substantial amount of epidemiological and clinical data indicates that a high intake of plant foods and complex carbohydrates is associated with a reduced risk of several chronic diseases, especially coronary heart disease, certain cancers, hypertension, and diabetes.

The World Health Organization: Report on Diet, Nutrition and the Prevention of Chronic Diseases, 1990[31]

Carbohydrates are the main source of energy in most human diets worldwide: in Britain, for example, they provide an average 44% of total food energy. Plants make carbohydrates from the raw materials of carbon dioxide and water in the presence of sunlight. Plants use some carbohydrates to form their structural skeleton — substances known to us as fibre or roughage. Other carbohydrates are stored in fruits, seeds, roots and tubers, to provide nutrients for the seedling or an energy reserve for the plant throughout winter. Generally, fruits contain simple, soluble carbohydrates in the form of sugars, while seeds, roots and tubers contain complex carbohydrates in the form of starches. Sugars and starches have the same energy content of 4 Calories per gram.

FIGURE 2.1

TYPES OF CARBOHYDRATES FOUND IN FOOD

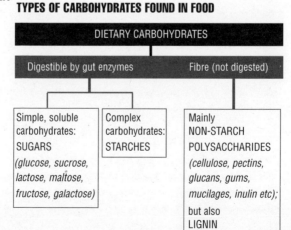

23

STARCHES

Starches are complex carbohydrates, consisting of long chains of glucose molecules joined together. When eaten these are broken down, by enzymes in the mouth and small intestine, mainly to glucose which is then absorbed into the bloodstream for distribution to all the body's tissues. Some carbohydrates are stored in the liver and muscles in the form of glycogen which, when required, is converted back to glucose for use as a fuel. This process is controlled by the hormones insulin and glucagon.

The sugars released from complex carbohydrates by digestion are generally absorbed into the bloodstream more slowly than when simple sugars are eaten, especially if unprocessed plant foods, containing fibre, are the source. The presence of fibre also modulates extreme changes in blood glucose (*see below*, **Fibre**). However, different kinds of complex carbohydrates produce different blood glucose responses — apples, lentils and fructose (fruit sugar), for example, cause only a quarter to a third the surge of blood sugar caused by glucose, parsnips and carrots[8].

SUGARS

Sugars are small, soluble carbohydrates and are a significant source of dietary energy. The common sugars in food, the sweetest listed first, are: fructose (in fruits and honey), sucrose (refined table sugar from cane and beet), glucose (in fruits and honey), maltose (in malted foods) and lactose (milk sugar).

Glucose is the basic unit of many sugars, and the form to which most sugars and starches are broken down during digestion. Each type of sugar is absorbed from the intestine at a different rate, and causes a different rise in blood sugar levels. Sucrose, derived from sugar beet or sugar cane, is highly refined and contains no other nutrients. Even raw brown sugar from cane or beet contains only small amounts of iron and B vitamins, although black molasses is a good source of iron.

FIBRE

Dietary fibre is found in plant foods, and consists mainly of fibrous or viscous non-starch polysaccharides, such as cellulose, hemicellulose, pectins, gums and inulin, as well as lignin (which is not a polysaccharide). These substances form the structure of plant cell walls.

The fibre in food is not digested by enzymes, although some is fermented by bacteria in the bowel (producing gases which can cause flatulence).

Being undigested, fibre provides no nutrients but nevertheless plays a very important role in health (*see **Fibre and health**, page 30*). Fibre occurs naturally in grains, pulses, nuts, seeds, fruit and vegetables which have not been refined or processed. Refining, processing and cooking may remove or break down the fibrous content of these foods.

RECOMMENDED CARBOHYDRATE INTAKES

The 1983 report of the National Advisory Committee on Nutrition Education (NACNE)[1], looking at the health of the British nation, recommended that carbohydrate intake (starches and sugars but not fibre) should increase from an average of 45% to a minimum of 50% total energy consumed. The 1994 COMA report on diet and heart disease[2] agreed with this target, and also suggested compensating for a reduced fat intake with more "complex carbohydrates, and sugars in fruits and vegetables . . ." The World Health Organization has recommended a total carbohydrate intake of 55%–75% of energy consumption[31].

Current British guidelines[26], published by the Department of Health in 1991, **recommend that total carbohydrates (sugars and starches) should provide 47% of our total energy consumption** (or 50% of *food* energy, ie. excluding the Calories provided by alcohol). The average carbohydrate intake by British adults is below this optimum, at about 42% of total energy consumption[24].

The UK Department of Health has made no specific recommendations for starch intakes, suggesting instead that starches plus natural plant sugars plus milk sugars should together contribute about 39% of total food energy[24].

Although sucrose consumption in Britain dropped during the 1980s, the estimated intake per person in 1987 was about 104g (3.7oz) sucrose — that is, *added* sugar — a day[27]. In addition, an average 16g honey plus glucose were consumed per person, and 23g lactose, making a total of 143g all sugars per person per day. In the British population as a whole, all sugars together contribute 17%–25% of food energy[3]. **The 1991 report of the UK Department of Health recommended that, because of their role in causing dental decay, the consumption of added sugars should be reduced from an estimated 16% of energy consumed, to 10%; or about 60g per day.**

During the last century fibre consumption in Britain has fallen by about two-thirds to its present level[24] of 18.6g a day in women, and 24.9g in men — compared with the 50–150g eaten by rural Africans, who rarely suffer from bowel and other complaints associated with low fibre intakes. The UK NACNE Report[1] proposed significant increases, further suggesting that extra fibre should be eaten in foods such as whole grains, fruit and vegetables, rather than added as bran.

The 1991 UK Department of Health report[26] re-defined 'fibre' and refers to non-starch polysaccharides. Non-starch polysaccharides (NSPs) are the main, but not the only, component of dietary fibre, so the recommended intakes of NSPs are lower, at 12–24g a day. This is equivalent to a fibre consumption of 20–40g daily. The average British consumption of non-starch polysaccharides is 11–13g a day (equivalent to a fibre intake of 18–22g). Therefore many people are not eating enough fibre to maintain good health.

CARBOHYDRATES AND VEGAN DIETS

Investigations between 1954 and 1967 found the consumption by vegans of starch plus sugars (excluding fibre) varied between 54% and 82% of food energy consumed[9]. Values taken from several studies[7,10,25,29] during the 1980s and '90s yield an average carbohydrate consumption by vegans of 53% of energy (see *Table 2.1*, *opposite*). Two other studies[11,12] have also recorded higher carbohydrate intakes in vegans compared with age- and sex-matched omnivores. Vegans thus easily achieve and indeed exceed the recommended intake of 47%–50%, in contrast to fish-eaters and omnivores (there are negligible amounts of carbohydrate in fish and meat). Even vegetarians, as a group, only just achieve the recommended carbohydrate intake.

The carbohydrate (starches plus sugars) intake recommended in UK guidelines is higher than that presently consumed by omnivores in the UK and is achieved only by vegans and vegetarians as dietary groups.

STARCHES AND VEGAN DIETS

Few studies of vegans have measured starch intakes separately from total carbohydrate intakes. One which did, published in 1993, recorded a mean consumption of 152g starch (31% of food energy), compared with 139g (27%) for lacto-ovo-vegetarians and 137g (26%) for fish-eaters[25]. All these levels exceed the British average for starch intake, which is 24% of food energy[24]. An international investigation of starch consumption and bowel cancer has shown that starches may offer more protection than fibre against this type of cancer[32].

TABLE 2.1

STARCH PLUS SUGAR INTAKES BY DIFFERENT DIETARY GROUPS

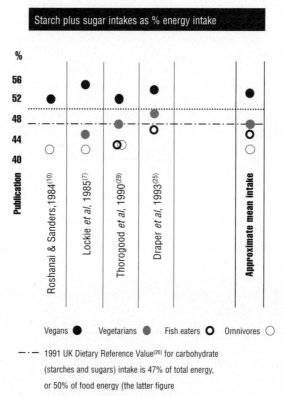

Starch plus sugar intakes as % energy intake

Vegans ●   Vegetarians ●   Fish eaters ◎   Omnivores ○

— · — 1991 UK Dietary Reference Value[26] for carbohydrate
(starches and sugars) intake is 47% of total energy,
or 50% of food energy (the latter figure
excludes alcohol from the calculations).

········· UK NACNE, 1983[1] recommendations: 50% of total energy consumed.

WHO recommendations[32]: 55%–75% of total energy consumed.

SUGARS AND VEGAN DIETS

A plant-based diet containing ample fruit and vegetables is likely to provide plenty of natural sugars, and published surveys suggest this is so. A Swedish study[5] of six middle-aged vegans found that glucose and fructose figured more prominently than in the omnivorous diet, while sucrose was eaten in slightly smaller amounts. This was not unexpected since this particular group of vegans used no added sugar, and indeed a greater difference might have been predicted. The men consumed twice as much sucrose as the women in the sample. Although the total intake of sugars of all sorts by these vegans was higher than that of a comparable omnivorous group, because they were taken in natural form, in association with fibre and water, over-eating and stress on the pancreas are less likely to occur.

An investigation of ten British vegans[6] also analyzed sugar intake separately from total carbohydrate consumption, revealing again that the intake of *all* sugars by the vegans was higher, at 20.6% total energy, than that by either vegetarians (15.2%) or omnivores (17.7%). The relatively high total sugar consumption by the vegans was due in part to natural sugars in fruit and vegetables, although another report of the same study[7] showed that the vegans in this group also ate more added sugar than the vegetarians and omnivores. As a proportion of total carbohydrate intake, sugar intake was relatively less in the vegans than in the other dietary groups analyzed.

A 1993 report[25] compared the nutrient intakes of 52 lacto-ovo-vegetarians and 38 vegans in Britain. Total sugar consumption (natural and added) was 23% of total food energy intake in vegans compared with 22% in vegetarians — similar to the national average in amount, although not in composition.

Twenty British children, life vegans aged 5.8 to 12.8 years, had a mean sugar intake of 15.6%[28] — considerably lower than the 17%–25% of typical omnivore children. The sugars in the vegan children's diets were mainly provided by fresh and dried fruits, and by soft drinks, particularly fruit juices. Confectionery, added sugars and preserves accounted for very little of their sugar consumption.

There is some variability in consumption of sugars by vegans. High-carbohydrate plant foods such as fruits and root vegetables, containing natural sugars, figure more prominently in a vegan diet, and may contribute to a slightly higher consumption of total sugars by vegans com-

pared to that of omnivores. However the proportion contributed by refined sugar is considerably less than average in vegan diets

SUGAR AND DENTAL DECAY

Natural plant sugars are not associated with dental decay, the main cause of which are added sugars (most commonly sucrose) found in processed foods. The frequency with which sugars are eaten, and the type of sugar, are thought to be the two main factors affecting the amount of decay caused, although amount of sugar also plays a part.

In unrefined wholefoods, sugars are combined with plant fibre and diluted with water, as well as coming 'packaged' with important nutrients such as vitamins and minerals. But extracted, refined, concentrated and added to foods such as cakes, biscuits, sweets and soft drinks, sucrose has become the main cause of tooth decay — a problem which has been exported to some third world countries such as Nigeria, where dental caries increased by 65% each year between 1982 and 1987.

Levels of dental decay in vegans have not been properly assessed, although Tom Sanders and Joan Manning reported that 18 British vegan children in their study had good teeth with little dental decay[28]. Since vegan diets tend to contain less refined sugar and more natural sugars — which are not thought to cause decay — it might be predicted that life-long vegans would have healthier teeth.

SUGAR AND OTHER DISEASES

The connections between sugar and diseases such as diabetes, heart disease, some cancers, Crohn's disease (an inflammatory condition of the gut) and gallstones are less well understood.

Some population studies in a number of countries have suggested a link between a high-sugar intake and the onset of non-insulin-dependent **diabetes**, while others have failed to show this connection. It seems likely that it is a combination of high-sugar and high-fat intakes which predispose towards diabetes. Epidemiological surveys in 41 countries show that populations which eat a lot of sugar also eat a lot of fat. Sugar makes fat more palatable and is frequently combined with it in cakes, biscuits, confectionery and many processed foods. The two ingredients together provide a concentrated source of Calories, which contributes to obesity, and it's now thought that obesity is a key factor in the development of adult-onset (non-insulin dependent) diabetes.

Some research has indicated a link between sugar and heart disease, but the evidence is not conclusive. The most likely connection is through sugar's contribution to overweight and obesity, which are risk factors for heart disease. The 1994 COMA Report[2] on diet and heart disease acknowledged this, and recommended that people who are overweight or becoming overweight could restrict their intake of added sugars; and that obesity should be avoided by means of appropriate food intake and physical activity.

A recent investigation showed that countries where sugar figures prominently in the diet have higher rates of **breast cancer** but, again, it has not been possible to separate the influences of sugar and fat. These two foods are also associated with the development of **large bowel cancer**, this disease being more common in people whose diet is high in fat, sugar and Calories, but low in fibre, and who become overweight[4].

FIBRE AND VEGAN DIETS

Recent surveys[6,10–13,25,29,30] of amounts of fibre eaten by vegans have shown that their average intake is 45g a day, compared with 22g for omnivore subjects, 33g for fish-but-not-meat eaters, and 37g for vegetarians. Although 45g of fibre sounds a lot, it is actually similar to the fibre intake of everyone in Britain only 100 years ago; and in African communities whose diet is based on maize, fibre intakes of 50–150g/day are still common. The current British recommendations for fibre are 20–40g/day.

Vegans and vegetarians equal or exceed the fibre intake recommended by nutrition advisory committees.

FIBRE AND HEALTH

The most obvious role of fibre in the diet is to provide bulk for intestinal muscles to work on, thus helping food pass though the gut easily and without straining. This effect is emphasized by fibre's ability to hold water, increasing its bulk further. Adequate fibre in food induces a feeling of fullness and hence reduces the likelihood of over-eating. **Irritable bowel syndrome** and **constipation** account for between one-third and two-thirds of new consultations at gastroenterology clinics in Britain, yet adequate dietary fibre prevents constipation, and consequently the likelihood of **varicose veins** and **haemorrhoids** is decreased. A 1986 study[13] confirmed that the transit time (the time taken for food to pass right through the digestive system) in vegans is shorter than in omnivores, and that the former pass softer faeces, more frequently.

Diverticular disease is characterized by pouching and inflammation of the wall of the bowel, and several studies have suggested that a high-fibre diet can help prevent it. In 1979, Oxford researchers showed that diverticular disease was consistently more common in omnivores than in vegetarians at all ages[14]. Moreover there was a major correlation between fibre intakes and occurrence of diverticular disease in the two groups, cereal fibre seeming to be the most important protective factor. Diets providing 30g fibre or more each day are beneficial in treating diverticular disease.

Many factors are involved in the development of **bowel cancer**, including the amount and type of fat in the diet, as well as fibre intake. Bowel cancer is less common in populations whose diets are high in fibre[15], and here fibre may help both by diluting the presence of mutagens (substances which cause mutations, and may therefore pose a cancer risk) in the faeces, and by hastening their transit through the gut. A comparison of 12 omnivores, six vegetarians and 11 vegans[16] showed significantly lower levels of mutagens in the faeces of the vegans and vegetarians.

A 1987 laboratory investigation of 12 male volunteers[17] who were housed in a metabolic ward while following 20-day experimental diets, showed that while on a vegan diet the level of bile acids in their faeces fell lower than when they were on an omnivore or a vegetarian diet. A high concentration of bile acids is associated with risk of bowel cancer, as is the concentration of cholesterol in the faeces, which was also lowest while volunteers were on a vegan diet. The authors noted that a higher mortality from bowel cancer has been reported for omnivores than for vegetarians and vegans.

Sufficient dietary fibre can help prevent the recurrence, and possibly the development, of **duodenal ulcers**. In one study[18], 73 patients with recently-healed duodenal ulcers were randomly allocated to a low- or high-fibre diet for six months, the fibre being provided mainly by wholemeal bread, unleavened bread, whole grains and vegetables. Eighty per cent of the low-fibre group suffered a recurrence of their ulcers, while only 45% of the high-fibre group did so.

Several factors may cause **gallstones**. A study examining these risk factors and comparing the prevalence of gallstones in vegetarian and omnivorous women was published in 1985[19]. Whereas one in four of the omnivores had gallstones, only one in eight of the vegetarians did. Taking into account differences in age and body weight between the two groups, it was found that omnivores were twice as likely to have gallstones as vegetarians. The main protective factor is fibre, and the main risk factors are fat, sugar, cholesterol and Calorie consumption; the vegetarians ate less saturated fat and more fibre than the omnivores.

Numerous studies have shown that a high-fibre diet, or added fibre, reduces the surge in blood glucose which follows a meal. This simple measure can enable many type-2 (non-insulin dependent or maturity-onset) **diabetics** to stop taking insulin, and can improve some aspects of blood glucose control in type-1 (insulin-dependent or juvenile-onset) diabetics[20–22]. Such a diet can also reduce pancreatic stress in non-diabetics.

In studies of human populations, high intakes of dietary fibre or complex carbohydrates are dietary factors strongly related to lower rates of **coronary heart disease**[2]. Large amounts of viscous fibre such as pectin and guar cause major reductions in blood cholesterol, a known risk factor for heart disease, and a 1987 investigation[23] has confirmed that vegans have lower levels of low-density-lipoprotein cholesterol and total cholesterol in their bloodstream than vegetarians and omnivores. The researchers predicted that lifelong vegans might show a 57% reduction in coronary heart disease compared to meat-eaters.

CARBOHYDRATES — SUMMARY

Nationally and internationally, nutrition experts have recommended an increase in the consumption of complex carbohydrates from legumes, whole grains, fruits and vegetables. Vegans, as a dietary group, are most likely to achieve the carbohydrate intake recommended.

It is also recognized that intake of dietary fibre by the general population is too low. Animal foods – such as meat, milk or eggs – are devoid of fibre, and in contrast to the average omnivore, vegans' and vegetarians' consumption of fibre meets or exceeds recommended intakes. Vegans and vegetarians also suffer less often from chronic illnesses associated with low-fibre diets.

A few studies suggest that vegans eat more natural sugars in fruits and vegetables than do omnivores, but probably less added, refined sugar which is the major cause of tooth decay.

REFERENCES

1 National Advisory Committee on Nutrition Education (1983). *Proposals for Nutritional Guidelines for Health Education in Britain*. London: Health Education Council.

2 Committee on Medical Aspects of Food Policy (1994). *Nutritional Aspects of Cardiovascular Disease*. Reports on Health & Social Subjects no. 46. London: HMSO.

3 Department of Health (1989). *Dietary Sugars and Human Disease*. Reports on Health & Social Subjects no. 37. London: HMSO.

4 Bristol, J.B., Emmett, P.M., Heaton, K.W. & Williamson, R.C.N. (1985). Sugar, fat and the risk of colorectal cancer. *Br. Med. J.* 291:1467–1470.

5 Abdulla, M., Andersson, I., Asp, N-G., Berthelsen, K., Birkhed, D., Dencker, I., Johansson, C-G., Jägerstad, M., Kolar, K., Nair, B.M., Nilsson-Ehle, P., Nordén, Å., Rassner, S., Åkesson, B. & Öckerman, P-A. (1981). Nutrient intake and health status of vegans. Chemical analyses of diets using the duplicate portion sampling technique. *Am. J. Clin. Nutr.* 34:2464–2477.

6 Carlson, E., Kipps, M., Lockie, A. & Thomson, J. (1985). A comparative evaluation of vegan, vegetarian and omnivore diets. *J. Plant Foods* 6:89–100.

7 Lockie, A.H., Carlson, E., Kipps, M. & Thomson, J. (1985). Comparison of four types of diet using clinical, laboratory and psychological studies. *J. Roy. Coll. Gen. Pract.* 35:333–336.

8 Jenkins, D.J.A., Taylor, R.H. & Wolever, T.M.S. (1982). The diabetic diet, dietary carbohydrate and differences in digestibility. *Diabetologica* 23:477–484.

9 Ellis, F.R. & Mumford, P. (1967). The nutritional status of vegans and vegetarians. *Proc. Nutr. Soc.* 26:205–212.

10 Roshanai, F. & Sanders, T.A.B. (1984). Assessment of fatty acid intakes in vegans and omnivores. *Hum. Nutr.: Appl. Nutr.* 38A:345–354.

11 Rana, S.K. & Sanders, T.A.B. (1986). Taurine concentrations in the diet, plasma, urine and breast milk of vegans compared with omnivores. *Br. J. Nutr.* 56:17–27.

12 Sanders, T.A.B. & Key, T.J.A. (1987). Blood pressure, plasma renin activity and aldosterone concentrations in vegans and omnivore controls. *Hum. Nutr.: Appl. Nutr.* 41A:204–211.

13 Davies, G.J., Crowder, M., Reid, B. & Dickerson, J.W.T. (1986). Bowel function measurements of individuals with different eating patterns. *Gut* 27:164–169.

14 Gear, J.S.S., Fursdon, P., Nolan, D.J., Ware, A., Mann, J.I., Brodribb, A.J.M. & Vessey, M.P. (1979). Symptomless diverticular disease and intake of dietary fibre. *Lancet* i:511–514.

15 Doll, R. (1979). Nutrition and cancer: a review. *Nutr. & Cancer* 1:35–45.

16 Kuhnlein, U., Bergstrom, D. & Kuhnlein, H. (1981). Mutagens in feces from vegetarians and non-vegetarians. *Mutation Res.* 85:1–12.

17 van Faassen, A., Bol, J., van Dokkum, W., Pikaar, N.A., Ockhuizen, T. & Hermus, R.J.J. (1987). Bile acids, neutral steroids, and bacteria in feces as affected by a mixed, a lacto-vegetarian, and a vegan diet. *Am. J. Clin. Nutr.* 46:962–967.

18 Rydning, A., Aadland, E., Berstad, A. & Ødegaard, B. (1982). Prophylactic effect of dietary fibre in duodenal ulcer disease. *Lancet* ii:736–739.

19 Pixley, F., Wilson, D., McPherson, K. & Mann, J.I. (1985). Effect of vegetarianism on development of gall stones in women. *Br. Med. J.* 291:1–12.

20 Anon. (1981). High-fibre diets and diabetes. *Lancet* i:423–424.

21 Simpson, H.C.R., Lousley, S., Geekie, M., Simpson, R.W., Carter, R.D., Hockaday, T.D.R. & Mann, J.I. (1981). A high carbohydrate leguminous fibre diet improves all aspects of diabetic control. *Lancet* i:1–5.

22 Anon. (1983). High carbohydrate, high fibre diets for diabetes mellitus. *Lancet* i:741–742.

23 Thorogood, M., Carter, R., Benfield, L., McPherson, K. & Mann, J.I. (1987). Plasma lipids and lipoproteins in groups with different dietary practices within Britain. *Br. Med. J.* 295:351–353.

24 Gregory, J., Foster, K., Tyler, H. & Wiseman, M. (1990). *The Dietary and Nutritional Survey of British Adults*. London:

HMSO.

25 Draper, A., Lewis, J., Malhotra, N. & Wheeler, E. (1993). The energy and nutrient intakes of different types of vegetarian: a case for supplements? *Br. J. Nutr.* 69:3–19.

26 Department of Health (1991). *Dietary Reference Values for Food Energy and Nutrients for the United Kingdom.* Reports on Health & Social Subjects no. 41. London: HMSO.

27 Central Statistical Office (1989). *Annual Abstracts of Statistics.* London: HMSO.

28 Sanders, T.A.B. & Manning, J. (1992). The growth and development of vegan children. *J. Hum. Nutr. Diet.* 5:11–21.

29 Thorogood, M., Roe, L., McPherson, K. & Mann, J. (1990). Dietary intake and plasma lipid levels: lessons from a study of the diet of health conscious groups. *Br. Med. J.* 300:1297–1301.

30 Lamberg-Allardt, C., Kärkkäinen, M., Seppänen, R. & Biström, H. (1993). Low serum 25-hydroxyvitamin D concentrations and secondary hyperparathyroidism in middle-aged white strict vegetarians. *Am. J. Clin. Nutr.* 58:684–689.

31 World Health Organization (1990). Diet, nutrition and the prevention of chronic diseases. Report of a WHO Study Group. *Technical Report Series* 797. Geneva: WHO.

32 Bingham, S. (1994). How important is nutrition to health? *MRC News* 61:8–11.

FATS

We conclude from the present study that a strict vegan diet, which is typically very low in saturated fat and dietary cholesterol and high in fiber, can help children and adults maintain or achieve desirable blood lipid levels.

Dr Ken Resnicow PhD and colleagues, of the American Health Foundation in New York, reporting on the effect of vegan diets on fats in the bloodstream, 1991[27]

The main constituents of all fats are the fatty acids, which may be saturated, monounsaturated or polyunsaturated, depending on the number of double bonds between the carbon atoms in the molecule. The more of these bonds in a fatty acid, the less it is saturated with hydrogen. There are more than 40 fatty acids found in nature (*see Figure 3.1, page 38*).

TYPES OF FATS

Fats containing a high proportion of saturated fatty acids are solid at room temperature. These are commonly known as saturated fats and most are from animal sources such as lard, suet and butter, although coconut and palm fats are also highly saturated. Most plant fats are high either in polyunsaturated fatty acids, such as oils from safflower seeds, sunflower seeds, corn and soya; or in monounsaturated fatty acids, such as olive oil.

The second component in a fat is glycerol: most dietary fat is made of three molecules of fatty acid joined to one molecule of glycerol, and this structure is technically called a triglyceride.

A fat (or triglyceride) = 3 molecules of fatty acid + 1 molecule of glycerol

Cholesterol is a related fatty substance found in all animal tissues, although eggs are the only common cholesterol-rich food. Cholesterol is a member of the sterol family of substances, and several plant sterols occur in vegan diets. Cholesterol itself, however, is only found in trace amounts in plant foods.

Saturated and monounsaturated fatty acids can be made in the human body, and so they are not necessary in the diet. Neither are trans fatty acids, which mainly come from the hydrogenation of fats in the manufacture of margarine, but are also found in dairy milk and related products, and in beef and lamb. Trans fats are solid at room temperature and may

FIGURE 3.1

TYPES OF DIETARY FATTY ACIDS FOUND IN FOOD

Saturated fatty acids (SFAs)	Monounsaturated fatty acids (MFAs)	Polyunsaturated fatty acids (PUFAs)	
The major fatty acids in palm & coconut oils; also in hydrogenated oils, butter, meat & lard	The major fatty acids in olive, peanut & rapeseed (canola) oils; also in walnuts, peanuts & avocados	The major fatty acids in safflower, sunflower, soya, sesame, corn & fish oils	
Saturated fats are usually solid at room temperature	These oils are liquid or viscous at room temperature	These oils are liquid even at cool temperatures	
Can be made in the body, so are not essential in diet	Can be made in the body, so are not essential in diet	There are many PUFAs; only two are essential in diet	
SFAs tend to increase risk of heart disease	MFAs may decrease risk of heart disease	PUFAs tend to decrease risk of heart disease	
SFAs include palmitic acid, stearic acid, lauric acid	The main MFA is oleic acid	Two essential PUFAs are: • Linoleic acid	• Alpha-linolenic acid
Vegans eat much less than omnivores	*Vegans eat average amounts*	*Vegans eat 1.5-4 x average*	*Vegans eat average amounts*

act in the body like saturated fats. For example there is some evidence that they can increase cholesterol levels in the blood, and may be statistically associated with heart disease or cancer — although the link is not yet proven. Vegan margarines free of trans fats are available in the UK, usually labelled as 'contains no hydrogenated fats'.

FUNCTIONS OF FATS

Fats are a major source of dietary energy, and contain 9 Calories per gram compared to the 4 Calories per gram provided by proteins and carbohydrates. In the small intestine, fats are emulsified by bile and then digested by enzymes released from the pancreas. In the cells lining the intestine, the released fatty acids are recombined into triglycerides and, mainly via the lymph system and then the bloodstream, these are carried to the tissues (especially body fat and skeletal muscle), where they are either oxidized as fuel or incorporated into body fats.

In the bloodstream are a number of carrier substances called lipoproteins, which transport cholesterol and fats: high-density lipoproteins (HDLs), low-density lipoproteins (LDLs) and very low-density lipoproteins (VLDLs). HDLs remove excess cholesterol from the tissues, while high levels of LDLs lead to cholesterol accumulation. Thus HDL-cholesterol is known as the 'good' type of cholesterol, while LDL-cholesterol is generally referred to as the 'bad' kind. VLDLs transport triglycerides to the tissues via the circulation. Levels of cholesterol in the bloodstream are determined more by the amount of saturated fat than by cholesterol in the diet, although the latter does have a small effect.

Apart from being a source of energy, in adipose tissue fat acts as insulation and provides support and protection for organs such as the heart and kidneys. Cholesterol is a constituent of nerves and some hormones and is used for the synthesis of bile, but is not necessary in the diet as the body can make enough for its requirements.

Two polyunsaturated fatty acids (PUFAs) which cannot be made in the body, lino*leic* acid and alpha-lino*lenic* acid, must be provided by the diet and are known as essential fatty acids. Within the body both can be converted to other PUFAs which are vital components of the cell membranes, especially in the brain (*see* **Polyunsaturated Fats and Vegan Diets**, *page 43*). PUFAs are also precursors of the prostaglandins which regulate many body processes, including inflammation and blood clotting. Another requirement for fat in the diet is to enable the fat-soluble vitamins A, D, E and K to be absorbed from food.

RECOMMENDED FAT INTAKES

The need for dietary fat varies with age. Infants, for example, require a relatively high fat intake for rapid growth, and 50%–55% of the Calories in human breast milk come from fat. Current nutritional recommendations for reducing fat intake apply mainly to adults and older children.

Eating too much or the wrong kind of fat is linked to a number of serious diseases, most notably cardiovascular disease. The 1990 Dietary and Nutritional Survey of British Adults[20] indicated that the average Briton's consumption of fat is 38% of total energy (Calorie) intake, while the 1991 National Food Survey[19] estimated it at 41% — both figures being much higher than the recommended amount of 30%–33%. The ratio of PUFAs to saturated fatty acids (known as the P/S ratio) in the general British diet has increased since the 1950s, with consumption of saturated fats decreasing and that of PUFAs increasing.

It is generally recognized that Western consumption of total fat and saturated fat should be decreased, in particular because of their effect in raising blood levels of cholesterol. The UK 1994 COMA report[1] on diet and heart disease proposed a target fat consumption of 35% of energy as "a significant reduction which is potentially achievable". The 1983 NACNE report[2] suggested a long-term reduction in fat consumption to 30% of energy intake. Similar recommendations have been made by American committees on nutrition and health.

The UK Department of Health's 1991 recommendations[23] are for a maximum total fat intake of 33% of all energy consumed, and the COMA report[1] set a realistic target of 35%.

The major sources of **saturated fatty acids** in the average British diet[19] are spreading fats (eg. butter, margarine, low-fat and dairy spreads) and vegetable and salad oils — together accounting for 27.4% of saturated fat consumption; milk and milk products (26.5%); meat and meat products (25.5%); and cereal products, including cakes, biscuits and breakfast cereals (12.8%). Vegetables contribute only 2.5% of saturated fats, and fruits only 1%. In the UK, the 1994 COMA report[1] and the Department of Health[23] recommended that saturated fats should account for no more than about 10% of energy consumed, and the 1983 NACNE report[2] concurred.

Polyunsaturated fatty acids (PUFAs) and monounsaturated fatty acids are both believed to reduce the risk of heart disease, and plant foods are the richest sources of these kinds of fats. The Department of Health[23] recommended that PUFAs should continue to account for about 6% of energy consumption, and monounsaturated fats about 12%.

There is some evidence that the consumption of **trans fatty acids**, especially those found in margarines containing hydrogenated vegetable oils, may be linked with heart disease. Until the evidence is clearer, the UK Department of Health[23] recommended that consumption of trans fatty acids should not increase above the present average of 2% of dietary energy. The 1994 COMA report[1] on diet and heart disease also suggested a maximum of 2%, but recommended that ways of decreasing people's consumption of trans fats should be found.

Scientific opinion in the 1990s is that **dietary cholesterol** has less effect on blood cholesterol levels than was once thought. However a very low consumption of cholesterol may reduce blood levels, and the 1994 COMA report[1] on diet and heart disease suggested that intakes of cholesterol should not rise above the current British average of 245mg/day.

The UK Department of Health's 1991 Report[23] on food energy and nutrients recommended that, for adults, saturated fatty acids should provide 10% of total energy (ie. including alcohol in the calculations) obtained from the diet; that monounsaturated fatty acids should continue to provide, on average, about 12%; that polyunsaturated fatty acids (PUFAs) should continue to provide about 6%; and that trans fatty acids should not increase above the estimated average intake of 2% of total dietary energy.

The sum total of *fatty acid* **intake should therefore be 30% of total dietary energy (including alcohol), while total** *fat* **intake (ie. fatty acids plus glycerol) is recommended not to exceed 33% — a level still well below the estimated average for the British population, which is between 38% and 41%.**

TOTAL FATS AND VEGAN DIETS

Numerous studies[5–9,27,29,32] show that the average total fat consumption of vegans is about 33.9% of total energy intake, as shown in **Table 3.1** (*page 42*). The comparable figure for the vegetarian and omnivore subjects in these studies is 37.9%–38.3%. Thus only vegans as a group approach the recommended total fat consumption of 33%–35% of energy intake.

Of all dietary groups, only vegans have a total fat consumption which approaches current national and international recommendations.

SATURATED FATS, MONOUNSATURATED FATS AND CHOLESTEROL IN VEGAN DIETS

A study[30] of British male vegans, using a four-day diary method, estimated that saturated fats comprised 6.2% of their total dietary energy, compared with 12.9% for matched male omnivores (both groups consumed the same amount of total dietary energy). Similarly, the Oxford

TABLE 3.1

AVERAGE DAILY TOTAL FAT CONSUMPTION OF VEGANS, VEGETARIANS AND OMNIVORES

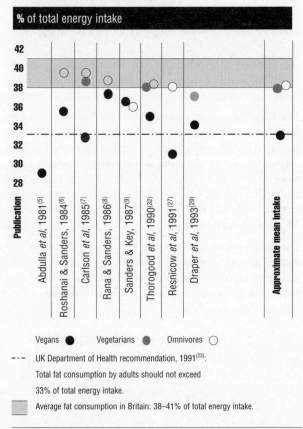

% of total energy intake

Vegans ● Vegetarians ● Omnivores ○

– – – UK Department of Health recommendation, 1991[23]:
Total fat consumption by adults should not exceed
33% of total energy intake.

Average fat consumption in Britain: 38–41% of total energy intake.

Vegetarian Study found that saturated fat intake as a percentage of energy was 6.8% in vegans, compared with 13.2% in vegetarians, 12.9% in fish-eaters and 13.7% in meat-eaters[32]. The P/S ratio (1.81) of the vegans was more than double those of the other dietary groups.

Vegans in the same investigation had an apparent cholesterol intake of 5.5mg. Cholesterol may be found in trace quantities in vegetable oils, but most studies over-estimate vegans' consumption of cholesterol. This is because the computer programs used to analyze diet diaries are written on the assumption that cakes, biscuits, bread and pasta are made with eggs or dairy products.

The dietary composition of six Swedish middle-aged vegans was analyzed in detail[5]. The P/S ratio was very high at 3.7, compared to 0.18 in Swedish omnivores. Total sterol intake was 381mg, of which only 28mg was measured as cholesterol. An American investigation[10] of 23 vegans calculated a P/S ratio of 1.9 and a 'cholesterol' intake of less than 10mg.

A British study[7] of 10 vegans also showed a low 'cholesterol' intake of 29mg, compared to 296mg in vegetarians and 357mg in omnivores, and another[9] measured a P/S ratio for fatty acids of 1.1 in vegans and 0.4 in omnivore subjects. A very detailed analysis[6] of fat consumption by 22 British vegans was published in 1984. There was little difference in total fat intake between the vegan subjects and age- and sex-matched omnivores, but the vegans ate only 18g saturated fatty acids a day, compared to 31g for the omnivores. Intakes of monounsaturated fatty acids were similar in both groups, at 33g a day.

Vegan Seventh Day Adventists ate an average 12g saturated fats and 44mg 'cholesterol' daily, compared with matched omnivore controls who consumed 38g saturated fats and 376mg cholesterol each day[27]. The vegans' average intake of monounsaturated fats was 27g daily compared to the omnivores' average consumption of 35g.

A 1993 report[29] confirmed that **vegans consume significantly less saturated fat, and similar amounts of monounsaturated fats, compared to other dietary groups. Cholesterol is found in plant foods only in trace amounts, and consumption by vegans is extremely low. This very low intake of cholesterol in food may have beneficial effects on vegans' blood levels of cholesterol.**

POLYUNSATURATED FATS AND VEGAN DIETS

In a wholefood vegan diet featuring grains, pulses and nuts, the 'hidden' fat is mainly in the form of polyunsaturated rather than saturated fatty acids. In addition, vegan alternatives to animal fats — such as vegetable oils, vegetable margarines or spreads made from nuts or seeds — contribute to the higher proportion of PUFAs found in vegan compared to omnivore diets.

The two main dietary polyunsaturated fatty acids (PUFAs) are linoleic acid and alpha-linolenic acid. Because they cannot be made in the body, these two are known as **essential fatty acids** which must be provided by food.

Food sources of linoleic acid include spreading fats and vegetable oils, vegetables, fruit, nuts, grains, and eggs; while alpha-linolenic acid is common in meat, spreading fats and vegetable oils, green leafy vegetables and grains. Within the body these fatty acids can be converted to longer-chain PUFAs such as arachidonic acid, or eicosapentaenoic acid and docosahexaenoic acid (*see Figure 3.2, below*). In the body, PUFAs are important for maintaining the membranes of all cells; for making prostaglandins, which regulate many body processes; and for regulating cholesterol metabolism.

A 1984 study[6] showed that vegans and omnivores had similar intakes of

FIGURE 3.2

POLYUNSATURATED FATTY ACIDS — DIETARY SOURCES AND CONVERSIONS IN THE BODY

Polyunsaturated fatty acids (The omega-6 family)	Polyunsaturated fatty acids (The omega-3 family)
LINOLEIC ACID In vegetables, fruit, nuts, grains & seeds; in safflower, sunflower, evening primrose & corn oils; in eggs, chicken, duck & turkey	**ALPHA-LINOLENIC ACID** In flaxseeds, mustard seeds & pumpkin seeds; in soya bean, walnut & rapeseed (canola) oils; in green leafy vegetables & grains; in meat & meat products
↓ *Converted in the body to:*	↓ *Converted in the body to:*
GAMMA-LINOLENIC ACID (GLA) In oils of blackcurrant, borage and evening primrose	**EICOSAPENTAENOIC ACID (EPA)** In marine fish oil
↓ *Converted in the body to:*	This conversion is limited if there is a large intake of linoleic acid ↓ *Converted in the body to:*
ARACHIDONIC ACID (AA) In marine fish oil; also in breast milk, but not in most infant formula feeds	**DOCOSAHEXAENOIC ACID (DHA)** In marine fish oil and some algae; also in breast milk, but not in most infant formula feeds

alpha-linolenic acid, but that vegans ate 26g of linoleic acid a day compared with only 10g eaten by the omnivores. In 1990 the intake of PUFAs by 18 vegan men was estimated as 10.3% of dietary energy, but only 7.2% in omnivore men[30]. A 1993 comparison[29] between vegans, lacto-ovo-vegetarians and fish-eaters showed that vegans consumed slightly less alpha-linolenic acid and related (omega-3) fatty acids, but considerably more linoleic acid and related (omega-6) fatty acids than the other groups, and twice as much as omnivores. Measured with the duplicate portion technique[5], the diets of six Swedish middle-aged vegans contributed 30g linoleic acid, which represented 50%–60% of their total fatty acid consumption.

The other main PUFAs can also be obtained from food, or made in the body from linoleic and alpha-linolenic acids (see **Figure 3.2**, *opposite*). These include arachidonic acid (AA), eicosapentaenoic acid (EPA) and docosahexaenoic acid (DHA); marine fish oils are rich sources of these. However, analyses of vegan diets did not find any EPA or DHA[6,31] , and vegans do have lower levels of DHA in their body fat, red blood cells, platelets and breast milk[12,21,31]. Platelets — small blood cells involved in clotting — contained higher proportions of linoleic acid and lower proportions of arachidonic acid, DHA and EPA than those of matched omnivores.

Alpha-linolenic acid — present in plants, especially in flaxseeds, walnuts, soya bean oil, rapeseed oil, soya beans, tofu, pumpkin seeds, seaweeds and purslane — is converted in the body to EPA and DHA, although many factors affect the rate of conversion. One factor seems to be a high food intake of linoleic acid, which is typical of vegan diets and may suppress the body's ability to convert alpha-linolenic acid to DHA. Vegans can achieve a better balance of PUFAs in their body tissues by using less sunflower, safflower and corn oils, and more oils containing alpha-linolenic acid — such as rapeseed (canola) oil, or soya bean or walnut oils. This would encourage their tissues to make more DHA.

Interestingly, there is at least one plant source of pre-formed DHA, according to a study published in 1993[22]. With a view to finding a source of essential PUFAs for use in infant formula feeds, researchers discovered that an alga called *Isochrysis* is a rich and easily-produced source of DHA.

In vegan diets polyunsaturated fatty acids (PUFAs), which have a beneficial effect on blood cholesterol levels, are more abundant than saturated fatty acids. Other characteristics of the PUFA content of vegan diets compared to omnivore diets are an absence of eicosapentaenoic acid (EPA) and docosahexaenoic acid (DHA); considerably more linoleic acid; but approximately similar levels of alpha-linolenic acid.

The human body can convert linoleic acid and alpha-linolenic acid — the two essential PUFAs — into arachidonic acid, EPA and DHA. However, some of the body tissues of vegans have been found to contain less DHA and EPA than those of other dietary groups. The consequences of this difference, if any, are not known.

FATS AND VEGAN INFANTS

The fatty-acid composition of breast milk is determined by a mother's current diet and by the composition of her own body's fat stores. So, as expected, the relative amounts of polyunsaturated fatty acids (PUFAs) differ in the breast milks of vegan, vegetarian and omnivore women. In particular, in vegan breast milk there is more of both linoleic acid and alpha-linolenic acid, less docosahexaenoic acid (DHA) and similar levels of arachidonic acid, compared to the breast milk of omnivores[21] . This leads to differences in the levels of PUFAs in the red blood cells of vegan and omnivore infants. DHA is important in the development of the nervous system and vision. Our bodies can usually make DHA from dietary PUFAs, but an exception may be premature babies who may require a food source of DHA. This topic is discussed in more detail in **Vegan Mothers and Children**.

No-one yet knows if these differences in the fat composition of breast milk and infants' tissues are significant, or whether they are within the 'normal' range. Certainly, there is no evidence that neural or intellectual functions of vegan children breast-fed by vegan mothers are affected[21].

Infant formula feeds and the breast milks of vegans, vegetarians and omnivores contain differing proportions of various polyunsaturated fatty acids. These differences are reflected in some body tissues of infants. It is not yet known exactly what, if any, effect these variations may have on the growth and development of infants.

FATS AND HEART DISEASE

A high fat consumption is associated with a number of serious and common diseases, as shown mainly by population studies. The relationship between fats and **coronary heart disease** has been reviewed by the UK Royal College of Physicians[3], Department of Health[23], Committee on Medical Aspects of Food Policy[1] and the World Health Organization[4].

Coronary heart disease still kills proportionately more men and women in the UK, especially in Northern Ireland and Scotland, than anywhere else in the world. Diet is a major factor in the development of heart disease whose basis is atherosclerosis, the narrowing of arteries by cholesterol-containing deposits (plaque), which can start in childhood. Thrombosis superimposed on atherosclerotic plaque is the usual trigger for a heart attack, and both these processes are affected by fat consumption.

More than 20 studies in 14 different countries have shown that, along with high blood pressure (hypertension), cigarette smoking and social class, certain cholesterols in the bloodstream are associated with heart disease[11]. The main dietary influence on total cholesterol and LDL-cholesterol in the bloodstream is the amount and type of fat eaten. Saturated fats and trans fats tend to raise levels, and PUFAs and monounsaturated fats lower them. There is some inconclusive evidence that trans fats, produced during the hydrogenation of vegetable oils in margarine production, for example, may increase the risk of heart disease.

There is also evidence from comparisons of different countries that with increasing dietary intake of linoleic acid, the risk of coronary heart disease decreases. Vegans eat more than average amounts of this essential PUFA. The long-chain PUFAs, eicosapentaenoic acid (EPA) and docosahexaenoic acid (DHA), also have beneficial effects on blood levels of fats and inhibit thrombosis. EPA and DHA are found mainly in marine fish oils, but not in vegan diets[6]. However vegan diets do provide plenty of alpha-linolenic acid, which is converted to EPA and DHA in the body (see **Figure 3.2**, page 44).

As noted above, vegans have a lower than average intake of fat and a high proportion of their consumption is in the form of PUFAs, so it would be expected that levels of total cholesterol and LDL-cholesterol in their bloodstream would be lower than average, while HDL-cholesterol would be about the same as in omnivores. Investigations have shown this to be the case, and also that vegans (and vegetarians) are at less risk of heart disease than meat-eaters.

A British report[12] in 1978 found that total plasma cholesterol in vegan subjects was 4.1mmol/l compared with 6.1mmol/l for omnivore subjects. The proportion of linoleic acid in all tissues studied was higher in the vegans, implying a higher intake in the diet, while the proportion of alpha-linolenic acid in tissues of vegans was lower than in omnivores. A 1985 comparison of plasma cholesterol levels in various dietary groups revealed[7] an average level of 3.9mmol/l in vegans, compared with

4.3mmol/l in vegetarians and 5.3mmol/l in omnivores. The difference was significant between the two vegetarian groups compared to the omnivores. A detailed analysis of the fatty acid composition of substances in the bloodstream of vegetarians, vegans and omnivores showed that linoleic and alpha-linolenic acids were predominant in the first two groups compared with the omnivores[13].

A 1987 British publication[14] arising from the Oxford Vegetarian Study compared the levels of total cholesterol, LDL-cholesterol and HDL-cholesterol in the bloodstream of vegans, vegetarians, fish-eaters and meat-eaters. After adjustments made for differences in age and sex of the subjects, it was found that total cholesterol and LDL-cholesterol (both being risk factors for heart disease) were highest in meat-eaters and lowest in vegans compared with other groups. HDL-cholesterol (which helps protect against heart disease) was higher in fish-eaters than in other groups. Vegans had the lowest LDL/HDL ratio, which helps maintain a healthy heart and circulation.

The authors speculated that dietary causes of these characteristics in vegans, apart from lower intakes of saturated fats, might be plant protein, fibre, total carbohydrate or high P/S ratio for fatty acids. They suggested that, because of their low plasma cholesterol, British lifelong vegans and vegetarians might show reductions of 57% and 24% respectively in coronary heart disease, compared with meat-eaters.

A 1990 report[32] of the ongoing Oxford Vegetarian Study revealed plasma total cholesterol levels for the dietary groups as follows: 4.92mmol/l (vegans), 5.34mmol/l (vegetarians), 5.65mmol/l (fish-eaters) and 5.93mmol/l (meat-eaters). In particular, the vegans had the lowest levels of LDL-cholesterol. A 1994 publication[35] from the same study found that non-meat eaters (including lacto-ovo-vegetarians, vegans and fish-but-not-meat eaters) experienced only about three-quarters the heart disease deaths of matched, 'health-conscious' meat-eaters — even after accounting for differences in weight, smoking habits and socio-economic status. Although statistical analysis indicated that the result was not definite enough to draw firm conclusions from, it is in line with other findings of reduced risk of death from heart disease among vegetarians.

An earlier American investigation[10] also found that blood levels of VLDL-cholesterol and LDL-cholesterol in vegan men and women were lower than in omnivore men and women of similar age, and that they had a lower LDL/HDL ratio, which suggests a low risk of atherosclerosis. A later study in the US[15] looked at the effects of fat from dairy products on the plasma lipoprotein levels of strict macrobiotics (virtually vegans) and vegetarians. Dairy products were the main source of dietary saturated fat and cholesterol for the vegetarians, whose LDL-cholesterol was 24% higher than in the almost-vegan macrobiotics. HDL-cholesterol did not seem to be related to any dietary component, but analysis within and among the vegetarians suggested that fatty dairy products raise plasma LDL-cholesterol on a percentage basis about three times more than they raise the beneficial HDL-cholesterol.

American Seventh Day Adventists who were strict vegans had very low levels of total cholesterol in their bloodstream (average 3.4 mmol/l)[27]. They ate less total fat than matched omnivores (31% versus 38% of dietary energy), especially less saturated and monounsaturated fat; and also less protein and considerably more fibre. The authors of this study, published in 1991, commented that the vegans' diets were characterized by an increased consumption of nuts and nut butters, citrus fruits, soya milk and leafy green vegetables. They concluded that, being low in saturated fat and high in fibre, vegan diets can help people achieve and maintain healthy levels of fats in their bloodstream, which reduces their risk of heart disease.

A fatty diet and high intakes of saturated fats in particular are risk factors for coronary heart disease, causing damaging changes in levels of cholesterols in the blood. Numerous studies show that vegans eat the least total fat and saturated fat of all dietary groups, have a minimal dietary intake of cholesterol, and have the lowest levels of LDL-cholesterol as well as the lowest LDL/HDL-cholesterol ratio in their bloodstream. Their risk of coronary heart disease is thus likely to be much smaller than that of meat-eaters or even vegetarians.

FATS AND CANCER

It is generally accepted that a third of all **cancer** deaths may be attributed to dietary causes, although the development of any cancer is affected by a number of interacting factors. While all the connections between diet and cancer are not yet understood, there is some evidence that **cancers of the breast**[16,34], **womb**[28], **prostate**[23,30,33,36], **pancreas**[37] and **bowel**[17,24,25] **are linked with the consumption of meat, and animal fat and protein.**

A study of 620 women in Singapore, published in 1991, showed that those with more polyunsaturated fats (PUFAs) in their diets were less likely to develop breast cancer[34]. Interestingly, women who had habitually eaten more beta-carotene and more soya products were also less at risk of breast cancer, while those who ate a lot of red meat were more at risk.

Obesity and high-fat diets have been associated with **cancer of the womb**. Research in China revealed that women eating the most animal fat and animal protein had more than three times the risk of developing womb cancer[28]. Meat, eggs and fish were identified as food groups which increased cancer risk.

Links between a diet rich in animal fat and **prostate cancer** have also been found[23] by international correlation studies, as well as case-control and prospective studies. In 1993, American researchers studying nearly 48,000 men found that those who ate red meat five or more times a week were 2.6 times more likely to suffer prostate cancer than those who ate it only once a week[36]. In addition, the consumption of animal fat — but not vegetable fat — was linked with prostate cancer. A prospective study of 14,000 American Seventh Day Adventist men indicated that a decreased risk of prostate cancer was associated with increasing consumption of beans, peas, lentils, tomatoes, raisins, dates and other dried fruit, but not with avoidance of animal products *per se*[33]. It has been proposed that levels of the hormone testosterone in the bloodstream may affect the risk of men developing prostate cancer, and some studies have suggested that vegetarian diets can lower testosterone. However, a comparison of testosterone levels in the bloodstreams of vegan and omnivore men found no significant difference[30].

A cohort study of 17,500 men in the USA whose health was monitored for 20 years showed that, after adjustment for other risk factors such as smoking and alcohol consumption, those who ate the most meat were three times more likely to develop **cancer of the pancreas** than those with a low meat consumption[37].

An association between meat and animal fat intakes and **bowel cancer** has been demonstrated in international population studies, as well as in case-control and cohort studies. The largest and best-designed investigation to date confirmed that the risk of bowel cancer was greater among women who ate more meat and saturated fat[24]. Similar results have been found for men, with saturated fats increasing the risk of bowel cancer, and high fibre intakes decreasing the risk[25].

In a 1987 laboratory investigation[18], 12 male volunteers followed three experimental diets for 20-day periods while housed in a metabolic ward. While on a vegan diet the concentrations of bile acids and cholesterol in their faeces — factors both known to be positively linked with colorectal cancer — were lowest, while on a meat diet with its high levels of fat and low amounts of fibre, these potential risk factors were highest. Similar results were found in 1992, when 18 volunteers followed a raw-food vegan diet for a month, and a conventional omnivore diet for another month[26]. The results indicated that the raw-food vegan diet decreased bacterial enzymes and toxic substances in the gut, which could thereby decrease the risk of bowel cancer. Overall, there is good evidence for a protective effect of vegan diets against bowel cancer.

During 1989, several UK newspapers carried headlines linking low levels of blood cholesterol with cancer. These arose from a report in the *British Medical Journal*[38] that men who had developed lung cancer had lower blood cholesterol levels; it suggested that low blood cholesterol could increase the risk of cancer. Other scientists claimed that the Scottish research was flawed, and pointed out that much larger studies had not found such a link[39]. One theory to explain this contradictory finding is that a drop in blood cholesterol occurs after cancer develops, and is thus a consequence of cancer and not a cause. Although it's not yet clear what the explanation is, the result is outweighed by other studies.

FATS — SUMMARY

Numerous expert committees have recommended a reduced consumption of total fat by the general population. Only vegan diets generally comply with current guidelines that fat should not contribute more than 35% of the total energy intake of adults and older children.

Saturated fats contribute to high levels of cholesterol in the blood, a risk factor for atherosclerosis and heart disease, while polyunsaturated fats (PUFAs) have the opposite effect. Vegan diets, containing no meat and dairy fats, are low in saturated fatty acids and high in beneficial PUFAs. Vegans consume considerably more of the essential PUFA linoleic acid than do omnivores, and approximately similar levels of the other essential PUFA, alpha-linolenic acid.

Eicosapentaenoic acid (EPA) and docosahexaenoic acid (DHA), two non-essential PUFAs, do not occur in vegan diets. The human body can convert alpha-linolenic acid into EPA and DHA but, even so, some of the body tissues of vegans contain less DHA and EPA than those of other dietary groups. The consequences of this difference, if any, are not known.

Similarly, breast milks of vegans, vegetarians and omnivores contain differing proportions of various polyunsaturated fatty acids, and these differences are reflected in some body tissues of infants. It is not yet known what, if any, effect these variations may have on the growth and development of infants.

Monounsaturated fats occur in similar amounts in vegan and omnivore diets. Very small amounts of cholesterol may occur in vegan diets, but even so many studies over-estimate the amounts. This is because computer programs used to analyze diet diaries assume that cakes, biscuits and similar products are made with eggs and dairy products.

The blood of vegans has lower total cholesterol and LDL-cholesterol levels than are found in any other dietary group, and as a result they are likely to be less susceptible to coronary heart disease. Certain cancers are also associated with high-fat diets, in some cases particularly with animal fats.

REFERENCES

1 Committee on Medical Aspects of Food Policy (1994). *Nutritional Aspects of Cardiovascular Disease*. Reports on Health & Social Subjects no. 46. London: HMSO.

2 National Advisory Committee on Nutrition Education (1983). *Proposals for Nutritional Guidelines for Health Education in Britain*. London: Health Education Council.

3 Royal College of Physicians and British Cardiac Society (1976). Prevention of coronary heart disease. *J. Roy. Coll. Phys.* 10:213–275.

4 WHO Expert Committee (1982). Prevention of coronary heart disease. *WHO Technical Report Series 678*. Geneva: WHO.

5 Abdulla, M., Andersson, I., Asp, N-G., Berthelsen, K., Birkhed, D., Dencker, I., Johansson, C-G., Jägerstad, M., Kolar, K., Nair, B.M., Nilsson-Ehle, P., Nordén, Å., Rassner, S., Åkesson, B. & Öckerman, P-A. (1981). Nutrient intake and health status of vegans. Chemical analyses of diets using the duplicate portion sampling technique. *Am. J. Clin. Nutr.* 34:2464–2477.

6 Roshanai, F. & Sanders, T.A.B. (1984). Assessment of fatty acid intakes in vegans and omnivores. *Hum. Nutr.: Appl. Nutr.* 38A:345–354.

7 Carlson, E., Kipps, M., Lockie, A. & Thomson, J. (1985). A comparative evaluation of vegan, vegetarian and omnivore diets. *J. Plant Foods* 6:89–100.

8 Rana, S.K. & Sanders, T.A.B. (1986). Taurine concentrations in the diet, plasma, urine and breast milk of vegans compared with omnivores. *Br. J. Nutr.* 56:17–27.

9 Sanders, T.A.B. & Key, T.J.A. (1987). Blood pressure, plasma renin activity and aldosterone concentrations in vegans and omnivore controls. *Hum. Nutr.: Appl. Nutr.* 41A:204–211.

10 Burslem, J., Schonfeld, G., Howald, M.A., Weidman, S.W. & Miller, J.P. (1978). Plasma apoprotein and lipoprotein lipid levels in vegetarians. *Metabolism* 27:711–719.

11 British Medical Association Board of Science and Education (1986). *Diet, Nutrition and Health*. London: BMA.

12 Sanders, T.A.B., Ellis, F.R. & Dickerson, J.W.T. (1978). Studies of vegans: the fatty acid composition of plasma choline phosphoglycerides, erythrocytes, adipose tissue, and breast milk, and some indicators of susceptibility to ischemic heart disease in vegans and omnivore controls. *Am. J. Clin. Nutr.* 31:805–813.

13 Melchert, H.-U., Limsathayourat, N., Mihajlovic, H. & Eichberg, J. (1987). Fatty acid patterns in triglycerides, diglycerides, free fatty acids, cholesteryl esters and phosphatidyl choline in serum from vegetarians and non-vegetarians. *Atherosclerosis* 65:159–166.

14 Thorogood, M., Carter, R., Benfield, L., McPherson, K. & Mann, J.I. (1987). Plasma lipids and lipoproteins in groups with different dietary practices within Britain. *Br. Med. J.* 295:351–353.

15 Sacks, F.M., Ornish, D., Rosner, B., McLanahan, S., Castelli, W.P. & Kass, E.H. (1985). Plasma lipoprotein levels in vegetarians: the effect of ingestion of fats from dairy products. *J. Am. Med. Ass.* 254:1337–1341.

16 de Waard, F. (1986). Dietary fat and mammary cancer. *Nutr. & Cancer* 8:5–8.

17 Willett, W. (1989). The search for the causes of breast and colon cancer. *Nature* 338:389–394.

18 van Faassen, A., Bol, J., van Dokkum, W., Pikaar, N.A., Ockhuizen, T. & Hermus, R.J.J. (1987). Bile acids, neutral steroids, and bacteria in feces as affected by a mixed, a lacto-vegetarian, and a vegan diet. *Am. J. Clin. Nutr.* 46:962–967.

19 Ministry of Agriculture, Fisheries and Food (1992). *National Food Survey: Household Food Consumption and Expenditure 1991*. London: HMSO.

20 Gregory, J., Foster, K., Tyler, H. & Wiseman, M. (1990). *The Dietary and Nutritional Survey of British Adults*. London: HMSO.

21 Sanders, T.A.B. & Reddy, S. (1992). The influence of a vegetarian diet on the fatty acid composition of human milk and the essential fatty acid status of the infant. *J. Pediatr.* 120:S71–77.

22 Cocchi, M., Noble, R.C., Fallowfield, H., Speake, B. & Turchetto, E. (1993). The significance of n-3 fatty acids in fetal and neonatal development and some alternative

sources. *Proc. Nutr. Soc.* 52:224A

23 Department of Health (1991). *Dietary Reference Values for Food Energy and Nutrients for the United Kingdom.* Reports on Health & Social Subjects no. 41. London: HMSO.

24 Willett, W.C., Stampfer, M.J., Colditz, G.A., Rosner, B.A. & Speizer, F.E. (1990). Relation of meat, fat and fibre intake to the risk of colon cancer in a prospective study among women. *New Engl. J. Med.* 323:1664–1672.

25 Giovannucci, E., Meir, J., Colditz, G.A., Rimm, E.B. & Willett, W.C. (1990). Relation of diet to the risk of colorectal adenoma in men. *Am. J. Epidemiol.* 132:783.

26 Ling, W.H. & Hanninen, O. (1992). Shifting from a conventional diet to an uncooked vegan diet reversibly alters fecal hydrolytic activites in humans. *J. Nutr.* 122:924–930.

27 Resnicow, K., Barone, J., Engle, A., Miller, S., Haley, N.J., Fleming, D. & Wynder, E. (1991). Diet and serum lipids in vegan vegetarians: a model for risk reduction. *J. Am. Diet. Assn.* 91:447–453.

28 Xiao, O.S., Wei, Z., Potischman, N., Brinton, L.A., Hatch, M.C., Gao, Y.T. & Fraumeni, J.F. (1993). A population-based case-control study of dietary factors and endometrial cancer in Shanghai, Peoples Republic of China. *Am. J. Epidemiol.* 137:155–165.

29 Draper, A., Lewis, J., Malhotra, N. & Wheeler, E. (1993). The energy and nutrient intakes of different types of vegetarian: a case for supplements? *Br. J. Nutr.* 69:3–19.

30 Key, T.J.A., Roe, L., Thorogood, M., Moore, J.W., Clark, G.M.G. & Wang, D.Y. (1990). Testosterone, sex hormone-binding globulin, calculated free testosterone, and oestradiol in male vegans and omnivores. *Br. J. Nutr.* 64:111–119.

31 Sanders, T.A. & Roshanai, F. (1992). Platelet phospholipid fatty acid composition and function in vegans compared with age-and sex-matched omnivore controls. *Eur. J. Clin. Nutr.* 46:823–831.

32 Thorogood, M., Roe, L., McPherson, K. & Mann, J. (1990). Dietary intake and plasma lipid levels: lessons from a study of the diet of health conscious groups. *Br. Med. J.* 300:1297–1301.

33 Mills, P.K., Beeson, W.L., Phillips, R.L. & Fraser, G.E. (1989). Cohort study of diet, lifestyle, and prostate cancer in Adventist men. *Cancer* 64:598–604.

34 Lee, H.P., Gourley, L., Duffy, S.W., Estève, J., Lee, J. & Day, N.E. (1991). Dietary effects on breast cancer risk in Singapore. *Lancet* 337:1197–1200.

35 Thorogood, M., Mann, J., Appleby, P. & McPherson, K. (1994). Risk of death from cancer and ischaemic heart disease in meat and non-meat eaters. *Br. Med. J.* 308:1667–1670.

36 Giovannucci, E., Rimm, E.B., Colditz, G.A., Stampfer, M.J., Ascherio, A., Chute, C.C. & Willett, W.C. (1993). A prospective study of dietary fat and risk of prostate cancer. *J. Nat. Cancer Inst.* 85:1571–1579.

37 Zheng, W. *et al* (1993). A cohort study of smoking, alcohol consumption and dietary factors for pancreatic cancer. *Cancer Causes & Control* 4:477–482.

38 Isles, C.G., Hole, D.J., Gillis, C.R., Hawthorne, V.M. & Lever, A.F. (1989). Plasma cholesterol, coronary heart disease, and cancer in the Renfrew and Paisley survey. *Br. Med. J.* 298:920–924.

39 Vines, G. & Kingman, S. (1989). Angry response to low-fat link with cancer. *New Scientist*, 15 April, p17.

VITAMINS

The evidence for a protective effect of the antioxidant vitamins E and C is persuasive but not yet conclusive . . . We recommend a diet rich in vegetables and fruit, containing nuts and seeds, and with less saturated oils partly substituting for more saturated fats, which would increase intake of these nutrients and is conducive to general health.

The COMA Report on Nutritional Aspects of
Cardiovascular Disease, 1994[78]

Vitamins are nutrients required in relatively small amounts in the diet, but which cannot be made in the body in sufficient amounts. There are two main types: the fat-soluble vitamins A, D, E and K; and those soluble in water — the B-group vitamins and vitamin C.

The UK Department of Health has set dietary guidelines for nine vitamins, which are:

- Vitamin A
- Thiamin (B_1)
- Riboflavin (B_2)
- Niacin
- Vitamin B_6

- Vitamin B_{12}
- Folate
- Vitamin C
- Vitamin D

Also needed in the diet are four more vitamins, for which UK Reference Nutrient Intakes (RNIs) have not been set, but indications of safe levels have been given:

- Pantothenic acid
- Biotin

- Vitamin E
- Vitamin K

VITAMIN A (RETINOL AND BETA-CAROTENE)

Vitamin A or retinol is a fat-soluble vitamin found naturally only in animal foods such as liver, kidney, dairy produce and eggs. The carotenes, of which the most important is beta-carotene or pro-vitamin A, are found in orange-coloured and green leafy vegetables. In the body, beta-carotene is converted to vitamin A.

Beta-carotene in plant foods is the only natural source of vitamin A available to vegans, and is also one of the prime sources for omnivores. **Plant** foods rich in beta-carotene include carrots, dark green leafy vegetables such as spinach, parsley and watercress, sweet potatoes, dried apricots and mangoes. By law in Britain, vitamin A (as retinol or beta-carotene) is added to **margarine** which is a major source for the general population, and is also acceptable to vegans when the margarine contains no animal products.

Vitamin A is required for growth and normal development of tissues. It is essential for vision (especially in dim light), and is also necessary for healthy skin and surface tissues, especially those which secrete mucus. Beta-carotene is an antioxidant, able to inactivate 'free radicals' which can damage tissues. Free radicals are formed constantly in the body by natural metabolism, as well as by outside agents such as ozone, radiation, some drugs, alcohol and vehicle exhausts.

If free radicals are not controlled, they can damage the chromosomes, proteins (eg. in the lens of the eye, connective tissue, heart muscle and enzymes), and lipids (such as in cell membranes). There is also increasing evidence that free radicals play a substantial role in causing certain degenerative diseases, including cancer, cardiovascular disease and arthritis. At least 21 human studies have suggested that too little dietary beta-carotene may be linked with cancer, although in one rogue finding from a Finnish study, smokers who took beta-carotene supplements had more lung cancers than unsupplemented smokers[71]. The 1993 report of a European-wide case-control study demonstrated that men consuming more beta-carotene in their food had a reduced risk of heart attack[65].

The most obvious vitamin A deficiency symptom is dryness of the surface of the eyes, which can eventually lead to permanent eye damage. A high intake of retinol — the animal form of vitamin A — can be harmful, causing liver and bone damage, hair loss, double vision, vomiting and other problems. Excessive consumption by pregnant women of vitamin A, but not beta-carotene, has also been linked with an increased risk of birth defects.

Retinol and beta-carotene are measured together as retinol 'equivalents'. Thus 1 microgram (µg) of retinol equivalent is equal to either 1µg retinol or 6µg beta-carotene. The UK Department of Health[40] recommends Reference Nutrient Intakes (RNI) of 350µg retinol equivalents for infants, increasing with age to 600µg retinol equivalents for women and 700µg for men, and more for pregnant and nursing women (but not exceeding 3,300µg in the form of vitamin A itself). The RNI is the amount calculated to be adequate for 97% of people. The comparable recommendations of the US National Research Council[47] and the German authorities[51] are 1,000μg for men and 800μg for women.

Reports from the 1950s and '60s showed beta-carotene intake by vegans equalled or exceeded the recommended amounts[1–3]. A 1986 comparison of vegan and omnivorous diets[4] found that the former contained significantly fewer retinol equivalents than the omnivorous diet, while the following year[5], Tom Sanders and Tim Key found similar intakes in vegans and omnivores. Another British study[6] from the same decade found that vegans consumed nearly double the current RNI in the form of beta-carotene. Vegetarians (who obtain additional amounts from dairy produce and eggs) and wholefood omnivores consumed even more, while average non-wholefood omnivores only just exceeded the current RNI. Sixteen out of 18 lifelong vegan children in Britain had retinol equivalent intakes which met or exceeded their RNIs[66].

There have been no reports of vitamin A deficiency in vegans, who are likely to obtain plenty in the form of beta-carotene from plant foods.

THE B-GROUP VITAMINS

The chemical structure of each B vitamin is unique but, because they have several features in common, vitamins B_1, B_2, niacin, B_6, B_{12}, folate, pantothenic acid and biotin are usually considered as a group. Vitamin B_{12} is of particular significance to vegans, and so is discussed separately in a following section. The remaining B-group vitamins are water-soluble (and therefore some can be lost if cooking water is thrown away), tend to be found in the same foods and act as co-factors in various enzyme systems in the body.

VITAMIN B₁ (THIAMIN)

Thiamin is widely available in both animal and plant foods. Rich sources include offal, pork, milk and eggs, as well as **whole grains, wheatgerm, pulses, peanuts and potatoes** (*see Table 4.1, page 61*). Thiamin is found in the outer bran layer of wheat, so a wholefood diet containing grains provides plentiful amounts. When wheat is refined most of the thiamin is lost, and for this reason white flour is fortified with thiamin in many countries, including the UK. Cooking can also partly destroy the vitamin.

Thiamin is used by the body to release energy from carbohydrates, fats and alcohol. The more carbohydrate consumed, the more thiamin is required, and this can lead to deficiency if high levels of refined carbohydrates are eaten. Deficiency of thiamin causes palpitations and muscular weakness, and in severe cases beri-beri.

The UK Department of Health[40] recommends Reference Nutrient Intakes of 0.2–0.3mg thiamin daily for infants; 0.5–0.7mg for children; 0.7–1.1mg for teenagers, and 0.8–1mg for adults (pregnant or breast-feeding women need slightly more than the 0.8mg suggested for women). The American recommendations[47] for adults are greater, at 1.1mg for women and 1.5mg for men, and German values are in the same range[51].

Three analyses[4–6] indicate that the thiamin content of vegan diets is significantly higher than that of omnivore diets; and a 1993 report[41] measured the intake of vegans as 1.58–2.14mg daily when the contribution from supplements was included. Fifty-four per cent of vegans in this study sometimes used dietary supplements. Analysis of the diets of 18 lifelong vegan children aged 5.8–12.8 years showed that they all consumed their RNIs for thiamin[66].

Several reports show that vegans easily meet or exceed both US and UK recommendations for thiamin.

VITAMIN B₂ (RIBOFLAVIN)

Riboflavin is widely available in animal foods such as liver, kidney, dairy products and eggs, and in plant foods such as **yeast extracts, wheatgerm, whole grains and wholemeal bread, nuts, pulses, avocados and mushrooms** (see *Table 4.1*, *opposite*). Cooking can destroy 30%–40% of the riboflavin in vegetables.

Riboflavin is needed by the body to release energy from food, and the daily Reference Nutrient Intakes proposed by the UK Department of Health[40] are 0.4 mg a day for infants, 0.6–1mg/day for children, and 1.1–1.3mg/day for teenagers and adults (plus an additional 0.3–0.5mg for pregnant or nursing women). US recommendations[47] are slightly higher at 1.3–1.8mg for adults, broadly similar to the German recommendations[51].

A 1979 report[8] indicated that vegan subjects had a mean daily intake of 1.33mg riboflavin, compared to 2.45mg in omnivore subjects. There was less riboflavin in breast milk from vegan subjects, but levels were similar to those reported for pooled milk samples from omnivores in five different areas in the UK. An assessment of 23 British vegan pre-school children published in 1981 found that their mean intake of riboflavin exceeded the present Reference Nutrient Intakes of 0.6–0.8mg[9]. In a follow-up study of

TABLE 4.1

THIAMIN AND RIBOFLAVIN CONTENT OF SOME PLANT FOODS

	mg thiamin		mg riboflavin	
	per 100g food	per average portion	per 100g food	per average portion
Peas, fresh, boiled	0.7	**0.8** (4oz)	0.03	0.03 (4oz)
Oatmeal	0.9	**0.5** (2oz)	0.1	0.05 (2oz)
Wheatgerm	2.0	**0.3** (0.5oz)	0.7	**0.1** (0.5oz)
Soya flour	0.9	**0.3** (1oz)	0.3	**0.1** (1oz)
Peanuts, shelled	1.1	**0.3** (1oz)	0.1	0.03 (1oz)
Potatoes, boiled	0.2	**0.3** (6oz)	0.02	0.03 (6oz)
Marmite (yeast extract)	3.1	0.2 (0.2oz)	11.0	**0.6** (0.2oz)
Mushrooms	0.1	0.1 (3oz)	0.3	**0.3** (3oz)
Avocado, flesh only	0.1	0.1 (3oz)	0.2	**0.2** (3oz)
Almonds, shelled	0.2	0.1 (1oz)	0.8	**0.2** (1oz)
Soya beans, boiled	0.1	0.1 (3oz)	0.1	**0.1** (3oz)
Wholemeal bread	0.3	0.2 (2oz)	0.1	0.05 (2oz)
White bread (fortified)	0.2	0.1 (2oz)	0.1	0.03 (2oz)
Hazelnuts, shelled	0.4	0.1 (1oz)	0.2	0.05 (1oz)

100g = 3.5oz. Values taken from Holland *et al* [7].

1991 UK Reference Nutrient Intakes for adults: 0.8–1.1mg/day thiamin; 1.1–1.3mg/day riboflavin.

( ) = average portion

Average food portions providing substantial amounts of vitamin are shown in bold type.

the children aged 5.8 to 12.8 years, 12 out of 18 met or exceeded their RNIs, and all exceeded the Lower Reference Nutrient Intake[66].

Two dietary analyses[4,5] in the late 1980s showed vegan and omnivore subjects consuming the same amounts of riboflavin, between 1.7 and 1.9mg daily. Another study, published in 1985[6], indicated that the intake of vegan subjects was lower than that of vegetarians and omnivores, although still meeting the current RNI. Alizon Draper and colleagues measured an average intake by British vegans of 0.98mg riboflavin for women, and 1.37mg for men, compared to higher amounts for lacto-ovo-vegetarians and fish-eaters[41]. The vegan women's intake was below the UK RNI, but above the Estimated Average Requirement, while the vegan men's intake equalled the RNI.

Published reports suggest that vegan diets may contain less riboflavin than vegetarian and omnivore diets, although most British vegans consume the recommended amounts. However, the riboflavin intakes of some women and some children may be slightly lower. There have been no reports of riboflavin deficiency in vegans.

NIACIN (NICOTINIC ACID AND NICOTINAMIDE)

Nicotinic acid and nicotinamide are known collectively as niacin. Most of the nicotinic acid in grains is in a bound form which is largely unavailable for use by the body. However the amino acid tryptophan, found in protein foods, is converted to nicotinic acid in the body. Sixty milligrams of tryptophan is considered equivalent to 1mg niacin. The total amount of niacin 'equivalents' in a diet is thus the sum of milligrams of niacin, plus $\frac{1}{60}$ x milligrams of tryptophan.

Rich food sources of niacin include meat, fish, cheese and eggs. Of foods acceptable to vegans, average portions of **yeast extract, whole grains, wheat bran and wholemeal bread, some pulses, peanuts and some vegetables** contain substantial amounts (*see Table 4.2, page 64*). Cooking destroys 30%–40% of the niacin in vegetables.

Niacin, like thiamin and riboflavin, is needed by the body to release energy from food, and deficiency causes pellagra, characterized by muscular weakness, dermatitis and, in severe cases, digestive and mental disorders. The British Reference Nutrient Intakes[40] are 12–18mg niacin 'equivalents' per day for adults and children aged 7 years and over, and 3–11mg a day for children up to 6 years old. The US[47] and German[51] RDAs are similar.

Dietary analyses of the 1980s[4,5] indicated that niacin intake by vegans is not significantly different from that of omnivores, while a comparative study[6] showed that subjects in four dietary groups all met recommended amounts, with vegans, vegetarians and non-wholefood omnivores eating nearly double official requirements, and wholefood omnivores consuming smaller, but still adequate amounts. Lifelong vegan children in Britain, at ages 5.8–12.8 years, all consumed their RNIs for niacin[66].

A 1993 study[41] comparing intakes among British vegans, lacto-ovo-vegetarians and fish-eaters again demonstrated that all groups consumed similar amounts of niacin, which was two to three times the recommended level when the contribution of supplements, used by about half of each group, was included.

Several reports have shown that vegans consume plentiful amounts of niacin.

VITAMIN B₆ (PYRIDOXAL, PYRIDOXINE, PYRIDOXAMINE)

Vitamin B_6 is a mixture of related substances called pyridoxal, pyridoxine and pyridoxamine. It is found widely in the same sorts of foods as the other B-group vitamins: meat, liver, fish and eggs, as well as in plant foods such as whole grains, wheatgerm and wholemeal flour, peanuts, avocados and nuts. Processed foods such as fats, oils and sugar contain none. Even though cooking destroys up to 40% of the vitamin, and some of the B_6 in vegetables is not available to the body, potatoes and other vegetables are the main source of the vitamin for the general population because they are eaten frequently in substantial portions. Some vitamin B_6 is made by intestinal bacteria, and some of this is absorbed by the body. Taking too much of the vitamin can be harmful; deficiency is very rare.

In the body, vitamin B_6 is essential for the metabolism of amino acids (from protein), and so our requirements are related to our protein intake — those who eat more protein need more of this vitamin.

The UK Department of Health has set Reference Nutrient Intakes of 1–1.5mg/day for adults and children over the age of 7 years, and 0.2–0.9mg/day for infants and younger children[40]. These recommendations assume a protein intake equivalent to 15% of total Calories consumed. Since vegans tend to eat slightly less protein than this (about 11% of energy intake), their requirement for vitamin B_6 would be slightly less. The US RDAs[47], set in 1989, are 1.6mg a day for women, and 2mg for men, while German recommendations are fractionally higher[51].

Some researchers have looked at amounts of this vitamin in vegan diets. One analysis published in 1986 recorded a daily vitamin B_6 intake of 1.9mg in vegan subjects compared to 1.5mg for omnivores[4]. Twelve American vegan men had a calculated average B_6 consumption of 2mg a day, equalling the US RDA[67]. A 1993 report[41] found that British vegans ate significantly more of the vitamin (3.25mg/day) than lacto-ovo-vegetarians (2.25mg/day) or fish-eaters (2.4 mg/day). British children who were lifelong vegans all consumed their RNIs for vitamin B$_6$[66].

Since most vegans have a moderate consumption of protein, **their need for vitamin B$_6$ will be easily met by these intakes, which equal or exceed recommended amounts.**

TABLE 4.2
NIACIN AND VITAMIN B$_6$ CONTENT OF SOME PLANT FOODS

	mg niacin equivalents		mg vitamin B$_6$	
	per 100g food	per average portion	per 100g food	per average portion
Wheat bran	29.6	**4.2** (0.5oz)	1.4	**0.2** (0.5oz)
Peanuts, shelled	13.8	**3.9** (1oz)	0.6	**0.2** (1oz)
Wholemeal flour	5.7	**3.3** (2oz)	0.5	**0.3** (2oz)
Mushrooms, raw	3.2	**2.7** (3oz)	0.2	**0.2** (3oz)
Wholemeal bread	4.1	**2.3** (2oz)	0.1	0.1 (2oz)
Marmite (yeast extract)	58.0	**2.3** (0.2oz)	1.3	0.1 (0.2oz)
Peas, fresh, boiled	1.8	**2.1** (4oz)	0.1	0.1 (4oz)
Potatoes, boiled	0.5	0.8 (6oz)	0.3	**0.6** (6oz)
Wheatgerm	4.5	0.6 (0.5oz)	3.3	**0.5** (0.5oz)
Avocado, flesh only	1.1	0.9 (3oz)	0.4	**0.3** (3oz)
Soya beans, boiled	0.5	0.4 (3oz)	0.2	**0.2** (3oz)
Hazelnuts, shelled	1.1	0.3 (1oz)	0.6	**0.2** (1oz)
Soya flour	2.2	0.6 (1oz)	0.5	0.1 (1oz)
Apricots, dried	2.3	1.3 (2oz)	0.1	0.1 (2oz)
Cashews, shelled & roasted	1.3	0.4 (1oz)	0.4	0.1 (1oz)
Sesame seeds or tahini	5.0	0.7 (0.5oz)	0.8	0.1 (0.5oz)

100g = 3.5oz. Values taken from Holland *et al* [7].

1991 UK Reference Nutrient Intakes (adults): 12–18mg niacin equivalents per day; 1–1.5mg vitamin B$_6$ per day.

( ) = average portion

Substantial amounts of vitamin provided *per average portion* of food are shown in bold type.

FOLATE (FOLIC ACID, FOLACIN)

Folate is a collective term for a number of related substances which occur in small amounts in many foods. The richest sources are liver and, for vegans, average portions of **green leafy vegetables, yeast extracts, whole wheat, wheatgerm, wheat bran, nuts and beans** contain useful amounts. Most fruits, meat and dairy produce contain little, and heating food destroys 20%–50% of its folate content. Folate is required for the metabolism of certain amino acids and, in conjunction with vitamin B_{12}, for rapidly dividing cells such as those in the bone marrow which form red blood cells. A deficiency of folate leads to megaloblastic anaemia.

The UK Department of Health[40] now estimates that a daily Reference Nutrient Intake of 200µg folate is enough, or more than enough, for virtually all teenagers and adults. The exceptions are pregnant (300µg daily) and breast-feeding women (260µg daily), who need more folate to protect their unborn children from neural tube defects such as spina bifida. They, and women hoping to conceive, should also be aware of official advice to take folate supplements in addition (*see Vegan Mothers and Children*). Infants and children are recommended to eat between 50 and 150µg daily, depending on age. The US official recommendation[47] is 200µg for men, 180µg for women; this rises to 400µg during pregnancy and 260–290µg during breast feeding. German RDAs, by comparison, are 150µg for women, and 300µg for men[51].

Dietary analyses conducted in the 1980s[4,5] showed the average intake of vegan subjects to be about 300µg, compared with nearer 200µg for omnivores. Another British study[61] demonstrated higher intakes of folate in vegans and vegetarians compared with omnivores. Swedish vegans were reported to consume greater amounts (averaging 545µg)[11], and a 1993 report[41] also confirmed higher intakes among vegans, with a significant difference between men and women (448µg and 298µg respectively). Blood levels of folate measured in 36 Israeli vegans of 5–35 years' standing were higher, at an average 14.4ng/ml, than those of omnivore subjects (9.9ng/ml)[56].

A study of British vegan pre-school children showed their intake of folate to be 161µg daily, well in excess of Reference Nutrient Intakes for their age groups[9]. A follow-up study, conducted when the children were aged 5.8–12.8 years, confirmed that they all met or exceeded their RNIs[66]. Bread, other grain products, and pulses were the most significant sources of folate in these children's diets.

TABLE 4.3
FOLATE CONTENT OF SOME PLANT FOODS

	microgms of folate	
	per 100g food	per average portion of food
Black eyed beans, boiled	210	180 (3oz)
Asparagus, boiled	155	177 (4oz)
Brussels sprouts, boiled	110	126 (4oz)
Soya flour	378	108 (1oz)
Kale, boiled	86	98 (4oz)
Spring greens, boiled	66	75 (4oz)
Marmite (yeast extract)	1010	52 (0.2oz)
Wheatgerm	331	47 (0.5oz)
Soya beans, boiled	54	46 (3oz)
Chick peas, boiled	54	46 (3oz)
Wheat bran	260	37 (0.5oz)
Peanuts, shelled	110	31 (1oz)
Hazelnuts, shelled	72	21 (1oz)

100g = 3.5oz.   ( ) = average portion

Values taken from Holland *et al* [7].

UK Reference Nutrient Intake: 200µg folate for teenagers and most adults;
300µg during pregnancy;
260µg during breast feeding.

Foods providing substantial amounts of folate *per average portion* are near the top of the list.

Many of these reports based their estimates of nutrient intake on standard food tables, but if the values for folate listed in these were derived from bacterial assays then they may not be entirely accurate. A modern method of measuring folate, called HPLC, gives more reliable results.

Folate is generally abundant in vegan diets, probably at higher levels than in omnivore diets.

PANTOTHENIC ACID AND BIOTIN

Pantothenic acid is found widely both in animal products and in **whole grains and pulses**, and is used by the body to release energy from fat and carbohydrate. Dietary deficiency of this vitamin is unlikely because it is widespread in food, but experimentally-produced symptoms in volunteers included fatigue, headache, dizziness, muscle weakness and digestive disturbances.

In Britain, the average consumption of pantothenic acid is 6.1mg a day for men, and 4.4mg for women. The UK Department of Health calculates that intakes of 3–7mg a day should be adequate, as cases of deficiency have not been recorded[40]. The US National Research Council, in the absence of precise information, has also not set an RDA but assumes a safe daily intake to be 4–7mg[47].

Biotin is a widely available vitamin, the richest food sources being offal, milk and egg yolk. Plant sources include **whole grains, fruits, vegetables and soya flour**. Biotin is **also made by bacteria in the intestine**, and some of this may be absorbed for use by the body. The vitamin is required only in very small amounts for the metabolism of fat and protein. The US-recommended safe intake for all ages and sexes was reduced to 30–100µg per day in 1989[47]. In the UK, similarly, there is no recommended optimal consumption, but the Department of Health[40] estimates that biotin intakes between 10 and 200µg a day are safe and adequate. Biotin deficiency is very rare; symptoms include scaly dermatitis, hair loss, nausea, loss of appetite, depression and hallucinations.

One 1986 study[4] found slightly less biotin in the diet of vegan subjects than in that of omnivores (19µg compared to 24µg), although both values were within current UK recommendations. A 1989 comparison of biotin levels in the blood and urine of American vegans, vegetarians and omnivores revealed that, for both adults and children, more biotin was excreted in the urine by vegans and vegetarians than by omnivores[38]. Vegan adults and children also had the highest average levels of biotin in the blood, although the difference was not statistically significant among the children. Partly because of a belief that biotin from plant sources may be less well absorbed by the body, the scientists were surprised to find this evidence that the biotin status of vegans was no worse and, indeed, better than that of omnivores.

Deficiencies of pantothenic acid and biotin are extremely rare in the general popuation, and have never been recorded among vegans.

VITAMIN B$_{12}$ (COBALAMINS)

The term vitamin B$_{12}$ encompasses a group of related substances called cobalamins, including hydroxocobalamin, adenosylcobalamin, methylcobalamin and cyanocobalamin. The vitamin is of special relevance to vegans, because it is commonly but inaccurately believed that animal foods are the only source. In fact, active B$_{12}$ is thought to be unique among vitamins in being made only by bacteria. The B$_{12}$ found in meat (especially offal), eggs and dairy milk derives from the activity of bacteria living within the animals. Prolonged cooking, including the boiling of cow's milk, destroys B$_{12}$.

To be absorbed effectively from food, B$_{12}$ relies on a number of 'shuttle molecules' to carry it through the body. The vitamin combines with the first 'shuttle' in the saliva during chewing. Then, it has to combine with a protein called intrinsic factor, which is produced in the stomach. The vitamin links up to intrinsic factor, which ferries it across the lining of the small intestine (terminal ileum) into the bloodstream. There, it hooks onto another special protein which carries it to all the tissues of the body.

The vitamin is needed, with folate (*see* **Folate**, *page 65*), by rapidly dividing cells such as those in the bone marrow which form the blood. Deficiency, which is rare, may lead to abnormally enlarged red blood cells which characterize megaloblastic anaemia. Vitamin B$_{12}$ is also crucial for a healthy nervous system, and a chronic lack can eventually cause neurological symptoms. In infants these include lethargy and developmental regression or retardation. In adults, early symptoms include sore tongue, weakness, tingling and numbness of fingers and toes, progressing to irreversible degeneration of the spinal cord, sometimes with abdominal pain and vomiting. Folate, a B vitamin which is plentiful in vegan diets, can protect against the anaemia of B$_{12}$ deficiency but not against the neurological degeneration.

Most cases of B$_{12}$ deficiency occur in the general population and are due to a lack of intrinsic factor, without which little of the vitamin can be absorbed. This type of deficiency leads to pernicious anaemia; causes include disorders of the small bowel, the effects of some drugs, smoking and alcohol, shrinkage of stomach tissues (atrophy) due to ageing, and some parasitic infections. Pernicious anaemia occurs in nearly 1% of the general population over the age of 60 years.

DAILY REQUIREMENT OF B$_{12}$

The UK Reference Nutrient Intakes for vitamin B$_{12}$ are 1.2–1.5 micrograms (µg) daily for teenagers and adults, and 2µg for breast-feeding women[40]. The adult recommendation of 1.5µg daily is intended to include extra to provide sufficient body stores to withstand a period of zero intake. Recommendations for infants are 0.3–0.4µg; and for children aged 1–10 years, the RNIs start at 0.5µg and increase to 1µg. Official recommendations have decreased in recent years, the body's needs having been previously over-estimated. Indeed, the Department of Health recognizes that some people have lower than average requirements for B_{12}, and for these individuals 1µg a day would suffice. A whole lifetime's requirement of B_{12} adds up to a 40-milligram speck of red crystals — about one-seventh the size of an average tablet of aspirin!

The World Health Organization's recommendation is 1µg daily for adults[42]. The US RDAs are higher at 0.7–1.4µg a day for children, 2µg for adolescents and adults, rising to 2.2µg during pregnancy and 2.6µg during breast feeding[47], although a leading American expert believes that 1µg of the vitamin daily will sustain most people[12]. Germany still retains a higher recommendation of 3µg daily[51]. Taking large doses of the vitamin by mouth is pointless, because 3µg is the most that can be absorbed at any one time.

Vitamin B_{12} is stored in the liver, which normally contains sufficient (2–5 milligrams) for a period of three to six years, even in the total absence of a food source. For this reason, although official recommendations are expressed as a daily amount, it is not actually necessary to consume the vitamin every day. A regular intake, at least three times a week, is adequate. Furthermore, since the main route of B_{12} loss is in bile, our bodies recycle the vitamin by re-absorbing it from the bile as it passes through the small intestine. The vitamin is also conserved in the kidneys. At times of lower dietary intake of B_{12}, its rate of absorption from food into the bloodstream goes up, thus maximizing available supplies[13]. These adaptations provide considerable leeway when dietary sources of B_{12} are scarce, and partly account for the fact that vegans of 20 years' standing and more, some with no obvious sources of dietary B_{12}, frequently show no signs of deficiency.

The UK recommendation of 1.5µg B_{12} a day for adults reflect several lines of research. Baker[14] studied five Southern Indian volunteers with B_{12}-deficiency anaemia by measuring their blood responses to different doses of the vitamin. He found that 0.07–0.25µg of dietary B_{12} a day was inadequate, but that 0.3–0.65µg was sufficient, and possibly more than sufficient, to return the subjects to normal health. He concluded that the minimum daily requirement is about 0.5µg B_{12}; and that 1µg would satisfy the needs of the vast majority of people and allow a wide safety margin.

Other evidence which has been used to assess dietary requirements of B_{12} include the absence of deficiency symptoms in Australian Seventh Day Adventist vegetarians, whose daily intake was estimated at 0.26µg[43], and in Swedish vegans whose daily B_{12} consumption was estimated to be 0.3–0.4µg[11]. Furthermore, patients with pernicious anaemia, who cannot absorb the vitamin from their food, recover after intravenous injections of as little as 0.1–0.2µg a day[44].

Measurement of the B_{12} content of various foods is complicated by the very tiny amounts involved, which are not easy to measure accurately; by the susceptibility of the vitamin to deterioration on cooking and storage; and, perhaps most importantly, by a confusion between active vitamin B_{12} and various related substances which resemble the vitamin but which the human body cannot use (*see below*, **Vitamin B_{12} look-alikes**).

Grains, nuts, pulses, vegetables and other natural plant foods do not contain the vitamin, unless they are contaminated with B_{12}-producing bacteria from the soil. Vegans using **lightly-washed home-grown** produce may obtain useful amounts of the vitamin in this way. In the 1950s a researcher investigated why a group of Iranian vegans did not develop B_{12} deficiency[54]. He discovered that they grew their vegetables in human manure, did not wash them carefully, and thus obtained the vitamin from bacterial contamination. Some drinking water may also contain B_{12}.

VITAMIN B_{12} LOOK-ALIKES

For many years it was thought that edible seaweeds (eg. nori, wakame and kombu), fermented soya foods (such as tempeh and miso), and a blue-green alga called spirulina, all contained high levels of B_{12}. However, the common methods of analysis, using bacterial growth as an indicator, actually measured a whole family of 'chemical look-alikes'. Not all of these are genuine, active vitamin which the human body can use[16]: the 'look-alikes', known as analogues, cannot play the role of vitamin B_{12} in the body.

A newer test, called a differential radioassay, is thought specifically to measure the forms of the vitamin which the human body can use, and re-analysis by this method indicates much lower levels of active B_{12} in many foods. For example **tempeh**, which was believed to contain several micrograms of B_{12} per 4-ounce portion, **was found on re-analysis to con-**

tain virtually no active vitamin[53,54].

Three brands of spirulina tablets when analyzed by differential radioassay had less than 20% of the B_{12} content predicted by the older bacterial test, the rest being B_{12} analogues[75]. The level of active vitamin in one brand, for example, was 1.1µg per six tablets rather than 6.4µg as measured by the older method. This would still be a useful intake of the vitamin, except that **there is a possibility that the presence of some analogues of B_{12} in spirulina may actually block the body's ability to use what genuine vitamin it contains.** When researchers took eight tablets of spirulina daily for 12 days, their blood levels of the vitamin did not rise. The content of active vitamin B_{12} found in spirulina tablets in that study was only 0–2% of the strength claimed on the label, 98%–100% being vitamin analogues[16].

Edible seaweeds such as nori and kombu, used extensively by macrobiotics, are now considered not to contain useful amounts of active vitamin. A 1987 report described how a macrobiotic mother, whose breast-fed baby had low levels of B_{12}, boosted the child's vitamin status to normal levels within two months apparently by increasing her consumption of seaweeds and fermented soya foods[15]. The published explanation was that her increased intake of B_{12} from these plant foods was passed to her infant in her breast milk. However, later it emerged[76] that the woman had also eaten fish and clam broth, which contain vitamin B_{12}. So it now seems that her consumption of clams, rather than seaweeds and fermented foods, was responsible for the improvement in her child's B_{12} levels.

The low B_{12} content of seaweeds and fermented soya foods has been confirmed by two studies which measured clinical signs of B_{12} status after consumption of these foods. One study involved 110 adults and 42 children who followed a largely vegetarian, macrobiotic diet. Levels of B_{12} in the bloodstream of those who ate seaweeds, tempeh or miso on a regular basis did not rise, suggesting that genuine vitamin B_{12} had not been available from these foods[69].

The second study[76] involved five vegan macrobiotic children with low blood levels of B_{12}, some of whom had slightly enlarged red blood cells (an early sign of B_{12}-deficiency anaemia). The children were given spirulina, nori, kombu or wakame seaweeds in an effort to improve their B_{12} status. After some months, although blood levels of the vitamin had apparently risen in the three children with the highest intake, the red blood cells in all five had enlarged further, indicating that the deficiency had continued unabated.

These two studies appear at first to contradict each other: in one, consuming seaweed did not boost bloodstream levels of B_{12}, while in the second it seemed to do so. Both investigations used the same technique for measuring B_{12}, so this could not account for the different findings. The most likely explanation relates to the investigational approaches used. In the first study, the adults and children ate their normal diet, to which they had adjusted over a long period of time, and which contained only small amounts of genuine vitamin, as well as modest amounts of B_{12} look-alikes. In the second study, children were deliberately fed larger amounts of seaweeds and, thus, more B_{12} analogues. High doses of B_{12} analogues can be absorbed into the bloodstream, but only when the genuine vitamin is not present in adequate amounts — the situation found in the second study. So, both the investigations support the theory that seaweeds are rich in non-active vitamin: the B_{12} analogues, which can be absorbed into the blood in some circumstances, but once there cannot perform the functions of the genuine vitamin.

The B_{12} story is still not fully unravelled, and more knowledge of the availability and function of different forms of the vitamin is urgently needed.

RELIABLE SOURCES OF B_{12}

Re-analysis of vitamin supplements using modern methods indicate that these are reliable sources of genuine vitamin. Fourteen out of fifteen American brands of multi-vitamin and mineral supplements were found to contain 88%–328% of the active B_{12} claimed on the label (the exception was one brand which had only 59%), as well as a small amount of inactive analogues[55].

There is active B_{12} in **nutritional yeast** as available in health food shops. However it derives from the B_{12}-enriched molasses medium on which the yeast is grown, and not from the yeast itself — which produces several inactive analogues but no true vitamin[54]. Nutritional yeast can be sprinkled on savoury dishes and has a slightly 'cheesy' taste.

Reliable sources of B_{12} also include products which are fortified with vitamin, such as yeast extracts, breakfast cereals, and some soya milks and margarines. Convenience meals and mixes using soya protein, such as vegetable 'sausages', vegetable burgers, soya minces and chunks, are sometimes fortified with B_{12} and this would be stated on the label.

TABLE 4.4

APPROXIMATE VITAMIN B_{12} CONTENT OF SOME VEGAN FOODS*

	micrograms of B_{12} per 100g or 100ml food
Yeast extracts (fortified)	Between 2–50
Margarines (fortified)	5.0
Granovita *Sojagen* (fortified, dried soya powder)	5.0
***Plamil* concentrated soya milk** (fortified)	3.2
***Plamil* ready-to-use soya milk** (fortified)	1.6
Breakfast cereals (fortified)	0.8
Unisoy *Gold* soya milk (fortified)	0.6
Farley's *Soya Formula* (fortified powdered infant formula)	1.1
Soya mince or chunks (fortified)	Label claims are probably reliable
Nutritional yeast (from enriched medium)	Label claims are probably reliable
Dried seaweeds:	
Nori	Uncertain (most seems to be B_{12} analogues)**
Spirulina	0–20% of label claim (most is B_{12} analogues)**
Wakame, kombu	Very little (most is B_{12} analogues)**
Soya bean tempeh	Very little (most is B_{12} analogues)**
Sourdough bread, shiitake mushrooms	Between 0.02–0.5 (of unconfirmed activity)
Soya sauce, miso, tofu, umeboshi plums	Between 0–0.02 (of unconfirmed activity)
Wines, ales, bitters, ciders	Unconfirmed
Sprouted pulses, sauerkraut	Unconfirmed

100g = 3.5oz.   UK Reference Nutrient Intake: 1.5µg a day for adults.

* Values are from various sources including references [15,54,55 & 68], and manufacturers' analyses.

** Unknown proportions of the vitamin in each food may be in the form of B_{12} analogues which are unavailable to the body, and may even block the body's ability to use what genuine vitamin is present in these foods.

All values are approximate because of variations in the accuracy of the methods of analysis used. The most reliable sources of the vitamin are shown in bold type. Brand names are shown in italics.

INTESTINAL BACTERIA AS A SOURCE OF B$_{12}$

There is some evidence that bacteria in our intestines make B$_{12}$ which our bodies can use. In a heroic experiment conducted in the 1950s, Sheila Callender collected the stools of vegan volunteers suffering from B$_{12}$ deficiency, made extracts of them and fed them to the volunteers[45]. This cured their deficiency. The experiment showed that bacteria in the intestines produce B$_{12}$, but that normally it is too low down the gut for it to be absorbed — otherwise the volunteers would not have become deficient in the first place. The fact that their deficiency was cured proved that adequate active B$_{12}$ is produced by intestinal bacteria, but generally in the colon where it cannot be absorbed, rather than higher up in the small intestine.

However some people certainly do have B$_{12}$-producing bacteria in their small intestine. In a study published in 1980, samples of bacteria were taken from the jejunum and ileum (small intestine) of healthy Southern Indian subjects, grown in the laboratory and analyzed for B$_{12}$-production using two microbiological assays, as well as chromatography[17]. A number of types of bacteria produced considerable amounts of B$_{12}$-like material in the test tube. Available intrinsic factor, necessary for the absorption of the vitamin, is known to be present in the small intestine; so if these bacteria also produce B$_{12}$ when inside the body, the vitamin could be absorbed.

Although only one out of every twenty B$_{12}$-like molecules found in human stools is the active form of the vitamin, this would be a more than adequate supply — about 5µg a day — if it were produced in the small intestine where it can be absorbed[54].

In some people, B$_{12}$-producing bacteria certainly exist in the small intestine where the vitamin manufactured can, in theory at least, be absorbed. Exactly what contribution this makes to the daily B$_{12}$ intake of vegans remains to be clarified.

VITAMIN B$_{12}$ — THE VEGAN EXPERIENCE

Because of a generally high level of awareness among vegans of the need for vitamin B$_{12}$, many individuals use fortified foods or supplements. Others make no special effort to incorporate these sources in their diets, and some vegan communities do not use supplements as a matter of policy. Therefore, generalizations about the B$_{12}$-content of vegan diets cannot easily be made.

KEY POINTS: VITAMIN B_{12}

• The UK recommendations for adults are an average daily intake of 1.5 micrograms of B_{12}, although for many people 1 microgram would be enough.

• The vitamin is produced only by bacteria, which live in the soil and in the intestines of humans and other animals.

• Liver stores of B_{12} mean that a *daily* consumption of the vitamin is not necessary, as long as the stores are not continually depleted.

• Our bodies have ways of conserving B_{12} by recycling it from the bile, decreasing loss from the kidneys, and increasing its rate of absorption from food.

• In the past, some edible seaweeds and fermented foods were thought to be rich in vitamin B_{12}. Modern measuring methods, as well as human studies, now suggest that this is mainly vitamin analogues or 'chemical look-alikes' which our bodies cannot actually use.

• It is possible that some of these analogues may partly block the use, by our bodies, of the small amounts of genuine vitamin present in these foods.

• Some people may be able to use B_{12} made by bacteria in their intestines, but this has not yet been confirmed.

• At the moment the most reliable vegan sources of B_{12} are foods fortified with the vitamin (*see **Table 4.4**, page 73*); or vitamin supplements (eg. tablets).

• The first obvious signs of vitamin B_{12} deficiency in adult vegans might be pins and needles or coldness in the hands and feet, fatigue and weakness, poor concentration or even psychosis.

• In infants, observable symptoms of deficiency would include losing the ability to sit up on their own, irritability, lethargy, stopping smiling and socializing, and loss of appetite.

A few investigations have documented the use of B_{12} supplements among British vegans. Tablets were used by 8%[19] and 18%[20] of vegans in groups studied in 1970 and 1978 respectively, but a 1986 survey[21] recorded tablet use by 41% of vegan runners.

Between 1967[18] and 1978[19,20] an average of 57% of vegans studied used foods fortified with B_{12}, while in a group of vegan runners informally surveyed, most individuals used fortified foods such as yeast extracts, soya milk and soya-based meat substitutes[21].

B_{12} INTAKES BY VEGANS

Dietary intakes of the vitamin by adult vegans have been measured in several studies, although by different methods — and so the values may not all be correct or even comparable. Three reports published in the 1980s indicate an average B_{12} intake (including fortified foods) by British vegans of between 1.2µg and 1.8µg[4-6]. A later study[41] of 38 vegans found the range of intakes to be 0–5.66µg/day, with a mean intake of 0.64µg. Of this, an average 0.25µg was supplied by supplements (which were, however, used only by a minority of vegan subjects during the three days of the study).

In a Swedish study in which subjects did not use fortified foods[11], an average intake of 0.35µg was recorded, and analysis of various foods used, including fermented vegetables, showed B_{12} contents of 10–70 nanograms per 100g of food. In the light of more recent developments, however, only a small proportion of this would have been active B_{12}.

In a 1981 report, British vegan pre-school children had a high average daily consumption of 2.7µg B_{12}[9]. All parents provided fortified soya milks, yeast extracts or textured soya protein, and in a few cases a vitamin B_{12} syrup was given. The children with the lowest intakes of the vitamin were those still receiving breast milk. Ten years later, 14 of 18 children had a daily intake of B_{12} (including supplements) which met or exceeded the UK Reference Nutrient Intakes, but one child was receiving less than the Lower Reference Nutrient Intake[66].

Similarly, at a vegan community called The Farm, in Tennessee, USA, where B_{12} was provided by supplemented soya milk and by nutritional yeast, *Saccharomyces cerevisiae* (used as a flavouring), the mean intake of 48 two- to five-year-old children was 15µg — ten times the US RDA[22].

BLOOD LEVELS OF B_{12}

There are four recognizable stages between normality and deficiency of B_{12}[77]. In early B_{12} depletion, low levels of the vitamin are seen in the serum. In the second stage there is, additionally, a decrease in stores of B_{12} in the body's cells, for example the red blood cells. These two stages of B_{12} *depletion* may be followed by early *vitamin deficiency*. This is recognized by biochemical changes, such as a rise in methylmalonic acid in the bloodstream. Finally, clinical symptoms of B_{12} deficiency occur. Megaloblastic anaemia is the classic deficiency symptom; but among vegans, neurological symptoms are more likely to occur first because vegans' high consumption of folate protects them from anaemia.

Thus, an early measure of the adequacy of B_{12} intake is the level of the vitamin found in the liquid component of the blood (serum). There is a wide range of 'normal' serum levels, from 100–900 picograms B_{12} per millilitre of blood. The UK Department of Health considers that 130pg/ml is the level at which dietary inadequacy can be assumed. Values below 80pg/ml indicate a deficiency of B_{12}, while between 80–140pg/ml there may or may not be symptoms of deficiency. In the USA, by contrast, researchers refer to blood levels of B_{12} below 200pg/ml as indicating vitamin depletion.

The discrepancies in defining what is a normal or low level of B_{12} reflect a genuine lack of knowledge, as well as individual variations. Lower than normal serum levels of the vitamin do not necessarily indicate deficiency, only a relative depletion, which can be reversed by boosting B_{12} intake. As already mentioned, vegans of more than 20 years' standing with no obvious source of the vitamin in their diets have only very rarely been found to have clinical symptoms of deficiency. Without the use of fortified foods or supplements, serum levels of B_{12} do generally fall after a number of years on a vegan diet, but they often stabilize at about 100pg/ml. Vegans who take supplements or fortified foods have higher serum levels of the vitamin. A further complication is that different methods of measuring B_{12} in the bloodstream have been used, and some are more accurate than others.

Consequently, surveys of vegans document a wide variation of serum levels of B_{12} (*summarized in **Table 4.5**, page 78*). One report[18] mentions values between 30 and 650pg/ml with a mean value (of 20 subjects) of 236pg/ml. These compare with a range of 120–740pg/ml, and a mean value of 441pg/ml, in matched omnivore subjects. There was no clinical evidence of B_{12} deficiency even in those vegans with the lowest serum levels, although one 80-year-old subject who had been a vegan for only two years had pernicious anaemia (ie. deficiency due not to dietary lack, but to lack of intrinsic factor and therefore an inability to absorb the vitamin). Three subjects who had been vegans for 17 years without taking supplements were healthy, with serum B_{12} levels of 150, 375 and 450pg/ml, and normal amounts of haemoglobin in the blood. Thirteen American vegans who followed a raw-food diet and took no supplements had blood levels of B_{12} between 90–219pg/ml[10].

TABLE 4.5
BLOODSTREAM LEVELS OF B_{12} IN VEGANS

	No. vegans in study	Duration of veganism (years)	Use of supplements	Mean blood stream B_{12} (pg/ml)	Range (pg/ml)
Ellis & Mumford, 1967[18]	20	up to 17	?	236	30–650
Sanders et al, 1978[20]	32	1–30	By 18%	257	94–675
*Campbell et al, 1982[30]	9	2–20	No	61	10–130
Dong & Scott, 1982[10]	13	1–49	By 8%	115	90–219
Crane et al, 1988[63]	47	1–29	No	n.a.	<100–850
**Bar-Sella et al, 1990[56]	36	5–35	No	164	65–>200
Gilois et al, 1992[46]	54	> 20	No	193	n.a.

These values are not all strictly comparable, as different methods of B_{12} analysis were used.

All subjects in these studies were healthy and without symptoms of B_{12} deficiency, except:

  * This was a study of vegans with evident B_{12} deficiency.
  ** Four of these subjects had some neurological symptoms of deficiency.

Normal levels of B_{12} in the blood are considered to be 140–900pg/ml.

The official UK criterion of B_{12} inadequacy is a blood level of 130pg/ml or below.

n.a. = Not available

Measurements of 32 vegans who had followed their diets for between one and 30 years revealed a range of serum B_{12} levels from 94–675pg/ml[20]. Most took B_{12} tablets or food fortified with the vitamin, and those who did had higher amounts of vitamin in their blood. There were three subjects who had been vegan for 6–13 years (long enough theoretically to exhaust liver stores of B_{12}) who had no obvious dietary source of B_{12}, and their serum levels were 120–230pg/ml. All the vegans were healthy, none showed symptoms of B_{12} deficiency and all had normal haemoglobin values. The same report lists other surveys of vegans which have not found symptoms of dietary deficiency of B_{12}.

Levels of B_{12} in the bloodstream of 47 vegan staff members at the Weimar Institute in California were measured[63]. They had been vegans for 1–29 years, and levels of B_{12} ranged between <100–850pg/ml. Forty-seven per cent (22 individuals) had blood levels of the vitamin above 180pg/ml, and 53% (25 individuals) had blood levels below 180pg/ml. None had symptoms of deficiency. In one case B_{12} injections were given because oral vitamin did not boost blood levels, suggesting an underlying absorption problem which may not have been related to diet.

Thirty-six Israeli vegans of 5–35 years' duration, aged 8–79 years, were examined for their serum levels of B_{12} and for signs of deficiency[56]. None used vitamin supplements, yet ten had "normal" levels (considered in this instance to be >200pg/ml) and 11 had "borderline" levels, defined in this study as 130–200pg/ml. Five (14%) of the vegans had blood levels of B_{12} lower than 130pg/ml, considered to be inadequate, and four of these complained of weakness, fatigue and poor concentration — probably neurological symptoms of B_{12} deficiency (*see Occasional B_{12} deficiency in vegan adults, page 80*). However, 12 of 16 subjects whose blood levels were in the "borderline" or "inadequate" range had no deficiency symptoms, either neurological or haematological. The researchers thought that absorption of B_{12} synthesized by bacteria in the intestine might have helped maintain blood levels in 13 of their subjects who had been vegan for more than 15 years.

Researchers looked at Asian vegans and vegetarians living in Britain, who had followed their diets for a minimum of 20 years and who used no vitamin supplements[46]. Average blood levels of B_{12} were lower but adequate in the 54 vegans (average 193pg/ml) and nine lacto-vegetarians (average 185pg/ml), compared with the 37 lacto-ovo-vegetarians (average 359pg/ml). Twenty of the subjects, vegans and lacto-vegetarians, had individual blood levels below 150pg/ml. Their average daily B_{12} consumption was estimated at 0.2µg, which is only one-seventh of the Reference Nutrient Intake. It may seem surprising for lacto-vegetarians to have such a low B_{12} consumption, but it's common in the Asian community to boil milk for a long time before use, and this could destroy much of its vitamin content. Despite low blood levels, thorough tests for blood and neurological abnormalities (visual evoked responses, somatosensory evoked potentials, and sensory and motor nerve conduction) showed all the vegans and lacto-vegetarians to be completely well. The conclusion of the researchers was that the average daily requirement for B_{12} may still be over-estimated, and that long-term vegans may adapt to a low food content of the vitamin.

Lower than normal serum levels of vitamin B_{12} do not necessarily indicate deficiency: at levels of about 100 picograms of B_{12} per millilitre of blood, some vegans may develop deficiency symptoms but most do not. Without the use of fortified foods or supplements, serum levels of B_{12} do generally fall after a number of years on a vegan diet, but they often stabilize at about 100pg/ml — possibly vitamin B_{12} synthesized by intestinal bacteria makes a contribution in some cases. Vegans who take supplements or fortified foods do have higher serum levels of the vitamin. However, vegans of 20–35 years' standing with no significant source of the vitamin in their diets have only very rarely been found to have symptoms of deficiency.

OCCASIONAL B_{12} DEFICIENCY IN VEGAN ADULTS

Cases of B_{12} deficiency in adult vegans, sometimes resulting in neurological symptoms, have been documented. Results are incomplete in four early reports[23-26] and the diagnoses of subacute combined degeneration of the spinal cord in these cases are not convincing, according to Sanders[27]. Fewer than 30 individual cases of B_{12} deficiency attributed to vegan and vegetarian diets worldwide had been described in the medical literature up to 1980[28]. In several of these reports, underlying disease of the stomach or small intestine, or other contributory factors which could cause deficiency, were not ruled out.

Fifteen cases of probable B_{12} deficiency in vegans have been published during the 1980s and '90s. In 1982, ten Rastafarian men who had been vegans for between two and 20 years were reported to be suffering from B_{12} deficiency[30]. All except two patients had very low serum levels of B_{12} (10–75pg/ml). Neurological and gastrointestinal symptoms were observed; eight patients had macrocytic anaemia and all had megaloblastic changes in their red blood cells. Of three patients with spinal cord degeneration, one died (of a heart attack), one made a full recovery and one still suffered physical effects after several months of treatment. Failure to absorb the vitamin from the gut was excluded as a cause of the condition, which was attributed by the investigators solely to dietary deficiency. However, it is surprising that serious B_{12}-deficiency symptoms should occur after only 2–3 years on a vegan diet, since liver stores are generally sufficient for 3–5 years without any dietary source at all. Furthermore, the subject with the highest blood levels of the vitamin had been a vegan for 20 years.

One case reported in 1987 concerned a 14-year-old girl in Israel, who had adopted a vegan diet after witnessing the slaughter of a cow on her farm. Neither she nor her parents had been aware of the need for vitamin B_{12}, and after eight years she had developed severe neurological disturbances including difficulties in walking, running and climbing stairs. Her serum level of B_{12} had fallen to only 50pg/ml. Following injections and supplements of B_{12} and the inclusion of fish and dairy products in her diet, the girl returned quickly to health[29], although this could also have been achieved on a vegan diet.

A study of 36 Israeli vegans of 5–35 years' duration revealed that four subjects, whose blood levels of B_{12} were very low at 65–90pg/ml, complained of weakness, muscle pain, fatigue and poor mental concentration[56]. Symptoms improved markedly after injections of the vitamin, but the researchers did not clarify whether a lack of B_{12} in the diet was the problem in all four cases, or whether inadequate absorption of B_{12} from food was also a contributing factor.

Dietary B_{12} deficiency in adult vegans is rare: some 15 cases have been recorded in the medical press worldwide since the 1980s. Not all cases are published, of course, but it is significant that B_{12} deficiency is so uncommon that single case reports are still thought worthy of publication in the medical journals.

OCCASIONAL B_{12} DEFICIENCY IN VEGAN INFANTS

A well-planned vegan diet provides adequate quantities of B_{12} for infants and children, but in cases where a mother has a low current intake of the vitamin, deficiency can develop after a few months in solely breast-fed infants. This is because a baby developing in the womb of a B_{12}-depleted woman does not receive enough of the vitamin to build up its own liver stores. At weaning, absence of the vitamin from weaning foods would also lead to deficiency in a child, but this is exceedingly rare. A brief summary follows, but the subject is dealt with in full in **Vegan Mothers and Children.**

DURING BREAST FEEDING

Some reports in the medical journals do not adequately specify the diets followed by parents, and early reports of vitamin B_{12} deficiency were not always rigorous in excluding other causes. Given these provisos, it seems that since 1978 there have been ten reports — from the USA, France, Germany, Switzerland, Israel, Australia and the West Indies — of serious vitamin B_{12} deficiency in exclusively breast-fed infants of vegan mothers[31–34,57,58,60,61,73,74]. In another instance[72], the baby of a vegan mother showed some signs of B_{12} deficiency, although the infant's blood levels of the vitamin were not very low. Additionally, the infant of a women who might have been a vegan (her diet was inadequately described in the report) showed early signs of B_{12} deficiency[62].

The general pattern has been as follows: symptoms were recognized at 3–15 months of age, when the infants regressed developmentally, for example losing the ability to sit up on their own. They often became irritable, lethargic, stopped smiling and socializing, and fed poorly. There was also megaloblastic anaemia, and developmental retardation — including poor movement control, muscle wasting, sight deterioration or brain shrinkage — which was not always completely reversible. All the mothers were healthy; most, but not all, had low blood levels of B_{12}. Occasionally, mothers whose own blood levels of the vitamin are just adequate for themselves may not have enough B_{12} in their milk for their infants.

Ten definite reports of serious B_{12} deficiency in breast-fed infants of vegan mothers have appeared in the medical literature worldwide since the late 1970s.

It is very important that vegan women ensure they have an adequate intake of B_{12} during pregnancy and breast feeding. The most reliable way to do this is to use foods fortified with the vitamin (*see Table 4.4, page 73*), or supplements. The first signs of B_{12} deficiency in breast-fed infants may not be recognized, and if developmental retardation should occur it may not be entirely reversible. Moreover mothers may have no symptoms of deficiency themselves.

However, B_{12} problems remain very rare, and thousands of children have been reared as healthy vegans.

WEANING

There have been only two reports[35,70] of vitamin B_{12} deficiency in infants weaned onto inadequate vegan diets, both occurring in the same community. Three cases of deficiency, two resulting in megaloblastic anaemia, were reported in 1979[70]. In 1982, a further nine infants with low blood levels of B_{12} were reported from the same community of black Hebrew Americans living in Israel[35], and five of these had signs of megaloblastic anaemia. The infants had been weaned onto a generally inadequate diet, and were suffering from multiple nutritional deficiencies.

Vitamin B_{12} deficiency in weaned vegan infants has been reported only in a single, atypical religious community.

VITAMIN B_{12} — SUMMARY

The body requires only a tiny amount of vitamin B_{12}, and is able to conserve it when supplies are scarce. There is persuasive evidence that, at least in some individuals, there are bacteria present in the small intestine which manufacture B_{12} that is available to the body.

Contrary to previous beliefs, seaweeds and fermented soya products are not now considered to be useful sources of active vitamin. However, there are numerous fortified foods which are acceptable to vegans, as well as dietary supplements. Without the use of fortified foods or supplements, serum levels of B_{12} do generally fall after a number of years on a vegan diet, but they often stabilize at about 100pg/ml. Vegans of 20–35 years' standing with no significant source of the vitamin in their diets have only very rarely been found to have clinical symptoms of deficiency. Vegans who take supplements or fortified foods have higher serum levels of the vitamin.

A dietary deficiency of this vitamin is rare, despite its notoriety. In the population as a whole, most cases of deficiency occur in omnivores who lack the intrinsic factor required for absorption of B_{12}.

The consequences of deficiency can be serious, especially in infants. Pregnant and breast-feeding women in particular should ensure they have an adequate intake of vitamin B_{12}, and after weaning parents should make sure their children have a regular intake of the vitamin, preferably from fortified foods.

VITAMIN C (ASCORBIC ACID)

Humans are one of only a few species (such as guinea pigs and monkeys) unable to make our own vitamin C, and therefore we need a dietary source. Small amounts are found in milk and liver, but almost all the vitamin C in the human diet comes from **vegetables and fruit, especially potatoes, green leafy vegetables, green peppers, blackcurrants, mangos, citrus fruits and tomatoes.** Although potatoes have a comparatively low content, because they are eaten often they constitute the major source of vitamin C in the average British diet. Vitamin C is easily destroyed during food storage, preparation and cooking, so a deficiency (eventually leading to scurvy) can occur.

We need vitamin C for the development and maintenance of connective tissues, haemoglobin, hormones, neurotransmitters, bones and teeth, and it plays a vital role in wound healing and in resistance to infection. Vitamin C also enhances the absorption of iron from food. Whether or not high doses are protective against cancer or reduce symptoms of the common cold is still under debate. Epidemiological evidence does suggest a protective effect of vitamin C for cancers of the stomach, mouth, oesophagus and pancreas[39]. The vitamin has antioxidant properties, scavenging free radicals which can otherwise cause tissue damage, and helping to regenerate vitamin E (*see **Vitamin A**, page 57, for more on free radicals*). These antioxidant activities could certainly offer some protection against cancers.

The UK Reference Nutrient Intakes are 25–30mg vitamin C for infants and children; 35mg for adolescents; and 40mg for adults, with an extra 10 and 30mg respectively during pregnancy and lactation[40]. The US RDAs[47] are higher at 60mg for adolescents and adults, with extra for pregnant women; while the German recommendation for adults is 75mg daily[51].

Given the food sources of vitamin C, **it is no surprise to find that vegan diets contain plentiful amounts of this vitamin.** Surveys[4–6,41] indicate that the vitamin C intake of adult vegans varies between 137 and 210mg a day, with an average of 159mg. The diets of lifelong vegan children in Britain provided 107mg vitamin C[66], again exceeding by far their RNIs.

Three-quarters of the children's consumption was provided by fresh fruit, potatoes and other fresh vegetables.

VITAMIN D (ERGOCALCIFEROL, D_2; CHOLECALCIFEROL, D_3)

Few foods naturally contain vitamin D, and those which do are animal products containing vitamin D_3 (cholecalciferol). The richest of these sources are cod liver oil, oily fish, eggs, butter and liver. Margarine is fortified with vitamin D by law in the UK and some other countries; some breakfast cereals are fortified; and in some countries, including the UK, supplements are available to pregnant and nursing women.

Natural plant foods do not contain vitamin D, but some **soya milks, margarines and breakfast cereals acceptable to vegans are fortified with vitamin D_2**, obtained from yeasts and other fungi. **Vitamin supplements** which contain D_2 (ergocalciferol) are also suitable for vegans.

Food sources of vitamin D are relatively unimportant, since the most significant supply comes from the action of ultra-violet B light on sterols in the skin. Most people[7], including infants[36], need little or no extra from food. Bright sunlight is not necessary: even the 'sky-shine' on a cloudy summer day will stimulate formation of some vitamin D in the skin, while a short summer holiday in the open air will increase blood levels of the vitamin by two or three times.

However, the effective light wavelength — ultra-violet B (UVB, 300–320 nanometers in wavelength) — is probably not present in winter sunlight (between October and February/March inclusive) in countries above latitude 52° north, which includes most of Britain[59]. Thus winter-time supplies of vitamin D depend on the previous summer's exposure creating adequate stores in the liver, or on dietary sources.

Vitamin D is a fat-soluble vitamin which acts like a hormone, regulating the formation of bone and the absorption of calcium and phosphorus from the intestine. It helps to control the movement of calcium between bone and blood, and *vice versa*. In infancy and childhood, a deficiency of vitamin D causes the deformed bones characteristic of rickets, while in adults a lack of the vitamin causes a softening of the bones known as osteomalacia. Deficiency is seen more often in northern countries, or where tradition dictates that the body is well covered by clothes, such as in parts of the Islamic world. An excess of the vitamin can cause loss of appetite, weight loss, nausea, headache, depression, and deposits of calcium in the kidneys.

The exact requirement for vitamin D is not known. As a dietary source is not usually necessary, UK Reference Nutrient Intakes[40] have only been set for certain "vulnerable" groups. For infants and children up to the age of 3 years, the dietary intake recommended is 8.5µg dropping to 7µg a day. The recommendation for pregnant and breast-feeding women, and for adults over the age of 65 years, is 10µg daily (10µg vitamin D is equivalent to 400 international units). Older people who do not go outdoors much, or who are housebound, would be more reliant on food sources of this vitamin.

VITAMIN D INTAKES BY VEGANS

An unpublished survey[21] indicated that 91% of British vegans who were keen runners obtained vitamin D from margarines and 54% used a proprietary soya milk fortified with the vitamin. Two studies[4,6] measured the food intake of vitamin D by vegans as 2.5µg and 3.2µg, compared with 3.7 and 3.5µg for omnivore subjects. A third[41] recorded a mean intake of 1.73µg for 38 vegans, while lacto-ovo-vegetarians and fish-eaters consumed 2.7µg and 3.1µg respectively. A 1993 report compared the vitamin D intake of four dietary groups in Finland[59]. The ten vegans had a lower food intake of vitamin D (less than 0.3µg/day) than the lacto-vegetarians (approximately 0.5µg daily), fish-eaters (approximately 2.3µg), and omnivores (4.5µg).

A 1981 study[9] of British vegan pre-school children found their average intake from food to be nearly a third of the current recommendations, similar to findings for omnivore children. Most parents were aware that exposure of the skin to sunlight is a good source of vitamin D, and some gave their children vitamin D supplements.

Most vegans meet their requirement for vitamin D from regular exposure to daylight, and from the use of fortified foods and supplements.

OCCASIONAL VITAMIN D DEFICIENCY

Rickets and osteomalacia can be a problem in the Asian vegetarian population in Britain (possibly because of restricted exposure to daylight), but seem to be very rare in Caucasian vegans[37]. The Finnish report mentioned above compared the vitamin D status of vegans, lacto-vegetarians, fish-eaters and omnivores in Finland[59]. The study was conducted in winter, when the sunlight in Finland contains none of the UVB light necessary to make vitamin D in the skin.

The vegans consumed less vitamin D in their food than the other dietary groups, and their bloodstream levels of the vitamin (as cholecalciferol) were lowest, at 11.3ng/ml, compared to 12.1ng/ml in lacto-vegetarians and 19.6ng/ml in omnivores. The Finnish researchers suggest that the vegans' blood levels indicated deficiency; but the UK Department of Health considers 8–35ng/ml as the normal range[40]. All the vegans in this study were healthy, with no clinical symptoms of osteomalacia.

Many expert committees recommend vitamin D supplements for breast-feeding mothers, regardless of their dietary preferences, since breast milk does not always contain adequate amounts. Infants who are solely breast fed after the ages of 4–6 months, and those who are dark-skinned, born in the autumn, or are seldom outdoors, may be particularly at risk. A very few isolated cases of rickets due to vitamin D deficiency have been reported in dark-skinned infants raised on vegan diets (*see* **Vegan Mothers and Children**).

Adult vegans obtain adequate vitamin D if they regularly spend time outdoors in spring, summer and autumn. A dietary intake of the vitamin can be ensured by consumption of fortified vegan margarines, soya milks and other vitamin D-fortified products. Vegan children, like all children, are especially vulnerable to vitamin D deficiency while their bones are growing.

In northern latitudes vegan women who are breast feeding should ensure their intake during winter by using fortified foods or taking supplements. Parents are advised to include vitamin D-fortified foods or supplements if they wean their infants during the winter months, especially if they are dark skinned. Osteomalacia has not been reported in adult vegans, and rickets is extremely rare in vegan infants.

VITAMIN E (THE TOCOPHEROLS)

Vitamin E comprises a number of substances called tocopherols, the most active being alpha-tocopherol. The vitamin is found widely in plant foods, the richest sources being **vegetable oils, wheatgerm, nuts, seeds and whole grains**; most other vegetables, fruits, meats and animal fats contain considerably less. Being a fat-soluble vitamin, vitamin E is stored in the body and so a daily intake is not essential. This, combined with its fairly wide availability, means that deficiency is very rare. One symptom of deficiency is neurological damage, such as loss of balance and muscle control.

The full role of vitamin E in the human body is not yet known, although its major function is likely to be as an antioxidant, protecting cell membranes from damaging free radicals. Free-radical damage may be involved in illnesses such as atherosclerosis, arthritis, cataract and cancer (*see under* **Vitamin A**, *above, for more on free radicals*). Vitamin E is believed to be essential for the nervous system and immune function.

In 1993, two reports of large prospective studies[46-47] showed that healthy men and women who took vitamin E supplements for at least two years were only two-thirds as likely to develop coronary heart disease, compared with those who did not take supplements. Five other epidemiological studies have also indicated beneficial effects of vitamin E in preventing heart disease, although three studies have not shown this link. The results suggest, but do not yet prove, a protective effect of the vitamin at higher doses, and ongoing research is expected to clarify the situation.

An individual's need for vitamin E depends on their dietary intake of polyunsaturated fatty acids. As this is very variable from person to person, the UK Department of Health has not set Reference Nutrient Intakes for vitamin E. Instead, it states that 3–4mg daily is probably adequate, and in Britain average intakes are between 6.7 and 9.3mg[48].

A recent dietary analysis[41] measured the average vitamin E intake of 38 vegans at 19.8mg daily (16.5mg for women, 23.1mg for men). Lacto-ovo-vegetarians and fish-eaters consumed an average of 16mg daily.

Vegans — especially those who eat a mainly wholefood diet — probably consume considerably more than the recommended amounts of vitamin E, and more than vegetarians, fish-eaters or omnivores.

VITAMIN K

This is another fat-soluble vitamin, and in the form of vitamin K_1 (phylloquinone) is widespread in plant foods such as **green leafy vegetables — spinach, broccoli, cabbage, lettuce — and vegetable oils, cauliflower, fruits and grains**. Vitamin K is provided in roughly equal proportions by diet and, in the form of vitamin K_2, by bacterial activity in the large intestine. Modest amounts of the vitamin are stored in the liver, and dietary deficiency is virtually unknown after the first few months of life. The use of antibiotics, which reduce gut bacteria, can occasionally cause deficiency. Vitamin K is crucial for normal clotting of the blood, and is also needed by a variety of the body's tissues.

Knowledge of our daily needs for this vitamin is limited, but estimates indicate that adults obtain about 80μg a day from food. The UK Department of Health[40] suggests that 1μg of vitamin K from food for each kilogram of body weight, per day, is a safe and adequate intake for adults; while infants should receive about 2μg of vitamin per kilogram of body weight daily, as they have little or no liver stores of vitamin K, and are presumed to rely entirely on dietary sources. The American RDA[47] for adults and children is approximately 1μg per kilogram of body weight daily, which represents a total consumption of 55–80μg for adults. The comparable German figures are 60–80μg[51].

Vitamin K is common in plant foods and there have been no reports of deficiency in vegans.

VITAMINS — SUMMARY

A varied and balanced vegan diet contains all the vitamins necessary for good health. For vitamin B_{12} the most reliable sources are fortified foods, or supplements. Because of the serious effects of B_{12} deficiency, especially in infants, all vegans should give thought to how they and their children obtain the vitamin. Although some cases of B_{12} deficiency have been described in vegans, these are exceptional.

Adults and children can generally obtain sufficient vitamin D from the action of sunlight on the skin. Furthermore, many vegans use margarines and soya milk which are fortified with vitamin D. Other factors, such as poor nutritional status in the mother, dark skin, or inadequate exposure to daylight, were also involved in the two instances of rickets in vegan infants. There have been no reports of vitamin D deficiency in light-skinned vegans, although it can be a problem among vegetarians of Asian origin.

Vegan diets may contain less riboflavin than omnivore diets, but most vegans consume their RNI for riboflavin. A few vegan women and children have been found to eat slightly less than this recommended amount, but many plant foods are rich in the vitamin. A largely wholefood diet, as advocated by the Vegan Society, is the most likely to provide adequate levels of vitamins.

Vegans easily meet or exceed the recommended intakes of vitamin A (as beta-carotene), thiamin, vitamin B_6, folate, biotin, and vitamins C, E and K.

REFERENCES

1 Hardinge, M.G. & Stare, F.J. (1954). Nutritional studies of vegetarians: nutritional, physical and laboratory studies. *J. Clin. Nutr.* 2:73–82.

2 Hardinge, M.G. & Stare, F.J. (1954). Nutritional studies of vegetarians: dietary and serum levels of cholesterol. *J. Clin. Nutr.* 2:83–88.

3 Guggenheim, K., Weiss, Y. & Fostick, M. (1962). Composition and nutritive value of diets consumed by strict vegetarians. *Br. J. Nutr.* 16:467–474.

4 Rana, S.K. & Sanders, T.A.B. (1986). Taurine concentrations in the diet, plasma, urine and breast milk of vegans compared with omnivores. *Br. J. Nutr.* 56:17–27.

5 Sanders, T.A.B. & Key, T.J.A. (1987). Blood pressure, plasma renin activity and aldosterone concentrations in vegans and omnivore controls. *Hum. Nutr.: Appl. Nutr.* 41A:204–211.

6 Carlson, E., Kipps, M., Lockie, A. & Thomson, J. (1985). A comparative evaluation of vegan, vegetarian and omnivore diets. *J. Plant Foods* 6:89–100.

7 Holland, B., Welch, A.A., Unwin, I.D., Buss, D.H., Paul, A.A. & Southgate, D.A.T. (1991). *McCance and Widdowson's The Composition of Foods*. 5th edition. Royal Society of Chemistry and MAFF.

8 Hughes, J. & Sanders, T.A.B. (1979). Riboflavin levels in the diet and breast milk

of vegans and omnivores. *Proc. Nutr. Soc.* 38:95A.

9 Sanders, T.A.B. & Purves, R. (1981). An anthropometric and dietary assessment of the nutritional status of vegan preschool children. *J. Hum. Nutr.* 35:349–357.

10 Dong, A. & Scott, S.C. (1982). Serum vitamin B_{12} and blood cell values in vegetarians. *Ann. Nutr. Metab.* 26:209–216.

11 Abdulla, M., Andersson, I., Asp, N-G., Berthelsen, K., Birkhed, D., Dencker, I., Johansson, C-G., Jägerstad, M., Kolar, K., Nair, B.M., Nilsson-Ehle, P., Nordén, Å.Rassner, S., Åkesson, B. & Öckerman, P-A. (1981). Nutrient intake and health status of vegans. Chemical analyses of diets using the duplicate portion sampling technique. *Am. J. Clin. Nutr.* 34:2464–2477.

12 Herbert, V., Colman N. & Jacob, E. (1980). *Folic acid and vitamin B_{12}*. In: Goodhart, R.S. & Shils, M.S., eds. Modern nutrition in health and disease. 6th edition. pp229–259. Philadelphia, PA: Lea & Febiger.

13 Herbert, V. (1987). Recommended dietary intakes (RDI) of vitamin B_{12} in humans. *Am. J. Clin. Nutr.* 45:671–678.

14 Baker, S. J. & Mathan, V.I. (1981). Evidence regarding the minimal daily requirement of dietary vitamin B_{12}. *Am. J. Clin. Nutr.* 34:2423–2433.

15 Specker, B.L., Miller, D., Norman, E.J., Greene, H. & Hayes, K.C. (1988). Increased urinary methylmalonic acid

excretion in breast-fed infants of vegetarian mothers and identification of an acceptable dietary source of vitamin B-12. *Am. J. Clin. Nutr.* 47:89–92.

16 Herbert, V., Drivas, G., Chu, M., Levitt, D. & Cooper, B. (1983). Differential radioassays better measure cobalamin content of vitamins and 'health foods' than do microbiologic assays. *Blood* 62 (suppl.1):37a.

17 Albert, M.J., Mathan, V.I. & Baker, S.J. (1980). Vitamin B_{12} synthesis by human small intestinal bacteria. *Nature* 283:781–782.

18 Ellis, F.R. & Mumford, P. (1967). The nutritional status of vegans and vegetarians. *Proc. Nutr. Soc.* 26:205–212.

19 Ellis, F.R. & Montegriffo, V.M.E. (1970). Veganism, clinical findings and investigations. *Am. J. Clin. Nutr.* 23:249–255.

20 Sanders, T.A.B., Ellis, F.R. & Dickerson, J.W.T. (1978). Haematological studies on vegans. *Br. J. Nutr.* 40:9–15.

21 Langley, G.R. & Wilcox, J. (1987). *Nutrient sources and health profile of vegan and vegetarian runners.* Unpublished.

22 Fulton, J.R., Hutton, C.W. & Stitt, K.R. (1980). Preschool vegetarian children. *J. Am. Diet. Assn.* 76:360–365.

23 Badenoch, A.G. (1952). Diet and stamina (letter). *Br. Med. J.* 2:668.

24 Badenoch, T. (1954). The use of labelled vitamin B_{12} and gastric biopsy in the investigation of anaemia. *Proc. Roy. Soc. Med.* 47:426–427.

25 Wokes, F., Badenoch, J. & Sinclair, H.M. (1955). Human dietary deficiency of vitamin B_{12}. *Am. J. Clin. Nutr.* 3:375–382.

26 Smith, A.D.M. (1962). Veganism: a clinical survey with observations on vitamin B_{12} metabolism. *Br. Med. J.* 1:1655–1658.

27 Sanders, T.A.B. (1978). The health and nutritional status of vegans. *Plant. Fds. Man* 2:181–193.

28 McDougall, J.A. & McDougall, M.A. (1983). *The McDougall Plan.* p40. New Jersey: New Century Publishers.

29 Ashkenazi, S., Weitz, R., Varsano, I. & Mimouni, M. (1987). Vitamin B_{12} deficiency due to a strictly vegetarian diet in adolescence. *Clin. Pediatr.* 26:662–663.

30 Campbell, M., Lofters, W.S. & Gibbs, W.N. (1982). Rastafarianism and the vegans syndrome. *Br. Med. J.* 285:1617–1618.

31 Wighton, M.C., Manson, J.I., Speed, I. Robertson, E. & Chapman, E. (1979). Brain damage in infancy and dietary vitamin B_{12} deficiency. *Med. J. Australia* 2:1–3.

32 Sklar, R. (1986). Nutritional vitamin B_{12} deficiency in a breast-fed infant of a vegan-diet mother. *Clin. Pediatr.* 25:219–221.

33 Higginbottom, M.C., Sweetman, L. & Nyhan, W.L. (1978). A syndrome of methylmalonic aciduria, homocystinuria, megaloblastic anemia and neurologic abnormalities in a vitamin B_{12}-deficient breast-fed infant of a strict vegetarian. *New Engl. J. Med.* 299:317–323.

34 Close, G.C. (1983). Rastafarianism and the vegans syndrome (letter). *Br. Med. J.* 286:473.

35 Shinwell, E.D. & Gorodischer, R. (1982). Totally vegetarian diets and infant nutrition. *Pediatrics* 70:582–586.

36 Lawson, D.E.M. (1978). *Vitamin D.* p304. London: Academic Press.

37 Sanders, T.A.B. (1983). Vegetarianism: dietetic and medical aspects. *J. Plant Foods* 5:3–14.

38 Lombard, K.A. & Mock, D.M. (1989). Biotin nutritional status of vegans, lacto-ovo-vegetarians, and nonvegetarians. *Am. J. Clin. Nutr.* 50:486–490.

39 Block, G., Henson, D.E. & Levine, M. (eds) (1991). Ascorbic acid: biological functions and relation to cancer. Proceedings of a conference at NIH, Bethesda, 1990. *Am. J. Clin. Nutr.* 54 (suppl):1113S–1327S.

40 Department of Health (1991). *Dietary Reference Values for Food Energy and Nutrients for the United Kingdom.* Reports on Health & Social Subjects no. 41. London: HMSO.

41 Draper, A., Lewis, J., Malhotra, N. & Wheeler, E. (1993). The energy and nutri-

ent intakes of different types of vegetarian: a case for supplements? *Br. J. Nutr.* 69:3–19.

42 Food and Agriculture Organization (1988). Requirements of Vitamin A, Iron, Folate and Vitamin B_{12}. Report of a joint FAO/WHO Consultation. *FAO Food and Nutrition Series*, 23. Rome: Food and Agriculture Organization.

43 Armstrong, B.K., Davies, R.E., Nicol, D.J., Van Merwyk, A.J. & Larwood, C.J. (1974). Hematological vitamin B_{12} and folate studies on Seventh Day Adventist vegetarians. *Am. J. Clin. Nutr.* 27:712–718.

44 Sullivan, L.W. & Herbert, V. (1965). Studies on the minimum daily requirement for vitamin B_{12}. Hematopoietic responses to 0.1 micrograms of cyanocobalamin or coenzyme B_{12} and comparison of their relative potency. *New Engl. J. Med.* 272:340–346.

45 Callender, S. & Spray, G.H. (1962). Latent pernicious anemia. *Br. J. Haematol.* 8:230–240.

46 Gilois, C., Wierzbicki, A.S., Hirani, N., Norman, P.M., Jones, S.J., Ponsford, S., Alani, S.M. & Kriss, A. (1992). The hematological and electrophysiological effects of cobalamin — deficiency secondary to vegetarian diets. *Ann. N. Y. Acad. Sci.* 669:345–348.

47 National Research Council USA (1989). *Recommended Dietary Allowances*. 10th edition. Washington, DC: NAS.

48 Gregory, J., Foster, K., Tyler, H. & Wiseman, M. (1990). *The Dietary and Nutritional Survey of British Adults*. London: HMSO.

49 Stampfer, M.J., Hennekens, C.H., Manson, J.E., Colditz, G.A., Rosner, B. & Willett, W.C. (1993). Vitamin E consumption and the risk of coronary heart disease in women. *New Engl. J. Med.* 328:1444–1449.

50 Rimm, E.B., Stampfer, M.J., Ascherio, A., Giovannucci, E., Colditz, G.A. & Willett, W.C. (1993). Vitamin E consumption and the risk of coronary heart disease in men. *New Engl. J. Med.* 328:1450–1456.

51 Deutsche Gesellschaft für Ernährung (1991). *Empfehlungen für die Nährstoffzufuhr*. Frankfurt: Umschau Verlag.

52 Specker, B.L., Black, A., Allen, L. & Morrow, F. (1990). Vitamin B-12: low milk concentrations are related to low serum concentrations in vegetarian women and to methylmalonic aciduria in their infants. *Am. J. Clin. Nutr.* 52:1073–1076.

53 Herbert, V., Drivas, G., Manusselis, C., Mackler, B., Eng, J. & Schwartz, E. (1984). Are colon bacteria a major source of cobalamin analogues in human tissues? 24-hour human stool contains only about 5µg of cobalamin but about 100µg of apparent analogue (and 200µg of folate). *Trans. Assoc. Am. Physiol.* 97:161–171.

54 Herbert, V. (1988). Vitamin B-12: plant sources, requirements, and assay. *Am. J. Clin. Nutr.* 48:852–858.

55 Herbert, V., Drivas, G., Foscaldi, R., Manusselis, C., Colman, N., Kanazawa, S., Das, K., Gelernt, M., Herzlich, B. & Jennings, J. (1982). Multivitamin/mineral food supplements containing vitamin B_{12} may also contain analogues of vitamin B_{12}. *New Engl. J. Med.* 307:255–256.

56 Bar-Sella, P., Rakover, Y. & Ratner, D. (1990). Vitamin B_{12} and folate levels in long-term vegans. *Israel Med. Sci. J.* 26:309–312.

57 Stollhoff, K. & Schulte, F.J. (1987). Vitamin B_{12} and brain development. *Eur. J. Pediatr.* 146:201–205.

58 Kühne, T., Bubl, R. & Baumgartner, R. (1991). Maternal vegan diet causing a serious infantile neurological disorder due to vitamin B_{12} deficiency. *Eur. J. Pediatr.* 150:205-208.

59 Lamberg-Allardt, C., Kärkkäinen, M., Seppänen, R., & Biström, H. (1993). Low serum 25-hydroxyvitamin D concentrations and secondary hyperparathyroidism in middle-aged white strict vegetarians. *Am. J. Clin. Nutr.* 58:684–689.

60 Davis, J.R., Goldenring, J. & Lubin, B.H. (1981). Nutritional vitamin B_{12} deficiency in infants. *Am. J. Dis. Child.* 135:566–567.

61 Gambon, R.C., Lentze, M.J. & Rossi, E. (1986). Megaloblastic anaemia in one of monozygous twins breast fed by their vegetarian mother. *Eur. J. Pediatr.* 145:570–571.

62 Michaud, J.L., Lemieux, B., Ogier, H. & Lambert, M.A. (1992). Nutritional vitamin B_{12} deficiency: two cases detected by routine newborn urinary screening. *Eur. J. Pediatr.* 151:218–220.

63 Crane, M.G. & Sample, C.J. (1988). Vitamin B-12 in a group of vegans. *Am. J. Clin. Nutr.* 48:927.

64 Sanders, T.A.B. (1988). Growth and development of British vegan children. *Am. J. Clin. Nutr.* 48:822–825.

65 Kardinaal, A.F.M., Kok, F.J., Ringstad, J., Gomez-Aracena, J., Mazaev, V.P., Kohlmeier, L., Martin, B.C., Aro, A., Kark, J.D., Delgado-Rodriguez, M., Riemersma, R.A., van't Veer, P., Huttunen, J.K. & Martin-Moreno, J.M. (1993). Antioxidants in adipose tissue and risk of myocardial infarction: the EURAMIC study. *Lancet* 342:1379–1384.

66 Sanders, T.A.B. & Manning. J. (1992). The growth and development of vegan children. *J. Hum. Nutr. Diet.* 5:11–21.

67 Laidlaw, S.A., Schultz, T.D., Cecchino, J.T. & Kopple, J.D. (1988). Plasma and urine taurine levels in vegans. *Am. J. Clin. Nutr.* 47:660–663.

68 van den Berg, H., Dagnelie, P.C. & van Staveren, W.A. (1988). Vitamin B_{12} and seaweed. *Lancet* i:242–243.

69 Miller, D.R., Specker, B.L., Ho, M.L. & Norman, E.J. (1991). Vitamin B-12 status in a macrobiotic community. *Am. J. Clin. Nutr.* 53:524–529.

70 Zmora, E., Gordischer, R. & Bar-Ziv, J. (1979). Multiple nutritional deficiencies in infants from a strict vegetarian community. *Am. J. Dis. Child.* 133:141–144.

71 Nowak, R. (1994). Beta-carotene: Helpful or harmful? *Science* 264:500–501.

72 Frader, J., Reibman, B. & Turkewitz, D. (1978). Vitamin B_{12} deficiency in strict vegetarians. *New Engl. J. Med.* 299:1319.

73 Lacroix, J., Macher, M.A., Badoual, J. & Huault, G. (1981). Complications of a vegetarian diet in a breast-fed girl. *Arch. Fr. Pediatr.* 38:233–238.

74 Monfort-Gouraud, M., Bongiorno, A., Le Gall, M.A. & Badoual, J. (1993). Severe megaloblastic anemia in a breast-fed infant born to a vegetarian mother. *Ann. Pediatr. (Paris)* 40:28–31.

75 Herbert, V. & Drivas, G. (1982). Spirulina and vitamin B_{12}. *J. Am. Med. Ass.* 248:3096–3097.

76 Dagnelie, P.C., van Staveren, W.A. & van den Berg, H. (1991). Vitamin B-12 from algae appears not to be bioavailable. *Am. J. Clin. Nutr.* 53:695–697.

77 Herbert, V. (1994). Staging vitamin B-12 (cobalamin) status in vegetarians. *Am. J. Clin. Nutr.* 59 (suppl.):1213S–1222S.

78 Committee on Medical Aspects of Food Policy (1994). *Nutritional Aspects of Cardiovascular Disease.* Reports on Health & Social Subjects no. 46. London: HMSO.

MINERALS

Certain plant constituents appear to inhibit the absorption of dietary calcium, but within the context of the total diet, this effect does not appear to be significant. Calcium from low-oxalate vegetable greens, such as kale, has been shown to be absorbed as well as or better than calcium from cow's milk . . . Studies have shown that vegetarians . . . absorb and retain more calcium from foods than do non-vegetarians.

The American Dietetic Association position statement
on vegetarian diets, 1993[58]

There are several minerals known to be essential to the human body and which must be obtained from food. The major minerals — calcium, magnesium, phosphorus, sodium, chloride and potassium — are needed in the greatest quantities or are present in large amounts in the body.

The trace elements — iron, zinc, selenium, cobalt, copper, chromium, iodine, manganese and molybdenum — are equally necessary, but our daily requirements of these are less than 100mg. The three main functions of minerals are as constituents of the skeleton, as soluble salts which help control the composition of the body fluids, and as essential adjuncts to the action of many enzymes and other proteins.

THE MAJOR MINERALS

CALCIUM

For many years, Americans of all ages were advised to drink a quart of cow's milk daily to ward off imminent calcium deficiency. Professor Sherman of America's Columbia University had a great influence on the teaching of nutrition between 1920 and 1950, and his concerns about calcium deficiency were based on two lines of evidence[22]. Firstly, lack of calcium restricted the growth of young rats on experimental diets; and secondly, men and women often went into negative calcium balance when put on diets containing only moderate amounts of the mineral.

Later it became apparent that children were very different from rats, and maintained positive calcium balance on intakes as low as 200mg daily; while the negative calcium balance in volunteer studies proved to be a temporary phase — most people adapt to lower food levels of calcium. This became clear when it was found that in countries with a low calcium consumption, people's bones are normally calcified with no greater propensity to fracture.

Calcium is found in dairy milk, cheese and yoghurt, but only in tiny amounts in meat and fish (unless the bones are eaten, as with sardines); white bread and flour is fortified with calcium in Britain. Cereal products and vegetables provide 32% of the calcium intake of the average British omnivore, with milk and milk products contributing 47%[41].

Good plant sources of calcium include **tofu** (soya bean curd which, when prepared with calcium sulphate (check the label) contains more than four times the calcium of whole cow's milk), **green leafy vegetables, seeds and nuts** (*see Table 5.1, opposite*). **The calcium in green vegetables which are not high in oxalate, such as kale, is as well or better absorbed than the calcium from cow's milk**[58]. **Some proprietary soya milks are fortified with calcium.** Drinking **hard water** can provide typically 200mg calcium daily, sometimes up to 500mg, but soft water contains almost none[40]. Other foods which contain calcium, but which are usually eaten in small amounts, include black molasses, edible seaweeds, watercress, parsley and dried figs.

Calcium is the most abundant mineral in the body (on average 1000g), about 99% of it being in the bones and teeth in the form of calcium phosphates. As well as providing the structural substance of bones, the bone minerals are also a reservoir for other needs, and there is a continual movement of calcium between the bones and the blood (and hence to other parts of the body), which is under close control. The 5–10g calcium not in the bones and teeth are required for muscle contraction, the co-ordination of cell activities, the functioning of nerves, the activity of several enzymes and for blood clotting.

Children develop rickets if they have a deficiency of vitamin D, which is needed for absorption of calcium from food — calcium lack is thus secondary to a vitamin D deficiency. Women who develop vitamin D deficiency, and who have been unable to replace calcium lost from their bodies during repeated pregnancies and breast feeding, may develop osteomalacia (softened bones). Older people, especially women, often suffer from osteoporosis which is becoming endemic in Westernized societies and may be related to calcium intake (*see Osteoporosis, page 103*). However, actual deficiency of calcium in the diet is not common in Britain, especially as our bodies can adapt to low intakes.

Table 5.1

PORTIONS OF SOME PLANT FOODS PROVIDING *100mg* OF CALCIUM

Food	Weight of food providing 100mg calcium
NUTS (shelled) **Almonds**	42g (1.5oz)
Brazils	59g (2.1oz)
PULSES Tofu *(if prepared with calcium sulphate)*	20g (0.7oz)
Soya flour	44g (1.5oz)
Soya beans, boiled	121g (4.2oz)
GRAINS White bread *(fortified)*	91g (3.2oz)
Oatmeal	192g (6.7oz)
Wholemeal bread	185g (6.5oz)
SEEDS (shelled) **Sesame seeds or tahini**	#15g (#0.5oz)
Sunflower seeds	91g (3.2oz)
OTHERS Black molasses	20g (0.7oz)
Figs, dried	40g (1.4oz)
Parsley	50g (1.8oz)
Watercress	59g (2.1oz)
Spinach, boiled	63g (2.2oz)
Chinese leaves	65g (2.3oz)
Kale	67g (2.4oz)
Holland & Barrett fortified soya milk	*71 (**2.5)
Provamel fortified soya milk	*71 (**2.5)
Currants, dried	108g (3.8oz)
Plamil concentrated fortified soya milk	*119 (**4.2)

Foods rich in calcium are shown in bold print and, *for each food type, items near the top of each list contain the most calcium.*
\# Only about one-fifth of this calcium is absorbed because sesame seeds are high in phytate.
* This amount is in millilitres.
** This amount is in fluid ounces.

Values taken from Holland *et al* [21] and from manufacturers' analyses.

1991 UK Reference Nutrient Intakes for calcium: 700mg for adults, 550–1,000mg for children, depending on age.
US recommendations for adults: 800–1,200mg.

The UK Department of Health[40] recommends Reference Nutrient Intakes for calcium as follows: different values between 350 and 550mg a day for infants and children, according to age; 800mg/day for teenage girls; 1,000mg for teenage boys; 700mg/day for adult men and women; and an extra 550mg a day (total 1,250mg) for breast-feeding women. These intakes are believed to be adequate for the needs of virtually everybody in the population.

The 1989 US recommendations[39] are slightly higher at 400–600mg daily for infants aged 0–12 months, and 800mg for men and 1,000mg for women, aged 25–50 years. In 1994 the US recommendation for children aged 1–10 years was increased from 800mg to 1,200 mg daily, and for young adults aged 11–24 years it was increased from 1,200mg to 1,500mg[55]. During pregnancy and breast feeding, women in the USA are now advised to have 1,400mg calcium daily, and American men and women over the age of 50 years are advised to increase their calcium intake towards 1,500mg, because the intestinal absorption of calcium declines with age.

A dietary survey of the British population, published in 1990, indicated that the average calcium intake by women is 730mg, and by men 940mg daily[41], both of which meet the UK RNI.

MEAT, PROTEIN AND CALCIUM BALANCE

It is now widely accepted that a high protein intake, especially from animal foods, causes calcium to be excreted from the kidneys. The evidence for this has come from more than 16 human studies. For example, several volunteer studies lasting up to 95 days have shown that, on experimental diets with a constant calcium intake, loss of calcium in the urine increases markedly as protein intake goes up[1–3]. On a low-protein diet adults were in calcium balance regardless of whether calcium intake was 500, 800 or 1,400mg a day[4].

Calcium intake from food is only one aspect of calcium balance. This is clear from the fact that there are many populations whose diets are chronically poor in calcium, and yet who seldom suffer from osteoporosis. For example, among the Bantu of South Africa, whose diet is low in protein and high in phytate (which is supposed to decrease calcium absorption), very few individuals eat as much as 500mg of calcium a day; and the women have an average of six children, with prolonged breast feeding. Six pregnancies with long-term breast feeding are calculated to cause a cumulative calcium loss of 400–500mg, which would be about half the body's stores. Yet in 1965 osteoporosis was estimated to be rare, occurring in about 1 in 200 of the Bantu population[6].

Studies of traditional Inuit further implicated high protein intakes, especially from animal foods, in calcium loss and the development of osteoporosis. Elderly Inuit, whose diet was very rich in meat and animal protein, had less "bone mineral mass" than omnivore Caucasians of a similar age consuming a less meat-dominated diet, although at younger ages the two groups had bones of similar density[7]. Interestingly, a 1988 study showed that when soya milk and tofu (soya bean curd) were the primary sources of protein, calcium balance in the body was maintained even when calcium intake was low and protein intake relatively high[5].

The higher sulphur-to-calcium ratio of meat increases calcium excretion, and a diet rich in meat can cause bone demineralization. A report published in 1988 compared the amounts of calcium excreted in the urine of 15 subjects who followed experimental diets for 12-day periods[10]. The diets contained constant amounts of calcium (400mg/day) and protein (75g/day), but differed with respect to protein sources, which were: animal protein; vegetable and egg protein; and all-vegetable protein. The animal-protein diet caused greater loss of bone calcium in the urine (150mg/day) than either the mixed diet (121mg/day) or the all-vegetable protein diet (103mg/day). These findings suggest that diets providing vegetable, rather than animal, protein may actually protect against bone loss, and hence osteoporosis.

The American Dietetic Association, in its 1993 policy statement on vegetarian diets, pointed out that the calcium intakes recommended in the USA were increased specifically to offset calcium losses caused by the typically high protein consumption in that country[58].

Vegans, with a slightly lower protein intake than average omnivores and a meat-free diet, lose less calcium in their urine.

CALCIUM ABSORPTION FROM PLANT FOODS

Only 20%–30% of calcium in the average diet is absorbed. The availability to the body of calcium in food can be reduced if it binds to fibre, phytate or oxalate in the intestine. Vegan diets provide more than average amounts of these three factors, so do they restrict how well calcium is absorbed from plant foods?

Fibre is no longer thought to limit the availability of calcium from food, since calcium absorption from kale, a fibrous but low-oxalate vegetable, is higher than from cow's milk[63].

Phytate (or phytic acid) is a natural substance, found in grains, nuts and seeds, which can bind with calcium in foods, making it less absorbable. A sudden change to a diet containing more phytate can reduce calcium absorption, but this is unlikely to be permanent as our bodies are able to adapt. Moreover, the phytate in flour is reduced when bread is leavened, and our intestines can also break down phytate. There are many communities whose traditional diet is based on whole grains and contains enough phytate, theoretically, to bind *all* the calcium in their food!

Oxalate (or oxalic acid) is found in some fruits and vegetables, such as spinach, rhubarb and sweet potatoes. It can reduce the availability of calcium although, overall, these foods are unlikely to have a very marked effect.

Bearing in mind the content of phytate and oxalate in various foods, **particularly good sources of absorbable calcium include tofu (if prepared with calcium — check the label), turnip greens, mustard greens, kale, white beans, broccoli, almonds, green cabbage, watercress and Brussels sprouts.**

The American Dietetic Association[58] believes that fibre, phytate and oxalate do not have a significant effect on calcium intake overall — a view shared by the UK's Ministry of Agriculture, Fisheries and Foods[11] and Department of Health[40]. Numerous interacting factors can increase or decrease calcium absorption, but any single factor is unlikely to affect dramatically our bodies' ability to stay in mineral balance.

CALCIUM INTAKE BY VEGANS — ADULTS

Several surveys have recorded daily calcium consumption by vegans. Studies in the 1950s and 1960s found intakes of between 500 and 1,000mg[14]. In a 1985 report[15] the average intake of ten male and female vegans was lower, at 493mg, than that of matched omnivores. Although below the UK Reference Nutrient Intake (700mg/day), this level exceeds the Lower Reference Nutrient Intake (400mg/day) and is close to the Estimated Average Requirement (525mg/day). Two studies[16,17] of 18 and 22 British vegans, men and women, also showed their average calcium intakes, at 554mg and 585mg, to be lower than those of matched omnivores and below the RNI. However, none of these studies took into account the contribution made by drinking and cooking water in hard-water areas, which provide 200–500mg calcium daily[40].

An analysis[18] of the diet of six middle-aged Swedish vegans showed an average calcium consumption of 626mg. A 1987 report found a lower dietary intake of calcium in near-vegan women compared to omnivore women, but similar bloodstream levels of the mineral[12]. A 1993 study using weighed dietary intake showed that 38 British vegans consumed a mean of 540mg calcium daily (497mg women, 582mg men), again below the RNI but close to or above the Estimated Average Requirements[43].

Most recently, a study of eight vegan women aged 35–45 years revealed that with one exception all individuals exceeded the calcium RNI, and the woman with the lowest intake was close to the RNI (personal communication[59]). Everyone in the group exceeded the Estimated Average Requirement for calcium. The study included the contribution of drinking and cooking water to calcium consumption; fortified soya milks and tofu products were useful sources for some women. Four individuals used calcium supplements, but excluding the contribution of these did not markedly alter the average calcium intake of the vegan group as a whole.

Finnish male and female vegans had a lower daily calcium intake (about 500mg/day) than lacto-vegetarians (about 800mg/day), fish-eaters (about 890mg/day) and omnivores (about 970mg/day), but there was no difference in calcium levels in the bloodstream between any of these dietary groups[46].

Although the calcium intake of adult vegans tends to be lower than the recommended optimum, it is close to the Estimated Average Requirement. Also, it is known that the body can adapt to low calcium intakes, especially when the diet does not contain excessive protein. There have been no reports of calcium deficiency in adult vegans.

OSTEOPOROSIS

Osteoporosis — literally, porous or fragile bones — is the major cause of bone fractures in the elderly. In the UK, 40% of women and 13% of men aged over fifty are likely to suffer a bone fracture due to osteoporosis. It is characterized by a loss of bone 'mass', that is, a loss not only of calcium from the skeleton but also of all the other bone components, such as the protein matrix. Throughout the world every year about 1.7 million people, mostly post-menopausal women, suffer hip fractures mainly as a result of osteoporosis. One in four British women is affected by osteoporosis, which can lead to dowager's hump (due to collapse of the spinal bones), and painful fractures of the hip, spine, thigh or arm.

Osteoporosis is better prevented than treated. Prevention includes an adequate intake of calcium throughout life, but especially in childhood and young adulthood; and minimizing major risk factors such as smoking, heavy alcohol use and lack of physical exercise. The effect of inactivity on bone density is very clear in astronauts, whose bones quickly lose calcium in weightless conditions. Diets high in protein and in salt (sodium chloride) also increase calcium loss from the body, and may have an effect on osteoporosis. Post-menopausal women are more prone to osteoporosis because they produce less oestrogen, which protects the skeleton in younger women.

There has been considerable publicity about the role of dietary calcium in preventing osteoporosis, but the fact remains that it is *more* common in Westernized countries — where calcium intakes and consumption of dairy products are high — compared with the rest of the world. Osteoporosis is comparatively rare in rural subsistence cultures, even though calcium intakes are much lower. Lifestyle factors, such as physical activity, lower protein or salt intakes, little alcohol consumption and the rarity of smoking, may offer protection to people in these populations.

Dietary calcium is believed to be one important factor in preventing osteoporosis, particularly in the teens-to-twenties age group, when bone mass is being built up. There does not seem to be a direct link between an older adult's bone density and their current calcium intake. Rather, it seems that calcium consumption in youth may affect bone density in old age. Oestrogen treatment (hormone replacement therapy) can prevent, and possibly restore, bone loss in post-menopausal women, but a high intake of calcium on its own in this age group does not prevent bone loss. There is some evidence that a proportion of people have a hereditary susceptibility to osteoporosis, through the genes that control vitamin D activity.

BONE DENSITY IN VEGANS AND VEGETARIANS

To my knowledge only two studies have have assessed bone density in vegans. Eleven vegans were included in a study of 304 women aged 52–90 years[56]. The vegan women had the lowest average bone density, at 0.465 grams per cm^2, of all the dietary groups which included lacto-ovo-vegetarians (0.567g/cm^2); some who ate fish and chicken but not red meat (0.600g/cm^2), and others who also ate red meat occasionally (0.602g/cm^2). Although the occasional meat-eaters had the highest average bone density when all age-groups were combined, at the ages of 80–89 years the lacto-ovo-vegetarians' bones were denser. However, even in this age group the vegans had the least dense bones of all the groups. The second investigation, in 1989, indicated that bone mineral content and bone width of the forearm (radius) in post-menopausal women — omnivores (146 subjects), lacto-ovo-vegetarians (128 subjects) or vegans (16 subjects) — were similar at all ages[44]. Athough there were individual variations in current intakes of calcium, the average intakes of the dietary groups were not significantly different. There was also no clear link between estimated calcium intake (currently or previously) and bone mineral content or bone width.

Several researchers have measured bone density in vegetarians, and have often found older vegetarian women to have denser bones than their omnivore peers. Apart from the 1989 report just mentioned[44], a long-term study[8,9,56] compared more than 1,600 lacto-ovo-vegetarian and omnivore women aged 20–89 years. While no obvious differences were found in the younger women, increasing differences were found in bone mass between the ages of 50 and 89 years. By their 80s, omnivore women had lost twice as much mineral content from their bones as the lacto-ovo-vegetarians. Analysis in another report showed that 88 lacto-ovo-vegetarian women had denser arm bones (mid-radius) than 287 omnivore women aged 60–98 years; but no difference between the groups was found in measurements made nearer the wrist (distal radius)[62].

Some studies have suggested that the bones of vegetarian and omnivore women are similar. For example, the bone densities of 28 lacto-ovo-vegetarian and 28 omnivore post-menopausal women were similar at all sites measured, except the skull. Although the diets of the two groups differed in many respects, the researchers concluded that bone density was not affected by a lacto-ovo-vegetarian diet[53]. In a 1991 report, no differences were found in bone density in the lower spines of pre-menopausal lacto-ovo-vegetarian and omnivore women, aged 28–45 years old[47]. This supports the observation that when differences in bone density do occur, they happen after the menopause rather than before. In 1994 the results of a five-year prospective investigation of bone mineral density and mineral content in elderly American women was published[64]. At an average age of 81 years, there was no significant difference between the 140 omnivores and 49 lacto-ovo-vegetarians, even though the vegetarian women consumed about 150mg/day less calcium than did the omnivores. Interestingly, the study showed that maintaining weight through lean rather than fat body mass was the most important protective factor. This itself is linked to continuing physical activity in old age, such as sports, walking and gardening.

Given that poor calcium balance during adolescence and young adulthood is currently believed to increase the risk of osteoporosis in later years, it is prudent for people of every dietary persuasion to eat calcium-rich foods. At present, there is insufficient evidence to indicate whether vegans are more or less prone to osteoporosis, since the studies published so far have involved few vegan subjects.

Overall, research suggests that lacto-ovo-vegetarian women after the menopause are likely to have denser bones than omnivore women of the same age. Among younger women, no obvious differences in bone density between vegetarians and omnivores have been found. Thus a vegetarian diet probably helps protect against bone loss in older age groups, but the influence of a vegan diet is not yet clear.

CALCIUM AND VEGANS — INFANTS AND CHILDREN

Relatively few publications have reported on calcium intake by vegan children. British children who were vegan from birth consumed less calcium in food than the UK RNIs, but most met the Estimated Average Requirements, even though the calcium content of their drinking water was not taken into account[19,48]. All the children were well, with no signs of deficiency. The same was true for children brought up in a vegan community called The Farm, in Tennessee, USA. Their mean calcium intake, at 351mg, was less than the current US and UK recommendations but they were well and thriving[20].

To the author's knowledge, only three cases of possible calcium deficiency in vegan infants have been reported, and these were unusual. In Switzerland, a vegan mother who believed her infant son was allergic to cow's milk and could not suckle adequately, fed him with almond extract made at home, plus some cereals and a little fruit[42]. The child's calcium intake was less than the British Recommended Nutrient Intake and Estimated Average Requirement, and his bones were reported to contain too little of this mineral. Two infants from a black Hebrew vegan community in Israel also had fragile bones associated with low blood levels of calcium[66].

The calcium intake of vegans tends to be slightly below the recommended optimal amounts, but the body adapts to lower intakes and there have been no reports of calcium deficiency in vegan adults. The fact that vegans have a slightly lower protein intake and exclude meat from their diets encourages their bodies to retain calcium, so that their dietary needs may be lower than a typical omnivore's. The few published reports concerning the bones of vegans suggest that the likelihood of osteoporosis is no greater than for omnivores.

Only three likely cases of calcium deficiency in vegan infants have been reported. However, given the importance of calcium intake during childhood on the future risk of osteoporosis, all parents, including vegans, should ensure that their children's diets contain calcium-rich foods. Vegan sources suitable for small children include tofu (when prepared with calcium sulphate), mashed beans, green leafy vegetables such as kale and cabbage, home-made dried fruit spreads, fortified soya milks, nut and seed 'butters' using almonds or sesame seeds (tahini), and molasses.

MAGNESIUM

Magnesium is widespread in foods, particularly in **nuts, whole grains (including oats, millet, brown rice and wholemeal bread), wheatgerm, soya flour and yeast extracts**. About 60% of the body's magnesium is in the bones, and 40% in the cells. It is important in nerve and muscle activity, and is present in some 300 enzymes involved in metabolism. Deficiency is rare, the most likely cause being not dietary insufficiency but excessive loss through diarrhoea.

The Reference Nutrient Intakes in the UK[40], first published for magnesium in 1991, are 55–80mg daily for infants; 85–200mg for children; and 270–300mg for teenagers and adults, plus an extra 50mg a day for breast-feeding women. The US RDA is 6mg per kilogram of body weight daily for children aged 1 to 16 years; and for adults, a total daily intake of 280mg for women and 350mg for men[39]. German guidelines are very similar[45].

Less than half the magnesium eaten is absorbed from the intestine, and a high-fibre diet can theoretically cause some of the mineral to be unavailable to the body — although adaptation occurs[29]. In 1981 the magnesium intake of middle-aged Swedish male and female vegans averaged 542mg a day[18], and in 1987 the daily intake of British male and female vegans was reported to be significantly higher than that of matched omnivores, at 516mg compared with 398mg[17]. A Swedish study of 12 vegans recorded higher magnesium intakes than those of 19 subjects consuming the common omnivore diets[54]. In a recent report the average magnesium consumption by 38 British male and female vegans was 939mg/day and 538mg/day respectively, averaging 739mg daily — considerably higher than the intakes of the lacto-ovo-vegetarian and fish-eating subjects[43]. The findings of one study, that near-vegetarian macrobiotic women had higher levels of magnesium in their bloodstream than omnivore women, suggests that fibre does not reduce absorption of the mineral[12].

The average intake of magnesium by vegans is about double the UK Reference Nutrient Intake, and considerably higher than that of average omnivores. Thus, any binding effect of fibre is unlikely to be significant.

PHOSPHORUS

This mineral is present in nearly all foods, particularly good sources for vegans being **nuts, whole grains (including wholemeal bread) and yeast extracts.** It is the second most abundant mineral in the body after calcium, and is essential in all cells for the utilization of energy from food. In the form of phosphates it plays a vital structural role in the bones and teeth. Dietary deficiency of phosphorus is unknown. However, an excess supply of phosphorus over calcium in the first few days of life, as found in cow's milk and formula milks compared to breast milk, can cause muscular spasms in infants[11].

The UK Department of Health[40] suggests that intakes of phosphorus should be equal to those of calcium as measured in terms of molecular weights. This works out at 400mg phophorus a day for infants; 270–450mg/day for children; 625–775mg for female and male teenagers; and 550mg for adults, with an additional 440mg/day for breast-feeding women. The US RDAs are 1,200mg for young adults, and 800mg for the over-25s, with more for pregnant and nursing women[39]. German recommendations for phosphorus intake are one-third to three-quarters higher[45].

There are few reports on phosphorus intake by vegans. One, of children aged 2–5 years at The Farm, a vegan community in Tennessee, USA, showed that all age groups met or exceeded the recommended intake, except in the case of the 2- and 3-year-old girls whose intake was 94% of the 1980 US recommendations[20].

Although there have been few studies of phosphorus intake by vegans, phosphorus is widely available in plant foods and vegan diets are likely to contain adequate amounts.

SODIUM AND CHLORIDE

Sodium chloride (salt) levels are relatively low in unprocessed foods, but salt is added to many prepared foods. For example, bacon, sausages and other processed meat products have, on average, six times more sodium than fresh meat. Fresh fruits, vegetables and whole grains have less than half the amount of sodium found in fresh meat, eggs, fish and milk. However, salt is added to canned vegetables and most butter, margarine, cheese, bread and some breakfast cereals during manufacture; and many people add further salt in cooking and at the table. Sodium bicarbonate and monosodium glutamate are also dietary sources of sodium.

Sodium chloride is found in all body fluids, inside and outside the cells, and is involved in maintaining fluid balance. Sodium is also essential for muscle and nerve activity.

The UK Department of Health[40] proposed that 1.6g of **sodium** daily is adequate for adults (less for infants and children); and that **chloride** intake should be about 2.5g daily for adults. This recommendation translates into a **salt (ie. sodium chloride) intake of about 4g — or about one small teaspoonful — a day**. In 1994, the COMA report on nutrition and heart disease suggested that the British population should reduce its consumption from 9g to 6g of salt a day, with a similar proportionate reduction for children[65]. The US simply recommends a minimum intake of 0.5g sodium daily[39].

The recommended salt intake can be achieved from the sodium and chloride naturally present in food, without adding any in cooking or at the table. There is evidence that excessive sodium intakes can cause high blood pressure, itself a major risk factor for heart disease and strokes. The long-term decrease in salt intake suggested by the UK's National Advisory Committee on Nutrition Education, to 3g a day, might substantially reduce the prevalence of high blood pressure and deaths from it.

Intakes by 22 British vegans were 2.3g sodium and 3.3g chloride, compared to significantly higher levels for matched omnivores of 2.8g sodium and 4.5g chloride[17]. A similar sodium intake of 2.2g was found for a group of Swedish vegans[18]. These intakes are lower than those of the average British omnivore, but still higher than the UK recommendations. Vegans' lower-than-average consumption of sodium means that they are less likely to lose calcium in their urine.

Vegan diets tend to be lower in salt (sodium chloride) than omnivore diets, but may still contain more than is recommended.

POTASSIUM

The main sources of **potassium** in the average diet are **potatoes and other vegetables**, meat and milk, and **fruits and fruit juices**. Plant foods generally have a higher potassium-to-sodium ratio. There is consistent evidence that higher intakes of potassium are associated with lower blood pressure and fewer strokes, and the COMA report on nutrition and heart disease proposed that British adults should increase their potassium consumption from an average 3g/day to about 3.5g/day[65]. Our bodies closely control levels of this mineral, and excess is excreted by the kidneys. However, potassium deficiency can result from the use of some diuretics or from protracted diarrhoea, and in severe potassium depletion heart failure may result.

The Reference Nutrient Intakes recommended in the UK[40] are 0.8–2g/day for children, and 3.1–3.5g for teenagers and adults. In the US, a minimum requirement of 2g/day for adults has been set[39]. The potassium intake of a group of British vegans was 4.5g — significantly higher than that of matched omnivores, which was 3.7g[17]. In Sweden, the average intake of six vegans was 4g[18]. Eighteen British vegan children aged 5.8–12.8 years had an average daily consumption of 3.3g potassium[48].

Vegans probably consume more potassium than the general population, which may help protect them against high blood pressure and strokes.

THE TRACE ELEMENTS

Knowledge of the exact requirements for, and the functions of, some of the trace elements is incomplete, either because they have only relatively recently been found to be essential, or because dietary deficiencies of many are unknown, or because the utilization of one trace element may be affected by the amounts of other elements present. The trace elements include iron, zinc, selenium, iodine, copper, cobalt, chromium, manganese and molybdenum.

IRON

About one-fifth of the iron in an average diet comes from meat. Although eggs contain iron, because they are generally eaten in smaller amounts than bread, flour, other grain products, potatoes and vegetables, these latter are the more important sources. Of the plant foods, **dried fruits, whole grains (including wholemeal bread), nuts, green leafy vegetables, seeds**

and pulses are rich sources of iron. Other foods rich in iron, but which are usually eaten in smaller amounts, are **soya flour, parsley, watercress, black molasses and edible seaweeds.** The use of **iron pots and pans** contributes to dietary intake.

The human body normally contains 3–4 grams of iron, more than half of which is in the form of haemoglobin, the red pigment in the blood. Haemoglobin transports oxygen from the lungs to the tissues. Iron is a constituent of a number of enzymes. The muscle protein myoglobin contains iron, as does the liver — an important source during the first six months of life. The body's iron balance varies mainly according to dietary intake, as losses from the body are generally small — although women lose iron during menstruation. A lack of iron in the diet is partly compensated for by increased absorption rates, but in chronic dietary deficiency the body stores run down, resulting in iron-deficiency anaemia.

In 1991 the UK's Department of Health[40] recommended Reference Nutrient Intakes for infants of 1.7mg (at 0–3 months) rising to 7.8mg a day (at 12 months); 6.1–8.7mg for children; 11.3–14.8mg for teenagers; and 8.7mg for men and 14.8mg for women. The US Recommended Dietary Allowances[39] are similar at 10mg a day for adult men and post-menopausal women; 15mg for adolescents and pre-menopausal women; and an additional 15mg a day for pregnant women.

IRON BALANCE AND OTHER FACTORS

Up to 22% of the iron in meat is absorbed, while only 1%–8% is absorbed from eggs and plant foods. If body stores fall, the rate of iron absorption from foods goes up[23]. About 40% of the iron in animal foods is in a form called haem iron, while the remainder, and all the iron in plant foods, is in the less well absorbed non-haem form.

Absorption of iron from plant foods is improved by the presence in a meal of animal foods; vitamin C (ascorbic acid); and other organic acids such as malic acid (eg. in pumpkins, plums and apples) and citric acid (in citrus fruits). Iron absorption can be reduced by tannins (eg. in tea) and phytates (found in nuts, grains and seeds).

Of these factors, all are relevant to vegans with the obvious exception of animal foods. Laboratory research in which experimental meals were given to 299 volunteers has shown that the inclusion of foods (such as fresh salad, orange juice or cauliflower) providing 70–105mg of vitamin C in each meal increased the absorption of iron. A particularly pronounced

TABLE 5.2

PORTIONS OF SOME VEGAN FOODS PROVIDING *2mg* OF IRON

Food	Weight of food providing 2mg iron

	Food	Weight of food providing 2mg iron
NUTS (shelled)	**Pistachios**	14g (0.5oz)
	Cashews, roasted	32g (1.1oz)
	Pine nuts	36g (1.3oz)
	Almonds	67g (2.4oz)
PULSES	**Soya flour,** low fat	22g (0.8oz)
	Whole lentils, boiled	57g (2.0oz)
	Soya beans, boiled	67g (2.4oz)
	Chick peas, boiled	95g (3.3oz)
	Black eyed beans, boiled	105g (3.7oz)
GRAINS	**Wheat bran**	16g (0.6oz)
	Wheatgerm	24g (0.8oz)
	Wholemeal flour	51g (1.8oz)
	Oatmeal	53g (1.9oz)
	Rye flour, 100%	74g (2.6oz)
	Wholemeal bread	74g (2.6oz)
SEEDS (shelled)	**Sesame seeds** or **tahini**	19g (0.7oz)
	Sunflower seeds	31g (1.1oz)
OTHERS	**Papadums**, fried	18g (0.6oz)
	Black molasses	22g (0.8oz)
	Parsley	26g (0.9oz)
	Figs, dried	48g (1.7oz)
	Raisins	53g (1.9oz)
	Apricots, dried	59g (2.1oz)
	Chinese leaves	69g (2.4oz)
	Watercress	91g (3.2oz)
	Spinach, boiled	125g (4.4oz)
	Peas, fresh, boiled	133g (4.7oz)

Foods which are particularly good sources of iron are shown in bold print and, *for each food type, the best sources of iron are at the top of each list.*

Values taken from Holland *et al* [21].

1991 UK Reference Nutrient Intakes: 14.8mg for women, 8.7mg for men.

US recommendations: 15mg for women, 10mg for men.

effect was seen when 4.5oz cauliflower (containing 60mg vitamin C) was added to vegetarian meals, causing a more than three-fold increase in iron absorption[25]. Earlier studies have shown that, when iron intake from plant foods is relatively high (14–26mg a day), even large amounts of phytate do not adversely affect iron balance[26–28]. This level of iron intake is common among vegans (see **Iron in vegan diets — adults**, below).

There has been some concern that fibre in food, separate from the effect of phytate, can inhibit the absorption of iron. However a study with 12 volunteers showed that on diets containing about the same amount of iron (21.8mg and 26.4mg), iron balance was *more* favourable when fibre intake was 59g a day, than on a low-fibre regime of only 9g[29]. These experimental intakes of iron are similar to those in vegan diets, while the high-fibre regime exceeded the average 45g of fibre a day consumed by vegans. This suggests that the iron status of vegans is unlikely to suffer from a high fibre intake.

IRON IN VEGAN DIETS — INFANTS AND CHILDREN

As a general rule, iron-deficiency anaemia in infants is most likely to occur at the age of 4–6 months, when a child first becomes entirely dependent on dietary iron. Many infant feeding formulas and cereals contain added iron, and these contribute a large proportion of the intake of some infants. Iron-deficiency anaemia in infancy is more common in some ethnic minorities, particularly those in a poor socio-economic situation. This is thought to be due to weaning diets containing few iron-rich foods, and to over-reliance on cow's milk, which is not a good source.

The published information available shows that the diets of vegan children in the UK and USA generally provide the recommended amounts of iron, or more[19,20,48]. More details are in **Vegan Mothers and Children**, page 125.

IRON IN VEGAN DIETS — ADULTS

Studies of British vegans have reported average daily iron intakes of 22.4mg[15], 31mg[16], 20.5mg[17] and 16.9mg[43], while a group of middle-aged Swedish vegans had a mean intake of 16.5mg a day[18]. The average intake for British vegans is thus approximately double the recommended Reference Nutrient Intakes. At this level of iron consumption, any possible inhibitory effects of fibre and phytate on absorption are unlikely to be important (see **Iron balance and other factors**, page 111). As vegan diets contain about three to four times the British and US recommendations for vitamin C, absorption of iron is enhanced.

Iron deficiency is believed to be fairly common in the general population, and a 1985 survey[30] of young British omnivore women showed that, on average, they were consuming only just over half the current recommended intake. The Dietary and Nutritional Survey of British Adults, published in 1990[41], revealed that 4% of all women were anaemic, with low concentrations of haemoglobin in their bloodstream, and one-third of all women (42% of those under the age of 50 years) had low iron stores. Symptoms of iron deficiency anaemia include tiredness and breathlessness especially on physical exertion, giddiness, palpitations, headache and poor concentration.

A person's iron balance can be measured by several criteria. An early decrease in iron stores can be detected by a drop in ferritin (a complex of iron and protein) to less than 12μg per litre of blood. The next stage is characterized by changes in the content of red blood cells, and a drop in the amount of iron carried by the protein which transports it in the blood (transferrin saturation) — even though haemoglobin levels may remain normal. Finally, iron-deficiency anaemia is signalled by the presence of microcytic (abnormally small) blood cells and very low haemoglobin levels in the blood.

It is generally assumed that haemoglobin concentrations of less than 130g/l in men and 120g/l in women[23] are likely to indicate anaemia, but in 1986 the British Medical Association (BMA) stated that haemoglobin levels as low as 110g/l are not significant to health, and that the importance of maintaining haemoglobin at the previously recommended levels has been exaggerated[24]. The BMA also pointed out that a high level of haemoglobin in the blood has health hazards.

The Swedish vegans already mentioned[18] had haemoglobin levels in the normal range, with a mean of 143g/l (men) and 124g/l (women). Twenty-three out of 26 British vegans studied in 1970 had normal haemoglobin levels, similar to the findings for matched omnivores[31]. Thirty-four vegans had normal haemoglobin values of 143.5g/l in men and 135g/l in women, compared with 149g/l and 130g/l in omnivore men and women respectively[32]. Thirty-six Israeli vegans who had followed their diets for 5–35 years had an average haemoglobin level of 133g/l, compared to 134g/l in matched omnivore subjects[57]. One study reported that 10% of women who had recently adopted vegan diets had plasma ferritin levels below 10μg/l[50], a frequency lower than found among omnivore women in general. Signs of iron-deficiency anaemia were reported in a number of infants from an isolated community of Hebrew Americans living in Israel[51], but these cases were highly atypical. In addition, one breast-fed infant of a vegan mother was reported to have iron deficiency[60].

Vegans have a high dietary iron intake which is, on average, more than twice the recommended amount. Although iron from plant sources is less well absorbed than that from meat, vitamin C enhances iron absorption and vegan diets contain three to four times the recommended amounts of this vitamin. It has been shown that the fibre and phytate in plant foods are unlikely to interfere with iron absorption when dietary intake is as high as in a typical vegan diet. Studies show that the iron status of vegans is usually normal, and iron deficiency is no more common than in the general population.

ZINC

Zinc is present in a wide variety of foods, and meat and dairy products are very rich sources. Vegan sources of zinc include **wheatgerm, *whole* grains (such as wholemeal bread, rice, oats and cornmeal), nuts, pulses, tofu (soya bean curd), soya protein, miso (fermented soya bean paste) and some vegetables (eg. peas, parsley, bean sprouts).** An abundance or lack of zinc in the soil influences its content in plants.

Zinc is involved, directly or indirectly, with the major metabolic pathways in the body, and is required for growth, wound healing and immune function. It's also a component of several enzymes in the body, but most of this mineral is found in the bones. Less than half the zinc in food is absorbed, and this proportion may be lower in the case of plant foods containing fibre and phytates (*but see below*). A deficiency of zinc can cause stunted growth and delayed wound healing and, apart from dietary lack, possible causes of deficiency may include alcoholism, malabsorption, chronic kidney disease and certain drugs.

The 1991 UK Reference Nutrient Intakes[40] are 4–7mg a day for infants and children to the age of ten years; 9mg for adolescents; 9.5mg for adult men and 7mg for women (plus an extra 2.5–6mg daily during breast feeding). US Recommended Dietary Allowances are generally higher, at 12mg a day for women; 10–15mg for men; 15mg during pregnancy, and 16–19mg during lactation[39]. German recommendations are similar to these[45]. A representative survey of the British population, published in 1990, recorded an average zinc intake of 11.4mg daily for men, and 8.4mg for women[41], suggesting that most people achieve the RNI.

There is controversy over whether the fibre and phytate found in plant foods affect the body's ability to absorb zinc. Some research with omnivore volunteers has suggested that, in the short term, adding extra fibre to their diets caused their bodies to retain zinc less well. It is probable that the body adapts to phytate over a longer period of time, and some studies indicate that phytate does not have an inhibitory effect, especially at higher zinc intakes. According to the UK Department of Health[40], whole grains contain enough zinc to offset its limited bioavailability from this source, while white flour, for example, is a poor source.

In 1993, the average daily zinc intake of 38 British vegans was 10.1mg for men and 7mg for women[43]. Middle-aged Swedish vegans consumed 13mg (men) and 10mg (women), intakes which were a third higher than those typical of Swedish omnivores[18]. The calculated zinc intake of 11 American vegan men was 8.1mg daily[52]. The intakes measured in these studies are below the US recommendations but, with the exception of the American men, they satisfy or exceed UK RNIs.

The amount of zinc in the diets of 23 British pre-school vegan children varied from 1–8mg, with an average of 4mg a day, below current UK recommendations but similar to the intake of omnivore children[19]. A follow-up survey of these lifelong vegan children indicated that, at the ages of 5.8–12.8 years their mean zinc intake was 7.4mg, which exceeds the UK RNIs[48]. One case of zinc deficiency in a vegan infant from an isolated Hebrew American community living in Israel was reported in 1982, but this community was highly atypical[51].

Four studies have found slightly lower levels of zinc in the bloodstream of Caucasian vegetarians than in omnivores, and one unpublished study suggests that vegans may excrete less zinc (reviewed in [35]). This is probably the body's way of maintaining zinc balance, and need not suggest a deficiency. One American report indicated that female vegans, but not males, had rather low zinc intakes[49]. However, the zinc levels in the blood of the vegans were not significantly different from those of omnivores. At present, too few studies have been conducted to draw firm conclusions about the zinc status of vegans.

Intakes of zinc by vegans are similar to those of omnivores, and usually meet British recommendations; but may sometimes fall below the higher levels of zinc consumption recommended in the USA. When measured, zinc levels in the bloodstream of vegans have been in the normal range. There have been no reports of zinc deficiency in adult vegans, and only one atypical case in a vegan infant.

SELENIUM

Sources of selenium include meat, fish, **nuts (especially brazil nuts), seeds, soya beans, mushrooms, grains and bananas.** The amount of selenium in the soil, which varies widely within and between countries, is the main factor determining the level of this mineral in plants. In the UK, the soil contains relatively little selenium.

Selenium plays many roles in the body, and some are not fully understood. As part of an enzyme called glutathione peroxidase it has antioxidant activity and, in conjunction with vitamin E, helps protect against free-radical damage to tissues. Selenium is essential for normal immune function, and may help in the normal process of detoxification of chemicals. It has also been suggested that low levels of selenium in the bloodstream may be linked to increased risk of heart disease. Deficiency is not common, especially in countries where foods come from a wide variety of sources.

The 1991 UK Reference Nutrient Intakes[40] for selenium are as follows: 10–30µg/day for infants and children, depending on age; 45µg for adolescents; 70–75µg for young and adult men, and 60µg for women, with an extra 15µg daily during breast feeding. Recommended Dietary Allowances for selenium were established for the first time in the USA in 1989[39], at 10µg daily for infants up to 6 months, rising to 50µg for teenagers aged 15 to 18 years; 70µg for men; and 55µg for women, with an extra 10–20µg daily for pregnant and lactating women.

The few studies of selenium in the vegan diet have been from Sweden, whose soil has a low selenium content. Swedish middle-aged male and female vegans had variable intakes[18], whose mean was 9.6µg — compared with a mean intake of 25µg a day by average Swedish omnivores, and 65µg by Swedish lacto-vegetarians[36]. A later study[37] accurately measured dietary intakes of selenium by all three groups as well as levels of selenium in the bloodstream. Although selenium *intake* was lowest in the vegans and highest in lacto-vegetarians, the average *bloodstream level* of selenium in vegans was the same as that of the omnivores, while the lacto-vegetarians had significantly lower levels. The bloodstream levels of selenium in vegans were close to the mean of healthy omnivores from eight different countries.

Although population studies have shown that selenium intake has a major influence on blood levels of the mineral, other factors are also important, including the rate of turnover of blood proteins and loss of selenium in the urine. In the Swedish study[36], both lacto-vegetarians and vegans lost less than half the amount of selenium in their urine compared with omnivores, suggesting that their bodies were conserving supplies. Further research into selenium is needed before firm conclusions can be drawn.

Studies so far suggest that selenium may be present in smaller amounts in vegan diets, although bloodstream levels in vegans are similar to those of omnivores. The selenium content of plants varies according to the amount in the soil, and this will have a major effect on selenium intakes from food.

IODINE

The most reliable sources of iodine are seafoods, including **dried edible seaweeds such as nori, kelp, wakame and hijiki** which contain up to 500µg per 100g, and were used by an estimated 11%–16% of vegans in 1985[38]. Other vegan sources of iodine include **sea salt, iodized salt** and **Vecon** yeast extract, which contains seaweed powder[43]. There is iodine in **vegetables and grains**, and hence also in animal products, although amounts vary according to the iodine content of the soil and the fertilizers used. Because of the widespread use of iodides in animal feed, milk is the main source of iodine in the average British diet; meat and eggs also contain iodine.

Iodine is an essential component of hormones produced by the thyroid gland, and a deficiency leads to goitre. Deficiency is rare in Britain, but still common in many areas of the world, including some parts of Europe.

The 1991 UK Reference Nutrient Intakes[40] for iodine are 50–60µg/day for infants, rising through 70–130µg for children and adolescents, to 140µg for adults. The Department of Health also recommended a safe upper limit of 1,000µg a day, since too much iodine is toxic.

A report published in 1993 showed that average daily iodine intakes by 38 British vegans were 66µg for women and 98µg for men[43]. Thirty-six of the vegans said they included sea salt, *Vecon* or seaweed in their diets. These intakes were only half those of lacto-ovo-vegetarians and fish-eaters, and less than the UK RNI, but equal to the Lower Reference Nutrient Intake (LRNI). The LRNI is considered adequate only for a minority of people who have low needs. A study[18] of Swedish vegans reported a mean intake of 70µg, only a quarter of that found in the

Swedish omnivore diet. Forty-five British vegan men who did not use tablets or kelp powder had, on average, more thyroid stimulating hormone in their bloodstream than omnivore men[61]. This might indicate that their diets were low in iodine, but more research is needed to clarify this.

A single case study of iodine deficiency in a vegan/vegetarian family has been published[42]. In Switzerland, the 7.5-month-old infant of a vegan mother and lacto-vegetarian father had been breast fed for 2.5 months, and then fed on a home-prepared extract of almonds in water. The boy failed to thrive and developed a number of deficiencies, including that of iodine. There have been no other reports of iodine deficiency in vegans, to the author's knowledge.

To date, few studies have been published, but available results suggest that the iodine intake of vegans may be rather low. However, iodine deficiency does not appear to be more common among vegans than in the general population.

COPPER

Shellfish and liver are particularly rich sources of copper, but the main sources in the British omnivore's diet are meat (28%), **bread and other grain products** (24%), and **vegetables** (21%). Whole grains are a better source than refined grains (such as white flour and bread), and **wheatgerm** especially so. **Nuts and seeds** also contain useful amounts of copper, while cow's milk contains little. Households with copper piping may obtain some of this mineral from their drinking and cooking water.

Copper is necessary for a number of enzymes in the body, and for maintaining the bones. In the general population, deficiency has only occasionally been observed in malnourished infants, especially those who have been fed solely on cow's milk for a prolonged period, as it contains less copper than most foods. This particular problem would not arise with vegan infants.

The 1991 UK Reference Nutrient Intakes[40] for copper are 0.2–0.3mg a day for infants; 0.4–1mg for children and teenagers, and 1.2mg for adults, with an extra 0.3mg during breast feeding. The US Recommended Dietary Allowances range between 1.5 and 3mg per day for adults[39], while comparable German recommendations are 2–4mg[45]. The results of a representative survey published in 1990[41] indicated that the average British diet provides 1.43mg copper daily.

A 1993 study[43] of three dietary groups showed that of 38 British vegans, men consumed an average 3.4mg copper/day, and women 2.4mg. This was about 50% higher than the copper intakes of lacto-ovo-vegetarians and fish-eaters. However, at the time of writing confirmation is awaited from the UK Ministry of Agriculture, Fisheries and Foods that the copper content (1.7mg per 100g) attributed to tofu in food tables is incorrect, the more likely level being 0.2mg per 100g tofu. If so, this would reduce the intakes recorded for vegans in this report[43]. A study of Swedish vegans found their average copper intake to be 3.6mg[18].

Two studies indicate that adequate amounts of copper are provided by vegan diets. The copper content of tofu may have been over-estimated, which could affect the reliability of these reports.

CHROMIUM

Chromium is needed to enable the body to utilize glucose, to maintain nucleic acids and in gene expression. This mineral is fairly widely distributed in foods, but even so, chromium intake by the general population in the USA, UK and Finland has been found to be less than the US RDAs of 50–200µg a day[39]. German recommended intakes are also 50–200µg daily[45]. In the UK, no Reference Nutrient Intake has been set but the Department of Health believes a safe and adequate intake lies somewhere above 25µg a day. There is some evidence that a low chromium intake may be responsible for impaired glucose tolerance and raised insulin levels in subjects with mild hyperglycaemia, and that an increased intake may thus prevent maturity-onset (type-2) diabetes in some people. Since **whole grains, beans, brewer's yeast and nuts** are good sources of chromium, it is likely that most vegans have an adequate intake. However, **to the author's knowledge chromium intake by vegans has not been measured.**

MANGANESE

This mineral is a component of a number of enzymes; plant foods such as **nuts, whole grains and spices** are much better sources than animal products. In the UK, the Department of Health[40] recommends a safe and adequate intake of more than 1.4mg/day for adults. The US RDA is 2–5mg a day for adults[39]. **Tea** is very rich in this mineral, and probably provides half of the average daily intake.

COBALT

Cobalt is utilized by the human body only in the form of vitamin B_{12} (*see* **Vitamins**, *for a detailed discussion of this vitamin*).

MOLYBDENUM

This element is essential for some enzymes, and in the UK the safe adult intake is thought to lie between 50 and 400µg a day[40]. The US RDAs for molybdenum are between 75 and 250µg daily, depending on gender and age group[39].

To the author's knowledge there have been no studies of the levels of manganese, cobalt or molybdenum in vegan diets.

MINERALS — SUMMARY

A vegan diet provides all the minerals known to be needed by the human body. Some vegan children consume less calcium than the Reference Nutrient Intakes (as do many omnivore children), and parents are advised to ensure that calcium-rich foods are included in their children's diets. There have been no reports of calcium deficiency in vegans; the absence of meat and the slightly lower amounts of protein in their diets may help protect against this.

Vegans have a high dietary intake of iron which, combined with high amounts of vitamin C, appear able to counteract any effects of fibre or phytate in inhibiting iron absorption. Research shows vegans have adequate levels of iron in their bodies and rarely suffer from iron deficiency.

The lower level of sodium chloride found in the diets of vegans may help protect against high blood pressure and associated diseases. One study suggests that the level of selenium in the bloodstream of vegans is normal even when consumption is lower than average. For zinc, amounts in the vegan diet are adequate and no deficiency has been reported in vegans. Iodine may be lower than average in vegan diets, but again there have been no reports of deficiency. Further research on the trace minerals, in particular their presence in vegan diets, would be useful.

REFERENCES

1 Walker, R. M. & Linkswiler, H.M. (1972). Calcium retention in the adult human male as affected by protein intake. *J. Nutr.* 102:1297–1302.

2 Anand, C.R. & Linkswiler, H.M. (1974). Effect of protein intake on calcium balance of young men given 500g calcium daily. *J. Nutr.* 104:695–700

3 Allen, L.H., Oddoye, E.A. & Margen, S. (1979). Protein-induced hypercalcuria: a long-term study. *Am. J. Clin. Nutr.* 32:741–749.

4 Linkswiler, H.M., Zemel, M.B., Hegsted, M. & Schuette, S. (1981). Protein-induced hypercalcuria. *Fed. Proc.* 40:2429–2433.

5 Zemel, M.B. (1988). Calcium utilisation: effect of varying level and source of dietary protein. *Am. J. Clin. Nutr.* 48:880–883.

6 Walker, A.R.P. (1965). Osteoporosis and calcium deficiency. *Am. J. Clin. Nutr.* 16:327–336

7 Mazess, R.B. & Mather, W. (1974). Bone mineral content of North Alaskan Eskimos. *Am. J. Clin. Nutr.* 27:91–925.

8 Sanchez, T.V., Mickelsen, O., Marsh, A.G., Garn, S.M. & Mayor, G.H. (1980). *Bone mineral mass in elderly vegetarian and omnivorous females.* In: Mazess, R.B. ed. Proceedings of the 4th international conference on bone mineral measurement. pp94–98. Bethesda: MD NIAMMD.

9 Marsh, A.G., Sanchez, T.V., Mickelsen, O., Keiser, J. & Mayor, G. (1980). Cortical bone density of adult lacto-ovo-vegetarian and omnivorous women. *J. Am. Diet. Assn.* 76:148–151.

10 Breslau, N.A., Brinkley, L., Hill, K.D. & Pak, C.Y.C. (1988). Relationship of animal-protein rich diet to kidney stone formation and calcium metabolism. *J. Clin. End.*

66:140–146.

11 Ministry of Agriculture, Fisheries and Foods (1985). *Manual of Nutrition.* 9th edition. London: HMSO.

12 Specker, B.L., Tsang, R.C. & Miller, D. (1987). Effect of vegetarian diet on serum 1,25-dihydroxyvitamin D concentrations during lactation. *Obstet. Gynec.* 70:870–874.

13 Nielsen, F.H., Hunt, C.D., Mullen, L.M. & Hunt, J.R. (1987). Effect of dietary boron on mineral, estrogen, and testosterone metabolism in postmenopausal women. *FASEB J.* 1:394–397.

14 Ellis, F.R. & Mumford, P. (1967). The nutritional status of vegans and vegetarians. *Proc. Nutr. Soc.* 26:205–212.

15 Carlson, E., Kipps, M., Lockie, A. & Thomson, J. (1985). A comparative evaluation of vegan, vegetarian and omnivore diets. *J. Plant Foods* 6:89–100.

16 Rana, S.K. & Sanders, T.A.B. (1986). Taurine concentrations in the diet, plasma, urine and breast milk of vegans compared with omnivores. *Br. J. Nutr.* 56:17–27.

17 Sanders, T.A.B. & Key, T.J.A. (1987). Blood pressure, plasma renin activity and aldosterone concentrations in vegans and omnivore controls. *Hum. Nutr.: Appl. Nutr.* 41A:204–211.

18 Abdulla, M., Andersson, I., Asp, N-G., Berthelsen, K., Birkhed, D., Dencker, I., Johansson, C-G., Jägerstad, M., Kolar, K., Nair, B.M., Nilsson-Ehle, P., Nordén, Å., Rassner, S., Åkesson, B. & Öckerman, P-A. (1981). Nutrient intake and health status of vegans. Chemical analyses of diets using the duplicate portion sampling technique. *Am. J. Clin. Nutr.* 34:2464–2477.

19 Sanders, T.A.B. & Purves, R. (1981). An anthropometric and dietary assessment of the nutritional status of vegan preschool

children. *J. Hum. Nutr.* 35:349–357.

20 Fulton, J.R., Hutton, C.W. & Stitt, K.R. (1980), Preschool vegetarian children. *J. Am. Diet. Assn.* 76:360–365.

21 Holland, B., Welch, A.A., Unwin, I.D., Buss, D.H., Paul, A.A. & Southgate, D.A.T. (1991). *McCance & Widdowson's The Composition of Foods.* 5th edition. Royal Society of Chemistry and MAFF.

22 Passmore, R. & Eastwood, M.A. (1986). *Davidson and Passmore Human Nutrition and Dietetics*, p. 107. Edinburgh: Churchill Livingstone.

23 Herbert, V. (1987). Recommended dietary intakes (RDI) of iron in humans. *Am. J. Clin. Nutr.* 45:679–686.

24 Board of Science & Education, British Medical Association (1986). *Diet, nutrition and health.* London: BMA.

25 Hallberg, L., Brune, M. & Rossander, L. (1986). Effect of ascorbic acid on iron absorption from different types of meals. *Hum. Nutr.: Appl. Nutr.* 40A:97–113.

26 Walker, A.R.P., Fox, F.W. & Irving, J.T. (1948). Studies in human mineral metabolism. 1. The effect of bread rich in phytate phosphorus on the metabolism of certain mineral salts with special reference to calcium. *Biochem. J.* 42:452–462.

27 Cullumbine, H., Basnayake, V., Lemottee, J. & Wickramanayake, T.W. (1950). Mineral metabolism on rice diets. *Br. J. Nutr.* 4:101–111.

28 Hussain, R. & Patwardhan, V.N. (1959). The influence of phytate on the absorption of iron. *Ind. J. Med. Res.* 47:676–682.

29 Kelsay, J.L., Behall, K.M. & Prather, E.S. (1979). Effect of fiber from fruits and vegetables on metabolic responses of human subjects. II. Calcium, magnesium, iron and silicon balances. *Am. J. Clin. Nutr.* 32:1876–1880.

30 Barber, S.A., Bull, N.L. & Buss, D.H. (1985). Low iron intakes among young women in Britain. *Br. Med. J.* 290:743–744.

31 Ellis, F.R. & Montegriffo, V.M.E. (1970). Veganism, clinical findings and investigations. *Am. J. Clin. Nutr.* 23:249–255.

32 Sanders, T.A.B., Ellis, F.R. & Dickerson, J.W.T. (1978). Haematological studies on vegans. *Br. J. Nutr.* 40:9–15.

33 Anderson, B.M., Gibson, R.S. & Sabry, J.H. (1981). The iron and zinc status of long-term vegetarian women. *Am. J. Clin. Nutr.* 34:1042–1048.

34 National Advisory Committee for Nutrition Education (1983). *Proposals for Nutritional Guidelines for Health Education in Britain.* London: Health Education Council.

35 Sanders, T.A.B. (1983). Vegetarianism: Dietetic and medical aspects. *J. Plant Foods* 5:3–14.

36 Abdulla, M., Aly, K-O., Andersson, I., Asp, N-G., Birkhed, D., Denker, I., Johansson, C-G., Jägerstad, M., Kolar, K., Nair, B.M., Nilsson-Ehle, P., Nordén, Å., Rassner, S., Svensson, S., Åkesson, B. & Öckerman, P-A. (1984). Nutrient intake and health status of lactovegetarians: chemical analyses of diets using the duplicate portion sampling technique. *Am. J. Clin. Nutr.* 40:325–338.

37 Åkesson, B. & Öckerman, P.A. (1985). Selenium status in vegans and lactovegetarians. *Br. J. Nutr.* 53:199–205.

38 Langley, G.R. & Wilcox, J. (1987). *Health profile and nutrient sources of vegan and vegetarian runners.* Unpublished.

39 National Research Council USA (1989). *Recommended Dietary Allowances.* 10th edition. Washington, DC: NAS.

40 Department of Health (1991). *Dietary Reference Values for Food Energy and Nutrients for the United Kingdom.* Reports on Health & Social Subjects no. 41. London: HMSO.

41 Gregory, J., Foster, K., Tyler, H. & Wiseman, M. (1990). *The Dietary and Nutritional Survey of British Adults.* London: HMSO.

42 Kanaka, C., Schütz, B. & Zuppinger, K.A. (1992). Risks of alternative nutrition in infancy: a case report of severe iodine and carnitine deficiency. *Eur. J. Pediatr.* 151:786–788.

43 Draper, A., Lewis, J., Malhotra, N. & Wheeler, E. (1993). The energy and nutrient intakes of different types of vegetarian: a case for supplements? *Br. J. Nutr.* 69:3–19.

44 Hunt, I.F., Murphy, N.J., Henderson, C., Clark, V.A., Jacobs, R.M., Johnston, P.K. & Coulson, A.H. (1989). Bone mineral con-

tent in postmenopausal women: comparison of omnivores and vegetarians. *Am. J. Clin. Nutr.* 50:517–523.

45 Deutsche Gesellschaft für Ernährung (1991). *Empfehlungen für die Nährstoffzufuhr.* Frankfurt: Umschau Verlag.

46 Lamberg-Allardt, C., Kärkkäinen, M., Seppänen, R. & Bistrom, H. (1993). Low serum 25-hydroxyvitamin D concentrations and secondary hyperparathyroidism in middle-aged white strict vegetarians. *Am. J. Clin. Nutr.* 58:684–689.

47 Lloyd, T., Schaeffer, J.M., Walker, M.A. & Demers, L.M. (1991). Urinary hormonal concentrations and spinal bone densities of premenopausal vegetarian and nonvegetarian women. *Am. J. Clin. Nutr.* 54:1005–1010.

48 Sanders, T.A.B. & Manning. J. (1992). The growth and development of vegan children. *J. Hum. Nutr. Diet.* 5:11–21.

49 Freeland-Graves, J. (1988). Mineral adequacy of vegetarian diets. *Am. J. Clin. Nutr.* 48:859–862.

50 Helman, A.D. & Darnton-Hill, I. (1986). Vitamin and iron status in new vegans. *Am. J. Clin. Nutr.* 45:785–789.

51 Shinwell, E.D. & Gorodischer, R. (1982). Totally vegetarian diets and infant nutrition. *Pediatrics* 70:582–586.

52 Laidlaw, S.A., Shultz, T.D., Cecchino, J.T. & Kopple. J.D. (1988). Plasma and urine taurine levels in vegans. *Am. J. Clin. Nutr.* 47:66–663.

53 Tesar, R., Notelovitz, M., Shim, E., Kauwell, G. & Brown, J. (1992). Axial and peripheral bone density and nutrient intakes of postmenopausal vegetarian and omnivorous women. *Am. J. Clin. Nutr.* 56:699–704.

54 Abdulla, M. (1988). Dietary intake of inorganic chemical elements from vegetarian diets in Sweden. *Am. J. Clin. Nutr.* 48:926.

55 Rowe, P.M. (1994). New US recommendations on calcium intake. *Lancet* 343:1559–1560.

56 Marsh, A.G., Sanchez, T.V., Michelson, O., Chaffee, F.L. & Fagal, S.M. (1988). Vegetarian lifestyle and bone mineral density. *Am. J. Clin. Nutr.* 48:837–841.

57 Bar-Sella, P., Rakover, Y. & Ratner, D. (1990). Vitamin B12 and folate levels in long-term vegans. *Israel Med. Sci. J.* 26:309–312.

58 Havala, S. & Dwyer, J. (1993). Position of the American Dietetic Association: vegetarian diets. *J. Am. Diet. Assn.* 93:1317–1319.

59 Challis, J. Manuscript in preparation.

60 Frader, J., Reibman, B. & Turkewitz, D. (1978). Vitamin B12 deficiency in strict vegetarians. *New Engl. J. Med.* 299:1319.

61 Key, T.J.A., Thorogood, M., Keenan, J. & Long, A. (1992). Raised thyroid stimulating hormone associated with kelp intake in British vegan men. *J. Hum. Nutr. Diet.* 5:323–326.

62 Tylavsky, F.A. & Anderson, J.J.B. (1988). Dietary factors in bone health of elderly lactoovovegetarian and omnivorous women. *Am. J. Clin. Nutr.* 48:842–849.

63 Heaney, R.P. & Weaver, C.M. (1990) Calcium absorption from kale. *Am. J. Clin. Nutr.* 51:656–657

64 Reed, J.A., Anderson, J.J.B., Tylavsky, F.A. & Gallagher, P.N. (1994). Comparative changes in radial-bone density of elderly female lactoovovegetarians and omnivores. *Am. J. Clin. Nutr.* 59(suppl.):1197S–1202S.

65 Committee on Medical Aspects of Food Policy (1994). *Nutritional Aspects of Cardiovascular Disease.* Reports on Health & Social Subjects no. 46. London: HMSO.

66 Zmora, E., Gorodischer, R. & Bar-Ziv, J. (1979). Multiple nutritional deficiencies in infants from a strict vegetarian community. *Am. J. Dis. Child.* 133:141–144.

VEGAN MOTHERS
AND CHILDREN

To create a healthy body, ignorance is not bliss. The health-destroying practices of a 'fast-food childhood' must be replaced by accurate nutritional information given to children from informed parents and teachers. Using vegan nutrition to nourish the pregnant woman and growing child, as well as creating a satisfying and convenient dietary cuisine, is a major key to a long, healthy life for both parent and child.

Dr Michael Klaper MD,
Director of the Royal Atlantic Health Spa, Florida, 1987[70]

Our nutritional needs vary at different times of life. At conception and during pregnancy a woman's choice of foods may have profound effects on the development of her child, whose special requirements differ in many ways from an adult's.

During infancy, especially at the time of weaning, all children are nutritionally vulnerable. Despite generally low infant mortality rates in Westernized societies, there is no evidence that the overall health of young children is improving and, in fact, some chronic conditions such as asthma and insulin-dependent diabetes are on the increase.

Knowledge of the eating habits of British teenagers in general is sparse, but recent surveys suggest that their fat and sucrose intakes are much higher than recommended, while their consumption of starch and fibre is too low[60]. If these patterns of eating are carried into adulthood, then heart disease and cancers will continue to take a high toll in premature deaths.

Therefore the food children receive is vitally important for their health and wellbeing, not only during their childhood but also in years to come, as the next section explains.

LONG-TERM EFFECTS OF EARLY NUTRITION

Research during the 1990s has revealed that a pregnant woman's diet, and that of her infant during the first year of life, can affect the child's health in adulthood 40, 50 or even 60 years later. This means that the quality of nutrition in this particularly sensitive period in early life can modify the risks of developing illnesses decades later.

The studies used old records of the birth weights and one-year weights of thousands of babies born in the first half of the 20th century. In the 1980s and '90s, as middle-aged and elderly adults, they were contacted and asked to undergo a thorough health check. For those who had died, their health records and causes of death were noted. It was found that men who had weighed least at birth and at one year had the highest blood pressure and death rates from heart disease[12, 14], and were more likely to develop diabetes[16] or die of lung disease in middle or old age[17].

One theory which could explain these findings is that development in the womb and in the first year of life represents a critical period when a child's organs are particularly vulnerable to poor nourishment. For example, if the liver, lungs or pancreas do not develop fully, then in later years of life there may be a higher risk of disease in these organs. Of course, early diet is only one of many factors which affect our risk of illness, and the studies found that later diet and lifestyle could counteract early developmental effects.

Nevertheless, the research establishes the importance of good nutrition during pregnancy and infancy, not only for the health of the child, but because of long-term health consequences during adulthood.

CHILDREN'S PROTEIN AND ENERGY NEEDS

The UK Department of Health's 1991 recommendations[47] for protein and energy are lower than the 1979 standards[2] which they replace (*see Table 6.1*, page 131 *and Table 6.2*, *page 133*). This has been a general trend, although recommended protein intakes in the USA are very much higher. The UK Department of Health suggests that people whose main sources of protein are unrefined grains and other vegetables could, as a precaution, multiply the standard recommendations by a factor of 1.1, as shown in **Table 6.1**.

What small children primarily need is sufficient food energy (Calories), rather than protein *per se*[4]. Without a sufficient energy intake an individual will be in negative nitrogen balance (a measure of the adequacy of dietary protein) regardless of the amount of protein in the diet. Evidence for this has been provided by research into the type of diet best able to remedy oedema (bloating) caused by kwashiorkor in Jamaican children[22].

Also, in short-term studies with infant boys who had been malnourished but rehabilitated, nitrogen balance was similar whether the protein source was cow's milk, cottonseed and rice, soya beans, rice, soya beans and peanuts, soya beans and rice, cottonseed and peanuts, or cottonseed alone[23]. With these mixtures no effort was made to supply the 'limiting' amino acid in one plant protein by an excess in another (*see **Protein and Energy**, for an explanation of these terms*). Only peanut protein on its own was less well retained. In crossover studies lasting 2–3 months on each diet, babies fed rice and cottonseed or rice and peanuts as protein sources grew as well as infants fed wheat supplemented with lysine. All babies gained weight satisfactorily and at equivalent rates.

As long as children's energy needs are being met they will thrive on a diet in which protein is available from a mixture of plant foods.

VEGAN CHILDREN: PROTEIN, ENERGY AND GROWTH

Infancy and childhood are times of rapid growth and development when a satisfactory supply of nutrients is particularly important. Vegan children are usually breast fed for much longer than average, and breast-fed babies in general gain weight more slowly than those who are formula fed. Few formula feeds for babies are vegan; one available in the UK at the time of writing is Farley's *Soya Formula*. Ordinary soya milks are prepared for adult consumption and are not nutritionally adequate for infants.

Some nutritionists believe that a vegan diet may be inadequate for nursing women, or for young children. What do investigations show?

An American study published in 1980[26] reported on 48 pre-school children from The Farm, an 800-member vegan community in Tennessee which was virtually self-sufficient in food. The community's diet was based on beans and peas, a variety of grains and vegetables, soya milk and other soya products, some fruit, margarine, and yeast. Parents completed a three-day diet diary for their children, whose ages were 2–5 years, and each child was measured and weighed.

The authors reported that energy intake for all age groups and both sexes exceeded RDAs, with the exception of the 4-year-old girls whose mean energy intake of 1,621 Calories was slightly below the then US recommendation of 1,800 Calories for this group. The equivalent UK recommendation of 1,500 Calories was, however, exceeded and the authors pointed out that all the 4-year-old girls consumed more than two-thirds of the suggested energy allowances in the US.

Protein consumption in all groups exceeded the then current US recommended intakes; in the case of children aged 2, 3 and 5 years, by more than double. Although there were individual variations, mean intakes by the American vegan children of amino acids — cysteine, histidine,

TABLE 6.1

UK REFERENCE NUTRIENT INTAKES FOR WOMEN AND CHILDREN: PROTEIN

Group	Protein (grams/day)	
	Omnivore diet	Plant-based diet*
Women during pregnancy	51	56.1
Women breast feeding		
First 4 months	56	61.6
After 4 months	53	58.3
Infants and children		
0–3 months	12.5	13.8
4–6 months	12.7	14
7–9 months	13.7	15.1
10–12 months	14.9	16.4
1–3 years	14.5	16
4–6 years	19.7	21.7
7–10 years	28.3	31.1

From *Dietary Reference Values for Food Energy and Nutrients for the United Kingdom*, 1991[47].

* The official recommendations for an omnivore diet are calculated assuming the complete digestibility of protein. Since plant protein may be less digestible, the Department of Health recommends, as a precaution, that those whose protein is supplied primarily by unrefined grains and other vegetables should multiply the standard recommendations by 1.1, as shown in the second column.

isoleucine, leucine, lysine, methionine, phenylalanine, threonine, tryptophan and valine — were all higher than those recommended by the US National Academy of Sciences.

Average values for height and weight were below the national average among 3- to 5-year-old children, although not at 2 years, and all groups met or exceeded reference values for triceps skinfold thickness, except 4- and 5-year-old girls; the latter may be due to the slightly lower average age in the 5-year-old group compared with the reference 5-year-old population. Most, but not all, age groups exceeded the reference data for arm and arm muscle circumference. In interpreting the anthropometric data it should be borne in mind that hereditary factors were not taken into account in this study. A larger, follow-up study[50] of children at The Farm confirmed that their growth was close to the norm.

A different group of American vegan children was studied by Ken Resnicow and colleagues[62]. Aged between 5 and 17 years, eight of the nine children's weights and heights were in the normal range (one girl was noticeably shorter and heavier than average).

In 1981 a study of 23 British vegan pre-school children was published[24]. The children, born of vegan mothers, were aged 1–4.6 years and were located with the help of the Vegan Society, which also part-funded the study. Parents completed a 7-day diet diary for their children — one of the most accurate methods of measuring food intake. The average protein intake of the vegan children exceeded the UK recommendations at that time, and was more than double the 1991 recommendations. Wholegrain cereals and pulses each provided about one-third of the children's protein intake, with nuts contributing 18%.

The average energy consumption in each age group was slightly below 1979 and 1991 recommendations, but except for two children was within the normal range. Where energy consumption was low, the bulky nature of the diets was the probable cause. This is easily remedied by cutting down a little on the consumption of fruit and vegetables and increasing that of grains, pulses and nuts. Interestingly, by comparison, a 1992 report of energy intake by omnivore pre-school children aged 2–5 years revealed a wide variation among individuals, but a low average energy intake of only 60%–85% of their Estimated Average Requirements[64].

The British vegan children in the study were lighter in weight than average, but all were within the normal range for weight and height, with the exception of two children whose parents were of short stature. The Dugdale Index (an expression of weight for height) was a mean of 97 in the children, compared with a nominal value of 98–100, and head and mid-arm circumferences were normal. All the children had been breast fed for the first six months of life, and most well into their second year.

A follow-up survey of 20 British vegan children was published in 1992[44]. Their diets consisted mainly of bread and other grains and grain products; pulses, including soya products; fresh fruit and fruit juices; potatoes; and other vegetables. This and the 1981 study are unique in assessing prospec-

TABLE 6.2

UK ESTIMATED AVERAGE REQUIREMENTS FOR WOMEN AND CHILDREN: ENERGY (CALORIES)

Group	EARs (Calories/day)	
	Females	**Males**
Women		
19–50 years	1,940	n/a
Pregnancy* *(last three months)*	+200	n/a
Breast feeding*		
0–6 months	+450–570	n/a
6+ months#	+240–550	n/a
Infants and children		
0–12 months**	515–865	545–920
1–3 years	1,165	1,230
4–6 years	1,545	1,715
7–10 years	1,740	1,970
11–14 years	1,845	2,220

From *Dietary Reference Values for Food Energy and Nutrients for the United Kingdom*, 1991[47]. The values for adult women are for typically sedentary people.

n/a   Not applicable.

*   To be added to normal daily intake.

**   An infant's energy needs rise up through the range with increasing age.

\#   The higher value is for women whose breast milk is the main source of the infant's nourishment.

---

tively the health and development of children who have been vegans from birth, whose parents are vegans, and who live in the general community rather than in a self-selected communal group.

In this second survey the children, aged 5.8–12.8 years, continued to grow and develop normally and to enjoy good health. They were considerably leaner than the average child, although still within the reference range.

Their energy intake was 95% of the Estimated Average Requirement set by the UK Department of Health, similar to that of most British children. By way of comparison, a report published in 1986[25] showed that the energy intake of more than 3,000 omnivore schoolchildren in Britain averaged 90% of the then recommended amounts. The vegan children's protein consumption was also normal, at 12.4% of total Calories consumed, and the three most significant food groups for protein were pulses, bread, and other grain products. Possibly the children's leanness is explained by the theory that a high intake of fibre may slightly decrease the digestibility of nutrients such as fat and protein.

Although they are generally of lighter build than their omnivore friends, vegan children are within the normal ranges for height and weight. Infants and children reared on a varied vegan diet obtain adequate protein and energy, are healthy, and grow normally.

UNORTHODOX DIETS — PROBLEMS IN INFANCY

Reports in the medical press of vegan infants suffering from protein and energy deficiencies are extremely rare (*see below*). In some instances infants were weaned onto poorly planned fruitarian or macrobiotic regimes, rather than vegan diets. In other cases, parents had not adopted veganism but, instead, had eliminated foods from their infants' diets on a piecemeal basis and without seeking appropriate advice.

In 1979 four cases of malnutrition in infants raised on fruitarian and macrobiotic diets were reported[27]; these have often been described, incorrectly, as being vegan children. The first case concerned a 13-month-old boy who had been weaned onto a strict fruitarian diet, receiving no pulses or grains, but only breast milk and uncooked vegetables and fruit. Kwashiorkor was diagnosed and his diet was deficient in protein and Calories (as well as iron and vitamin B_{12}). After acute hospital treatment he was brought back to health on a vegan diet and at the age of two years was well, his weight and height being within normal limits.

The other three cases in this study were infants reared on inadequate macrobiotic diets which led to Calorie deficit and emaciation. Again, the parents were not vegans, but were following macrobiotic principles. Although there are similarities, there are also significant differences between vegan diets and these dietary regimes. The authors of the report failed to distinguish between them, consequently damning them all as "obviously inadequate for growing children", despite the fact that one infant was nursed back to health on a vegan diet.

Unfortunately, the authors also described all three diets as "cults" and "fads" and, apparently because one mother was suffering from post-natal depression, stated that the followers of "extreme faddist" diets may be mentally ill. Such generalized and inaccurate value judgments are out of place in a medical report; moreover, when parents follow a particular dietary philosophy which, when carefully implemented, is perfectly adequate and has been shown to offer some health benefits to children and adults alike, efforts to force the inclusion of ethically-offensive foods, such as meat and fish, are misplaced and can cause unnecessary anguish.

Two cases of kwashiorkor in infants in Cleveland, Ohio, were reported in 1975[28]. Although these children's diets, as described, contained no animal products, the parents were not vegans or vegetarians, but had restricted their children's diets because they believed that foods such as cow's milk were causing particular health problems. Both children were receiving a little cereal, fruit juices, baby fruit and in one case rice, and both were suffering from protein and energy deficiency.

Diet analysis[10] found that some Dutch vegetarian macrobiotic children, aged 4–18 months, were consuming less protein and Calories than the national recommendations, and were undersized[6]. They also learned to walk and speak more slowly than comparable omnivore children. The practice of sieving the grain porridge prepared for macrobiotic infants removes the bran, but some of the protein also remains behind in the sieve, and this contributed to the under-nutrition of these children. Further, water-based grain porridges are very glutinous if made thickly, and so tend to be over-diluted to make them palatable. The addition of vegetable oil would have reduced stickiness and improved the energy content, but giving fats to small children was discouraged among Dutch macrobiotics.

OCCASIONAL PROBLEMS WITH VEGAN INFANTS

Four reports of protein and energy deficiencies in infants raised on vegan diets have been published, two of them dealing with children from a community of black Hebrew Americans living in Israel[5,30]. The diet of this highly-atypical community's children was uniform and regulated by the group's leaders. It comprised fruits, vegetables, oats, yeast and home-made almond or soya milk, the latter forming the single most important dietary item for infants between 3 and 12 months of age.

Over three or four years, 29 infants showed evidence of protein and Calorie deficiency. All but one of these children had been weaned or partly weaned, and the main problem seems to have been that the plant

135

milks made by the community were over-diluted and the remaining foods were insufficiently energy-dense. Forty-seven infants under the age of 3 years from the community were well, although those aged between 4 and 18 months were small for their age. Catch-up growth meant that children older than 18 months were within the normal range for height and weight. Although, as superficially described, the diet given to infants in this community may appear adequate, the inclusion of more concentrated preparations of pulses, nuts and seeds, such as in spread or puréed form, would ensure adequate energy and protein intakes.

The second case involved a Swiss family, specifically the infant of a vegan mother and lacto-vegetarian father[41]. After being breast fed for 2.5 months, the child was fed largely on a home-prepared extract of almonds in water. By the age of 7.5 months he was failing to thrive, with muscular weakness and other symptoms caused by nutrient deficiencies, including a lack of Calories. Severe carnitine deficiency was thought to have been due to a reduced intake of the precursor amino acid, lysine, which was present in the almond extract only in low amounts. This case illustrates the drawback of over-restricting the variety of foods in vegan diets.

The fourth report[29] described a child in Chicago, Illinois, who was being given a diet of honey water (not vegan) and small amounts of cereal, bananas, fruit juices, soya formula and wheat germ oil. He was not receiving enough Calories and protein. The first reaction of medical staff was to try to introduce dairy or meat protein, but when this was resisted by the parents, the child was managed successfully on a vegan diet. As the authors pointed out, such a diet is obviously "nutritionally feasible". **Table 6.3** (page 139) suggests an outline diet plan for vegan infants and children.

These four reports of protein and Calorie deficiency in infants raised on vegan diets are isolated, but emphasize the general requirement for a variety of energy-dense foods to be included in the diets of young children.

Infants breast fed by women eating varied and balanced vegan diets thrive in early infancy[46]. The weaning period, often between six and 18 months for vegans, is a challenge for parents of any dietary persuasion because at this stage infants are nutritionally vulnerable. However, of various vegetarian-style diets — which can include macrobiotic, I-tal, fruitarian, vegetarian and vegan — the latter two have been associated with extremely few cases of protein or Calorie deficiency. After weaning, because infants have small stomachs which are easily filled, suitably-prepared energy-dense foods such as grains, pulses, and nut and seed 'butters' should figure

KEY POINTS: FEEDING VEGAN CHILDREN

• Introduce weaning foods gradually while still providing breast milk.

• Infants need plenty of energy (Calories). Home-prepared cereals should be made as a thick porridge, not as a thin gruel. Adding a little vegetable oil to the cooked grains increases their Calorie content, and improves palatability by making them less glutinous as they cool.

• Use more soya bean oil or rapeseed (canola) oil, and less sunflower, safflower or corn oils. The former may encourage the production of fatty acids which are important for development of the brain and vision.

• Don't let infants fill up with liquids before eating their meals.

• Spreading bread with margarine (fortified with vitamins D_2 and B_{12} if possible), or with tahini or smooth peanut butter, increases its energy density.

• Low-salt yeast extract is a good source of minerals and vitamins.

• Well-cooked and mashed pulses provide energy and protein.

• Ensure that foods fortified with vitamin B_{12} are provided *(see page 72)*.

• Use black molasses to boost iron and calcium intakes.

• Tofu (bean curd) prepared with a calcium salt (usually calcium sulphate, check the label) contains more calcium than cow's milk. It is also rich in protein. Green leafy vegetables (other than spinach) are also good sources of calcium.

• Soya flour, wheatgerm, millet, ground almonds, wholemeal bread, dried figs and dried apricots are particularly good sources of iron. Dried fruits can be soaked in a little water and well mashed, or liquidized, to form a thick spread.

• Include some citrus fruit, potatoes, green leafy vegetables or tomatoes in each meal, to enhance iron absorption.

• Make sure your child is in the open air regularly (not fully clothed, and not in direct sunlight at the hottest part of the day) to ensure a good vitamin D supply. In the winter, give vitamin D_2-fortified foods or a supplement.

• Use a soya milk which is fortified with calcium, and vitamins B_{12} and D_2.

regularly in their diets.

Some vegan children are smaller than average in this age group, but often catch up at ages 18 months to 4 years, when their nutritional needs per unit of body weight are less than in infancy. The ongoing British study by Tom Sanders indicates that the ages of 4–13 years present no special problems for vegan children, and protein and energy demands in adolescence can be met comfortably by vegan diets[44].

PROTEIN AND ENERGY — SUMMARY

Infants and children reared on a varied vegan diet obtain adequate protein and energy, and are healthy and grow normally. Although generally of lighter build than omnivore children, they are within the normal ranges for height and weight.

At weaning, vegan parents will want to ensure their children have an adequate intake of dietary energy, which can be achieved by using cooked and mashed pulses and grains, and ground seeds and nuts or nut and seed 'butters'. Mashed bananas and avocados are also suitable high-energy foods. These should be used as staples, with smaller amounts of bulky, less energy-dense fruits and vegetables, so that the children's small stomachs are not filled before they have eaten enough Calories. These guidelines are easy to follow, as demonstrated by the fact that thousands of children have been reared in good health on a vegan diet.

CARBOHYDRATES

Of all dietary groups, vegans most consistently eat the recommended amounts of carbohydrate (starches and sugars combined), which in the UK is 50% of food energy intake. So, pregnant and nursing vegan women are likely to have plenty of carbohydrates in their diets, especially in the form of starches.

Infants who are breast fed receive about 40% of their energy as sugar (lactose), but apart from this observation little is known about the carbohydrate consumption of children in general, and few studies of vegan infants and children have been conducted. One survey recorded that 18 British

TABLE 6.3
DIET GUIDELINES FOR VEGAN CHILDREN

	Approximate serving size	Daily servings per age group		
		6 mo–<1 yr	1–<4 yrs	4–<6 yrs
Bread	1 slice	1	3	4
Grains*	1–5 Tbsp	0.5 (ground & cooked)	1	2
Fats	1 tsp	0	3	4
Fruit				
citrus	0.25–0.5 cup	0	2 (juice/chopped)	2
other#	2–6 Tbsp	3 (puréed)	2 (chopped)	3
Protein foods¶	1–6 Tbsp	2 (cooked & sieved)	3 (chopped)	3
Vegetables**	0.25–0.3 cup			
green leafy/yellow		0.25 (cooked & puréed)	0.5 (chopped)	1
other		0.5 (cooked & puréed)	1 (chopped)	1
Soya milk (B₁₂ added)	1 cup	3	3	3
Miscellaneous				
molasses	1 Tbsp	0	1	1
wheatgerm	1 Tbsp	0	optional	optional
low-salt yeast extract (B₁₂ added)	1 tsp	0	1	1

* Grains include: bulghur wheat, wheat flakes, rice, millet, barley, wheat grains, oats. Serve as a thick 'porridge', not as a thin gruel.

\# Other fruits include: bananas, apples, peaches, pears, berries, apricots and grapes. Dried fruit spreads, including those made with dried peaches, bananas, apricots, raisins and figs, are high-energy foods, as are avocados.

¶ Protein foods include: nuts (almonds, peanuts, cashews, walnuts, pistachios); smooth nut 'butters'; pulses (soya beans, black-eyed beans, pinto beans, butter beans, peas, split peas, lentils etc.); miso (fermented soya paste); seeds (pumpkin, sesame and sunflower); seed 'butters'; and tofu. *To avoid risk of choking, nuts, grains, seeds and legumes should be ground or cooked and sieved for infants and small children.*

** Green leafy and dark yellow vegetables include: carrots, broccoli, spinach, kale, spring greens. Other vegetables include potatoes, tomatoes, lettuce, cabbage, corn, celery, onions, cucumbers, cauliflower and bean sprouts (mung, lentil and soya).

This table is based on one in Truesdell & Acosta, 1985[31].

children, lifelong vegans aged 5.8 to 12.8 years, obtained nearly two-thirds of their carbohydrate intake from bread, other grain products and potatoes, and had an average all-sugar intake of 15.6% of food energy[44]. The vegan children were lean, generally had good teeth and their level of dental decay was low, as might be expected since most of their sugar consumption was as fresh and dried fruits, and as soft drinks, particularly fruit juices. Confectionery, added sugar and preserves accounted for little. In contrast, all-sugar consumption by British omnivore children of a similar age range is an estimated 17%–25%, of which about half is provided by processed foods containing added sugar[61].

Concern has been expressed that a very high dietary fibre intake may interfere with the ability of infants and young children to absorb various nutrients. Studies with adult human volunteers have shown increasing faecal loss of nitrogen, carbohydrate, fat and energy as fibre intake rises to high levels. It has been speculated that for this and other reasons, a vegan diet may not be suitable for infants and small children[45]. However, although fibre may be a factor contributing to the noticeable leanness of vegan children, it is clear that vegan diets sustain good health in growing children. Indeed, relative leanness may well represent a health advantage in older children.

CARBOHYDRATES — SUMMARY

Vegans eat the recommended amounts of carbohydrates, unlike many omnivores. Few studies have looked specifically at carbohydrate consumption in vegan children, but evidence suggests that their diets contain plenty of complex carbohydrates, like those of their parents. Intake of refined sugar is probably low, and fibre intake is high.

FATS

During pregnancy women need fats in their diet both as an energy source and to provide the building elements for their child's developing nervous system and other organs. Infants require a relatively high fat intake for rapid growth, especially for the development of the brain and nervous system, so it's no surprise that human breast milk contains 50%–55% of its energy as fat. Sixty per cent of the brain is structural fats. Each brain cell makes between 6,000 and 10,000 connections with other brain cells, and every cell's membranes are manufactured from polyunsaturated fats.

The only fats which we must obtain from food are the essential polyunsaturated fatty acids lino*leic* acid and alpha-lino*lenic* acid. Our bodies can satisfy all our other requirements for fatty acids by modifying these two essential ones, with the possible exception of premature infants (*see below*). **Fats** (*page 35*) explains the function of different kinds of fats.

BREAST MILK AND INFANTS

The fat content of breast milk varies according to a mother's current diet and to the composition of her own body fat stores. Vegan diets are plentiful in the essential fatty acids linoleic acid and alpha-linolenic acid, but are believed not to contain any eicosapentaenoic acid (EPA) or docosahexaenoic acid (DHA). Both EPA and DHA are normally made in our bodies from alpha-linolenic acid, although a high intake of linoleic acid – as in most vegan diets — may reduce the efficiency with which we do this. Interestingly, DHA has been discovered in at least one plant, according to a 1993 publication[42] which reported that a primitive seaweed called *Isochrysis* is a rich and easily-produced source of DHA.

There are many different kinds of polyunsaturated fatty acids (PUFAs), and a study compared the amounts of different PUFAs in the breast milks of women from three dietary groups: vegans, vegetarians and omnivores[43]. Levels of arachidonic acid were similar, but the ratios of linoleic acid to alpha-linolenic acid were 15.6 in vegetarian breast milk, 17.5 in vegans, and 22.2 in omnivores. The proportion of DHA was lower, by nearly two-thirds, in the milk of vegans compared with that of omnivores. The PUFA content of formula feeds is also different from that of omnivore breast milk.

The study also compared the PUFAs found in red blood cells of three groups of 14-week-old infants: formula fed, breast fed by vegans or breast fed by omnivores. The proportion of linoleic acid was highest in the red blood cells of infants from the vegan group, and lowest in those of the bottle-fed infants. Conversely, the blood cells of the vegan infants contained the lowest proportions of DHA and EPA. It is possible that these infants would also have less DHA in their brain and nerve cell membranes. Although EPA and DHA can usually be made in the body from linoleic acid and alpha-linolenic acid, premature babies may require a food source of DHA to ensure optimum development of their brains and eyesight.

No-one yet knows to what extent the difference in fat content of breast milk and body tissues is important for the development of infants, or what is the 'normal' range. However, there is some evidence that children who were bottle fed are more likely to have neurological problems, such as poor co-ordination, than children who were exclusively breast fed.

There is nothing to suggest that the neurological, intellectual or visual functions of vegan children breast fed by vegan mothers are affected[43], although to date no published research has specifically addressed the possibility. Some studies have shown that children from vegetarian and macrobiotic communities have higher-than-average IQs, and although this may partly reflect the educational standing of the parents, it does demonstrate the capacity of such diets to support advanced mental development. The results don't rule out the possibility of subtle changes in visual or neural functions, and so the effects of different dietary PUFAs on the development of vegan infants remain unknown at present.

Different types and amounts of polyunsaturated fatty acids are found in formula feeds, and in the breast milks of vegan, vegetarian and omnivore women. These differences are reflected in the PUFAs found in the tissues of their infants. It is not yet known exactly what effect these variations may have on growth and development in early childhood.

VEGAN CHILDREN

The diets of vegan children tend to be lower in fat than average omnivore children. Their consumption of saturated fats is especially low, while they eat more of the healthy polyunsaturated fats. For example, the average fat intake of lifelong vegan children, aged 5.8 to 12.8 years, was 31.5% of dietary energy consumed[44]. The main fat-containing foods in their diet were fats themselves, followed by nuts and pulses.

Saturated fats contributed 4.8% of the children's dietary energy; the polyunsaturated fatty acid, linoleic acid, provided 8.8%; and alpha-linolenic acid accounted for 0.2%. This ratio of linoleic to alpha-linolenic acid is higher than average, and the authors speculated that it could decrease the body's ability to convert alpha-linolenic acid to docosahexaenoic acid (DHA)[44]. Since DHA is believed to be absent from vegan diets, vegans could use more soya bean or rapeseed (canola) oils instead of sunflower, safflower or corn oils for cooking. This would help boost intakes of alpha-linolenic acid, and thus possibly raise tissue levels of DHA, which is needed for vision and the function of the nervous system, and may be particularly important for infants and young children.

Official recommendations to reduce total fat consumption do not apply to children under the age of five years, because vegetable fats and oils make an important contribution to the food energy of infants, especially at the time of weaning. If fats are not given to small children they may not eat enough Calories. For example, Dutch vegetarian macrobiotic children aged 4–18 months, who were not given fats or oils until the age of two years because of the macrobiotic philosophy, were eating less than recommended amounts of energy in their diets[10]. It should be noted, though, that this dietary restriction is not a principle of veganism.

FATS — SUMMARY

The breast milks of vegan, vegetarian and omnivore women differ in the proportions of polyunsaturated fatty acids they contain. These differences are reflected in the tissues of their infants. It is not yet known exactly what, if any, effect these variations may have on the growth and development of infants, although some PUFAs, such as DHA, are required for development of the brain and vision. Research so far indicates that vegan infants and children develop normally. Their diets tend to be lower in fat than average omnivore children. Their consumption of saturated fats is especially low, while they eat more of the healthy polyunsaturated fats.

VITAMINS

During pregnancy and breast feeding, women are recommended by the UK Department of Health to eat more of most vitamins.

Beta-carotene is the plant form of **vitamin A**, and pregnant women should boost their consumption to 700µg a day; 950µg is recommended during breast feeding. Omnivore women are advised to avoid over-consumption of the animal form of vitamin A (retinol) during pregnancy, as an excess may increase the risk of birth defects. Beta-carotene is a much safer source of vitamin A, and vegans generally obtain plenty of beta-carotene from their diets.

Of the B-group vitamins, **thiamin (B_1), niacin, vitamin B_6** are present in vegan diets at or above the UK Reference Nutrient Intakes, which are shown in **Table 6.4** (*page 145*).

Reference Nutrient Intakes have not been set for **pantothenic acid** and **biotin**, both of which are plentiful in vegan diets. A 1989 comparison of

KEY POINTS: EXTRA VITAMINS RECOMMENDED DURING
PREGNANCY AND BREAST FEEDING

DURING PREGNANCY

- Vitamin A
- Thiamin
- Riboflavin
- Folate
- Vitamin C
- Vitamin D

DURING BREAST FEEDING

- Vitamin A
- Thiamin
- Riboflavin
- Niacin
- Vitamin B_{12}
- Folate
- Vitamin C
- Vitamin D

biotin levels in American vegans, vegetarians and omnivores revealed that, for both adults and children, there was more biotin in the bloodstream and the urine of the vegans[48]. This suggests that plenty of the vitamin was available in their bodies.

In a study published in 1979, the average concentration of **riboflavin** (vitamin B_2) in the breast milk of vegan women was lower than in that of the omnivore subjects, but similar to values reported for pooled milk samples from five different areas in the UK[11]. An assessment of 23 British vegan pre-school children published in 1981[24] found that the children's mean intake of riboflavin exceeded the current RNIs of 0.6–0.8mg. At ages 5.8 to 12.8 years, 12 out of 18 children met or exceeded their Reference Nutrient Intakes, and all exceeded the Lower Reference Nutrient Intakes[44].

One British study[3] found that some vegan women eat less riboflavin than the Reference Nutrient Intake which is 1.1mg daily, rising to 1.4mg during pregnancy and 1.5mg during breast feeding. They should note that good vegan sources of this vitamin include yeast extract, almonds, wheatgerm, hazelnuts, mushrooms, beans and dried apricots.

Pregnant women must ensure an adequate **folate** (folacin) consumption to protect their unborn children from neural tube defects such as spina bifida. In the UK, the 1991 recommendations for pregnant women were

TABLE 6.4

UK REFERENCE NUTRIENT INTAKES FOR WOMEN AND CHILDREN: THIAMIN, NIACIN AND VITAMIN B$_6$

Group	Thiamin (mg/day)	Niacin (mg/day)	Vitamin B$_6$ (mg/day)
Women during pregnancy	0.9	13*	1.2*
Women breast feeding	1	15	1.2*
Infants and children			
0–3 months	0.2	3	0.2
4–6 months	0.2	3	0.2
7–9 months	0.2	4	0.3
10–12 months	0.3	5	0.4
1–3 years	0.5	8	0.7
4–6 years	0.7	11	0.9
7–10 years	0.7	12	1

Recommendations of the UK Department of Health, 1991[47].

* These intakes are the same as those for adult women in general.

set at 300μg of folate a day, and for nursing women, 260μg daily.

However, on the basis of a more recent study, in 1992 the UK Department of Health[49] advised that all women who wish to conceive should also take a folate supplement of 400μg (0.4mg) daily, and continue this throughout the first 12 weeks of pregnancy. Women who have already had a child with a neural tube defect are advised by the Department of Health to take a daily dose of 5,000μg (5mg) while trying to conceive, and during the first three months of pregnancy[49]. Infants need 50μg of folate daily, rising to 70μg at ages 1–3 years, 100μg at ages 4–6 years, and 150μg at ages 7–10 years.

Studies suggest that folate is usually plentiful in the diets of adult vegans. British vegan children aged 1–4.6 years had an average folate intake of 161μg daily, exceeding their RNIs[24]. This was also the case in a follow-up study of the children at ages 5.8–12.8 years, the foods contributing the most folate being bread and other grain products, followed by pulses and then fresh vegetables[44]. In contrast, several studies of omnivore schoolchildren have shown that they often do not eat the recommended amounts of folate.

Bearing in mind the risk of neural tube defects, vegan women considering having a baby and those who are pregnant should note the Department of Health's advice to take a folate supplement, as well as consuming foods rich in the vitamin. These include wheatgerm, raw or lightly-cooked green leafy vegetables such as watercress, broccoli and spinach; yeast and yeast extracts, nuts, peas and other pulses, runner beans, oranges, dates, avocados and whole grains, including wholemeal bread.

VITAMIN B_{12}

Vitamin B_{12} demands a section to itself, having acquired legendary status among nutritionists and vegans alike.

According to UK recommendations, pregnant women do not require more than the average 1.5μg of **vitamin B_{12}** daily, although during breast feeding their intakes should increase to 2μg. This vitamin is unusual in being found very largely in animal foods — although micro-organisms, such as bacteria, are actually the original source of B_{12} even in meat. The body requires only a tiny amount of the vitamin and is able to conserve it when supplies are scarce. There is persuasive evidence that, at least in some individuals, there are bacteria present in the small intestine which manufacture B_{12} that is available to the body.

There are numerous fortified foods which are acceptable to vegans, such as some soya milks, margarines and breakfast cereals, nutritional yeast, yeast extracts, and soya mince and chunks, as well as vitamin supplements (*see page 72*). However, the value of unfortified foods such as seaweeds and fermented soya products as sources of active B_{12} now seems very doubtful.

Despite its notoriety, a dietary lack of this vitamin is extremely rare but the consequences of deficiency can be serious, especially in infants. Pregnant and breast feeding women in particular should ensure they have an adequate intake of vitamin B_{12} and, after weaning, parents should introduce B_{12}-containing foods into their infants' diets.

B_{12} DURING PREGNANCY

During pregnancy a woman's own laid-down body stores of B_{12} are not readily available to the fetus, who instead builds up a supply of her or his

TABLE 6.5
UK REFERENCE NUTRIENT INTAKES FOR WOMEN AND CHILDREN: VITAMIN B_{12}

Group	Vitamin B_{12}
	(µg/day)
Women during pregnancy	1.5
Women breast feeding	2.0
Infants and children	
0–6 months	0.3
7–12 months	0.4
1–3 years	0.5
4–6 years	0.8
7–10 years	1.0
11–14 years	1.2

Recommendations of UK Department of Health, 1991[47].

own from the mother's *current dietary intake* of the vitamin. If a woman's B_{12} intake is low during pregnancy, the fetus will not have adequate stores of the vitamin and this may lead to a deficiency some time after birth, even though the mother herself may have no clinical symptoms.

B_{12} AND BREAST FEEDING

Infants rely for their supplies of B_{12} on their own liver stores laid down while in the womb, and on B_{12} in their mothers' milk. After birth, if a woman's breast milk contains too little B_{12}, deficiency can then occur in her infant — not in the first few weeks of life, but after a few months when his or her own stores have run down.

A 1988 study measured the levels of methylmalonic acid (MMA) in the urine of breast-fed infants of vegan macrobiotic mothers, and in the urine of the mothers themselves[21]. High concentrations of MMA in the urine are considered to be an early indicator of impending vitamin B_{12} deficiency. The babies of the vegan mothers had more MMA in their urine than similar babies of omnivore mothers, although no deficiency signs were found.

Follow-up research confirmed that there was generally less B_{12} in the milk of vegan macrobiotic women than in that of omnivores, the average amounts being 300pg/ml versus 491pg/ml, respectively[55]. Women with the lowest amounts of B_{12} in their blood usually also had the least in their breast milk, and the highest amounts of MMA in their urine. Furthermore, the longer the women had followed their diets, the lower the B_{12} levels in their blood and milk tended to be.

There have been reports of B_{12} deficiency in infants, but some do not adequately specify the diets followed by parents, and some have not always been rigorous in excluding other causes. Given these provisos, it seems that since 1978 there have been ten reports — from the USA, France, Germany, Switzerland, Israel, Australia and the West Indies — of serious vitamin B_{12} deficiency in exclusively breast-fed infants of vegan mothers[32–35,51–54,58,59]. In another report[57], the baby of a vegan mother had signs of B_{12} deficiency, although the infant's blood levels of the vitamin were not very low. Additionally, a report[56] described how a routine screening programme identified elevated MMA in the urine of a breast-fed infant of a "strict vegetarian" mother. The mother and infant had low bloodstream levels of B_{12}, slightly enlarged red blood cells, and the baby had raised levels of MMA in its urine — factors suggesting an early stage of deficiency. It was not clarified whether the mother was a vegan.

In all reported cases, symptoms were recognized between 3–15 months of age, when the infants regressed developmentally, for example losing the ability to sit on their own. They often became irritable, lethargic, stopped smiling and socializing, and fed poorly. There was also megaloblastic anaemia, and developmental retardation — including poor movement control, muscle wasting, sight deterioration or brain shrinkage — which was not always completely reversible. All the mothers were healthy; most, although not all, had low blood levels of B_{12}.

Vitamin B_{12} problems in breast-fed infants of vegan families remain rare. Ten definite reports of serious B_{12} deficiency in infants of vegan mothers have been published in the medical literature worldwide since the late 1970s.

It is very important that vegan women ensure they have an adequate intake of B_{12} during pregnancy and breast feeding. The most reliable way to do this is to use foods fortified with the vitamin, or supplements.

The first signs of B_{12} deficiency in breast-fed infants may not be recognized, and should developmental retardation occur it may not be entirely reversible. Moreover mothers may have no symptoms of deficiency themselves. However, thousands of healthy children have been reared as vegans.

B_{12} AND WEANING

Vitamin B_{12} deficiency can occur after weaning if the foods provided do not contain adequate amounts of the vitamin to satisfy the needs of the infant. However, worldwide there have been only two reports of vitamin B_{12} deficiency in infants weaned onto inadequate vegan diets, both dealing with a community of black Hebrew Americans living in Israel[5,30]. Three cases of low serum B_{12}, two resulting in megaloblastic anaemia, were reported in 1979[5]. In 1982 a further nine infants with low blood levels of B_{12} were reported from the same group[30], and five of these had signs of megaloblastic anaemia.

The infants had been weaned onto a diet of over-diluted home-made soya and almond milks, oats, yeast, fruit and vegetables, and were suffering from multiple nutritional deficiencies including protein and energy malnutrition.

Levels of B_{12} in the bloodstream of 50 Dutch macrobiotic infants, aged 10–20 months, were reported in 1989[18]. Forty of the infants had been given no animal foods, ten had eaten some dairy products, but none had been given supplements. One-fifth of the infants had low levels of the vitamin in their blood (less than 125pg/ml), and changes in their red blood cells suggesting B_{12} deficiency. During examination, no obvious signs of neurological deterioration were found. Unlike these macrobiotic families, who did not approve of giving supplements, many vegan parents do give B_{12}-fortified foods or supplements to their children (*see below*).

B_{12} IN CHILDHOOD

In a 1981 report, British vegan pre-school children aged 1–4.6 years averaged a high daily consumption of 2.7µg B_{12}[24]. All parents provided fortified soya milks, yeast extracts or textured vegetable protein, and in a few cases a vitamin B_{12} syrup was given. The children with the lowest intakes of the vitamin were still receiving breast milk. When followed up ten years later, 14 of 18 children had a daily intake of B_{12} (including supplements) which met or exceeded the UK Reference Nutrient Intake, and only one child was below the Lower Reference Nutrient Intake[44].

Similarly, at a community called The Farm, in Tennessee, USA, where B_{12} was provided by supplemented soya milk and by the yeast *Saccharomyces cerevisiae* (used as a flavouring), the mean intake of 48 two-to five-year-old vegan children was 15μg — ten times the US RDA[26]. None of the vegan children in these studies showed any clinical signs of deficiency and all were healthy.

B_{12} deficiency due to vegan diets is very rare in infancy and childhood. However, because deficiency can have severe effects, and because natural plant sources of the vitamin are now in doubt, it is prudent for vegan families to use and to give their children B_{12}-fortified foods or supplements.

The UK recommendations[47] for **vitamin C** are 25mg daily for infants, 30mg for children to the age of ten, and 35mg for adolescents. The adult requirement of 40mg daily rises to 50mg during pregnancy, and 70mg while breast feeding. Since everyone's main sources of vitamin C are vegetables and fruits, vegan diets supply plenty of this vitamin. Vitamin C deficiency has never been recorded in fully breast-fed infants, regardless of their mothers' dietary practices. Lifelong vegan children in Britain, aged 5.8–12.8 years, exceeded their RNIs for vitamin C by consuming an average 107mg daily[44].

Vitamin D is not found naturally in plant foods. However, except in northern latitudes, most people obtain their vitamin D from exposure to sunshine, rather than from food. Consequently, the UK has only set a Reference Nutrient Intake for people most at risk of vitamin D deficiency, that is infants (8.5μg dropping to 7μg daily), pregnant and breast-feeding women (10μg), and people over the age of 65 years (also 10μg)[47].

Breast milk is not a rich source of the vitamin, so newborn infants rely on body stores which they built up while in the womb. Thus the vitamin D status of breast-fed infants depends primarily on how much vitamin was available in their mother's body during pregnancy, rather than during breastfeeding itself. Some soya milks, breakfast cereals and margarines are fortified with vitamin D_2 and are acceptable to vegans, as are vitamin D_2 supplements.

Vitamin D is essential for the formation of bones, and a deficiency during childhood can lead to the bone pain and deformity of rickets, as well as muscle weakness. In adults a deficiency of the vitamin leads to osteomalacia, a softening of the bones. Several official bodies have recommended that all pregnant women should take a vitamin D supplement; but women should also be aware that too much is toxic — even only five times the required dose, if taken over a prolonged period, can cause symptoms of toxicity.

An American study compared blood levels of vitamin D in near-vegetarian macrobiotic women, some of whom were breast feeding, and in omnivore women of similar age[15]. Bloodstream levels of the vitamin were the same in both dietary groups in the summer and autumn, but lower in the near-vegetarians in winter and spring, when the sunshine in northern latitudes (above 52°) contains little of the wavelength of light which allows vitamin D to be made in the skin.

Formula feeds contain sufficient vitamin D for infants, but breast milk may not supply adequate amounts after 4–6 months of age, especially in northern countries in the winter. Even in the general population, some autumn-born babies who are solely breast fed throughout winter may develop a deficiency, because the vitamin D content of their mother's breast milk is low. Nutritional rickets is more likely to occur under these conditions in dark-skinned people, especially if traditional clothing limits exposure to sunshine.

Weaning is a particularly sensitive time, as many weaning foods contain little of the vitamin and bone growth is rapid between the ages of six months and three years. However, brief daily exposure of the skin to daylight in spring, summer and autumn — although not at the hottest times of day, nor necessarily in direct sunshine — will ensure adequate vitamin D. Alternatively, vitamin D_2-fortified foods or supplements are an option for solely breast-fed infants and at weaning.

A very few isolated cases of rickets due to vitamin D deficiency have been reported in vegan and vegetarian infants. In a religious community of black, vegan Americans living in Israel, rickets was one of several deficiencies reported[5,30]. The infants were weaned early onto a diet which was also deficient in protein and Calories, and a 1986 study has suggested that certain forms of rickets may be associated with protein-energy malnutrition[39]. A report[40] of rickets in a black American infant weaned onto an inadequate vegan diet further supports the hypothesis that dark-skinned people may be more susceptible. The 20-month-old child had been weaned at nine months, after which he had been fed home-prepared soya milk, fruits and vegetables. His exposure to daylight was not mentioned in the report.

The fact that both these instances of rickets occurred in black-skinned children may be significant, as they are believed to be more susceptible to vitamin D deficiency. Asian vegetarian children are more prone to rickets, a possible factor being their heavy use of unleavened bread (chapattis) in which phytate has not been inactivated. This may affect the metabolism of vitamin D in the body.

All children need vitamin D for bone growth, but vegan infants are no more prone to rickets than omnivore children. In the spring, summer and autumn, regular exposure of the skin to daylight allows the body to manufacture adequate vitamin D. However, the necessary wavelength of light is missing from winter sunshine in northern latitudes, including most of Britain. Therefore vegan women who are breast feeding should ensure their intake during winter months by using fortified foods, or taking supplements. At weaning, infants should have regular exposure to daylight or receive D_2-fortified foods. Only two instances of rickets in vegan infants have been reported in the medical press worldwide.

No Reference Nutrient Intake for **vitamin E** has been set in the UK, but for adults 3–4mg daily is believed to be adequate. Human breast milk contains an average of 0.32mg per 100ml from the twelfth day onwards, so that a breast-fed infant consuming 850ml of milk a day would receive 2.7mg of vitamin E. Vegetable oils, wheatgerm, nuts, seeds and whole grains are rich sources of the vitamin, and these are common in vegan diets. Lifelong British vegan children aged 5.8–12.8 years, for example, had an average daily intake of 8.8mg[44].

Infants have little or no liver stores of the **vitamin K**, and are presumed to rely entirely on dietary sources. Therefore the UK Department of Health[47] suggests that infants should receive daily about 2µg of vitamin K for every kilogram they weigh. Haemorrhagic disease of the newborn has been linked with breast feeding, suggesting that some women's breast milk is low in vitamin K.

It is common in several countries for newborn babies to be routinely given an injection of the vitamin to prevent haemorrhagic disease. In the early 1990s two studies indicated that this could be linked to the later development of cancer in children, although other research found no such association[1]. Nevertheless, there is a move away from injections to giving vitamin K by mouth after birth. Vitamin K is common in green leafy vegetables, other vegetables and vegetable oils, fruits and grains, and pregnant and breast-feeding women should ensure they eat plenty of these foods.

VITAMINS — SUMMARY

During pregnancy or breast feeding, women are recommended to increase their intakes of beta-carotene, thiamin, riboflavin, niacin, folate, and vitamins B_{12}, C and D. Of these, beta-carotene, thiamin, niacin, folate and vitamin C are plentiful in vegan diets, which generally meet the UK recommendations for women.

Some vegan women eat less than the Reference Nutrient Intake for riboflavin, although vegans' breast milk contains amounts similar to that of omnivores in the UK. Vegan diets tend to be rich in folate, but given the importance of this vitamin in preventing birth defects, all pregnant women and those trying to conceive are recommended by the UK Department of Health to take additional supplements.

Understanding of food sources of vitamin B_{12} is still incomplete, but at the moment it seems that little active vitamin B_{12} is available naturally in plant foods. Therefore pregnant and nursing women are encouraged to use fortified foods or supplements, which should also be given to weaned infants. Most people obtain their vitamin D from the action of sunlight on the skin but, again, pregnant and breast-feeding women are generally advised by the authorities to take a vitamin D supplement, especially during the winter. As vitamin D is not present naturally in plant foods (although some are fortified with it), this advice is relevant to vegans.

Studies of vegan children suggest that their diets provide ample vitamins, either from natural content or from fortified foods or supplements, for example as with vitamin B_{12}. Cases of vitamin deficiency in vegan children are extremely rare, and are limited to vitamins B_{12} and D.

MINERALS

The UK Department of Health[47] does not suggest any increase in mineral intakes during pregnancy, but does advise a higher consumption of calcium, zinc, magnesium, phosphorus, copper and selenium during breast feeding.

The Reference Nutrient Intakes for **calcium** are 350–550mg a day for infants and children to the age of 10 years; 800mg/day for teenage girls; 1,000mg for teenage boys; 700mg for adult men and women; and an extra 550mg a day (total 1,250mg) for breast-feeding women. Additional calcium during pregnancy is not thought to be necessary.

Some vegans consume less calcium than the recommended optimum, but close to the Estimated Average Requirement. Also, it is known that the body can adapt to low calcium intakes, especially when the diet does not contain excessive protein. There have been no reports of calcium deficiency in adult vegans. Nevertheless, given the importance of calcium, vegan women should make a point of including plenty of calcium-rich foods in their diets on a daily basis.

Too little calcium in the tissues of young children can lead to stunted growth, and osteoporosis in older adults, especially women, may be linked to sub-optimal calcium intake during the teens and twenties.

In 1978, twenty-three British vegan children aged 1–4.6 years were consuming 298–331 milligrams of calcium a day[24]. This was lower than the UK Reference Nutrient Intakes (RNI, 350–450mg/day for 1–6 year-olds), but met the Estimated Average Requirements (EAR, 275–350mg/day) for these age groups. Moreover the study did not measure the amount of calcium contained in drinking water. None of the children showed signs of deficiency, and all were in good health. Eighteen children participated in a later follow-up study, aged 5.8–12.8 years[44]. All were consuming less calcium than the UK RNI, and one had an intake less than the Lower Reference Nutrient Intake. Again, the study did not measure the calcium provided in drinking water. The children were all well and had no signs of calcium deficiency.

The same was true for children brought up in a vegan community called The Farm, in Tennessee, USA. Their average calcium intake, at 351mg, was less than the current US and UK recommendations but they were well and thriving[26].

In Switzerland, a vegan mother who believed her infant son was allergic to cow's milk and could not suckle adequately, fed him with almond extract made at home, plus some cereals and a little fruit[41]. The child's calcium intake was less than the Recommended Nutrient Intake and the Estimated Average Requirement, and his bones were reported to contain too little of this mineral. Two infants from a black Hebrew vegan community in Israel also had fragile bones associated with low blood levels of calcium[5].

These three cases of possible calcium deficiency in vegan infants are highly unusual. However, given the importance of calcium intake during youth on the future risk of osteoporosis, vegan parents, like any other parents, should take care to ensure that the diets of their children include plenty of calcium-rich foods. From the plant kingdom, these include tofu (when prepared with calcium sulphate), mashed beans, home-made dried fruit spreads, fortified soya milks where available, green leafy vegetables, wholemeal bread, molasses, and nut and seed 'butters'.

Many of these foods are also rich in **iron**. The UK's 1991 recommendations[47] for infants' iron intakes are considerably higher than previously, reflecting the knowledge that iron-deficiency anaemia at this age can permanently affect brain development. The recommendations are 1.7mg daily (at ages 0–3 months), 4.3mg (ages 4–6 months), rising to 7.8mg a day (7–12 months). Children up to 10 years need between 6.1 and 8.7mg iron daily, depending on age; teenagers require 11.3–14.8mg; and 14.8mg iron daily is recommended for women. No extra iron is indicated in the UK for pregnant or breast-feeding women, because it is assumed that increased requirements can be offset against the cessation of menstrual iron loss. However the US Recommended Dietary Allowance for pregnant women is 30mg, double that of non-pregnant women.

Vegans should be aware that plant iron is less well absorbed than iron from animal foods. However, absorption is increased by vitamin C, by malic and citric acids (eg. in plums and apples; and in citrus fruits respectively), and by fruit sugars. Iron absorption can be decreased by tannins (eg. in tea), and by phytates (found in nuts, grains and seeds), although in the context of the diet as a whole these factors are unlikely to have a very significant permanent effect on iron absorption.

Infants can absorb up to 50% of the iron in human breast milk, but it is calculated that only 10% of the iron in formula milks is absorbed. As a general rule, iron deficiency is most likely to occur in infants at the age of 4–6 months. Many feeding formulas and cereals contain added iron, and these contribute a large proportion of the iron intake of some infants.

Iron-deficiency anaemia in infancy is more common in some ethnic minorities, particularly those in a poor socio-economic situation. This is thought to be due to weaning diets containing too few iron-rich foods, and to over-reliance on cow's milk, which is not a good source. There is increasing evidence that iron-deficiency anaemia in infancy may have longer-term effects on the mental and physical development of children.

A 1981 survey[24] of British vegan children aged 1–4.6 years found an average iron intake of 10mg a day (range 9–12mg), mainly from wheat and pulses, which considerably exceeds the British RNI of 6.1–6.9mg/day. A follow-up at ages 5.8–12.8 years confirmed that all the children were still consuming the RNI for iron[44]. A study of American children aged 2–5 years at The Farm, a vegan community in Tennessee, USA, indicated that all children achieved the then current US RDAs for iron except the 2- to 3-year-old girls, whose intake was 93% of the allowance before contributions from iron cookware were added[26].

Iron deficiency has seldom been reported among vegan children, although in a black Hebrew American community of vegans in Israel[30] some infants had low levels of iron in their bloodstream. Fifteen per cent of Dutch macrobiotic infants, aged 10–20 months, most of whom had not received any animal foods, did have signs of iron deficiency[18]. One breast-fed infant of a vegan mother was found to have iron deficiency[57].

All parents should ensure that suitably-prepared iron-rich foods — such as soya flour, seed and nut butters, black molasses, puréed dried figs or apricots, and cooked and mashed pulses — are regularly included in their children's food. Providing vitamin C-rich foods such as fresh citrus fruits and vegetables, at the same meal, markedly improves iron absorption. Vegans whose staple grain is wheat, as in wholemeal bread, are not particularly susceptible to iron-deficiency anaemia; but among Asian vegetarians in the UK and USA, who use less wheat and more rice, higher rates of anaemia are found, particularly among women and infants[63].

Other minerals of importance to vegans during pregnancy, breast feeding or infancy and childhood include zinc, phosphorus, magnesium, copper, selenium and iodine. The UK Department of Health does not recommend increased consumption of these during pregnancy, but does suggest larger intakes of the first five minerals during breast feeding (*see* **Table 6.6**, *opposite*).

Zinc is important for growth, wound healing and immune function, and there is evidence from the general population that malformations occur-

TABLE 6.6

UK REFERENCE NUTRIENT INTAKES FOR WOMEN AND CHILDREN: ZINC, PHOSPHORUS, MAGNESIUM, COPPER AND SELENIUM

	Zinc	Phosphorus	Magnesium	Copper	Selenium
	(mg/day)	(mg/day)	(mg/day)	(mg/day)	(µg/day)
Women, 19–50 years *(no increase during pregnancy)*	7	545	270	1.2	60
Women breast feeding	9.5–13	985	320	1.5	75
Infants & children					
0– 3 months	4	405	55	0.3	10
4–6 months	4	405	60	0.3	13
7–9 months	5	405	75	0.3	10
10–12 months	5	405	80	0.3	10
1–3 years	5	275	85	0.4	15
4–6 years	6.5	350	120	0.6	20
7–10 years	7	430	200	0.7	30

Recommendations of the UK Department of Health, 1991[47].

---

ring in some infants may be linked to zinc insufficiency in their mothers. Human milk is not a rich source of this mineral, and during breast feeding infants draw on their body reserves laid down during the last three months of pregnancy. Thus premature babies may be at particular risk of zinc deficiency.

The intakes of zinc by adult vegans are similar to those of omnivores. They usually meet British recommendations, but may fall below the higher amounts recommended in the USA. Zinc levels in the bloodstream of vegetarians and vegans, while generally within the normal range, may be slightly lower than those of omnivores.

The amount of zinc in the diets of 23 British vegan children aged 1–4.6 years varied from 1–8mg, with an average of 4mg a day[24], below current

UK recommendations but similar to the intake of omnivore children. A follow-up survey[44] of these lifelong vegan children indicated that, at the ages of 5.8–12.8 years their mean zinc intake was 7.4mg, which exceeds the UK RNI. A diet plan for vegan infants which provides adequate zinc has been published[31]. One case of zinc deficiency in an infant from a black Hebrew American community living in Israel was reported in 1982, but this community was highly atypical[30].

Controversy persists over whether the fibre and phytate found in plant foods affect the body's ability to absorb zinc. It is likely that the body can adapt to a high-fibre intake, and certainly the UK's Department of Health[47] states that unrefined grains, such as wheat, contain enough zinc to offset the effects of the fibre and phytate in the grains. Vegan sources of zinc include wheatgerm, whole grains (such as wheat, oats, millet, barley and rice), nuts, pulses, tofu (soya bean curd), soya protein, miso (fermented soya bean paste), brewer's yeast, yeast extracts and some vegetables (eg. peas, parsley, bean sprouts).

Phosphorus is common in all natural foods, so there have been few analyses of the phosphorus content of vegan diets. One, of children aged 2–5 years at The Farm, a vegan community in Tennessee, USA, showed that all age groups met or exceeded the recommended intake, except in the case of the 2- and 3-year-old girls whose intake was 94% of the 1980 US recommendations[26]. Vegan diets generally are likely to contain plenty of this mineral.

Several reports indicate that vegan diets contain more **magnesium** than average omnivore diets, providing roughly twice the UK Reference Nutrient Intake. One study showed that near-vegetarian macrobiotic women had more magnesium in their bloodstream than omnivore women, both generally and when breast feeding[15]. This suggests that the fibre in plant-based diets does not reduce the absorption of magnesium. Magnesium is widespread in foods, particularly in nuts, whole grains (including oats, millet, brown rice and wholemeal bread), wheatgerm, soya flour and yeast extracts.

Copper is found in many vegan foods, such as bread and other grain products (especially if unrefined), and in wheatgerm, vegetables, nuts and seeds. Studies suggest that vegan diets contain more than average omnivore diets, although there is a question over the copper content of tofu which may have been over-estimated.

Good vegan sources of **selenium** are nuts, grains, seeds, soya beans, mushrooms and bananas. Swedish vegans ate less selenium than Swedish omnivores and lacto-vegetarians[20, 36]. However the amount of selenium in the vegans' bloodstream matched that of the omnivores, and was close to the average of healthy omnivores from eight different countries[37].

The UK Reference Nutrient Intakes[47] for **iodine** are 50–60 micrograms (µg) a day for infants, rising through 70–130µg for children and adolescents, to 140µg for adults. The safe upper limit has been set at 1,000µg a day, since too much iodine is toxic. During the first three months of pregnancy the fetus needs iodine for development of the nervous system, but in the UK additional amounts of iodine are not considered necessary at this time.

Iodine is a mineral worth the attention of vegan parents, since a report published in 1993[3] showed that average daily iodine intake of 38 British vegans was less than the UK RNI, although equal to the Lower Reference Nutrient Intake (LRNI). The LRNI is considered adequate only for a minority of people who have low needs. A study[20] of Swedish vegans similarly indicated an average intake of only a quarter of that found in the Swedish omnivore diet. However, iodine deficiency does not appear to be more common among vegans than in the general population.

A single case study of iodine deficiency in a vegan/vegetarian family has been published[41]. In Switzerland, the 7.5-month-old infant of a vegan mother and lacto-vegetarian father was breast fed for 2.5 months, and then fed on a home-prepared extract of almonds in water. The boy developed a number of deficiencies, including that of iodine. His diet was grossly inadequate, being very low in Calories, calcium and iodine. There have been no other reports of iodine deficiency in vegans, to the author's knowledge.

The most reliable sources of iodine are seafoods, including dried edible seaweeds such as nori, kelp, wakame and hijiki which contain up to 500µg per 100g, and were used by an estimated 11%–16% of vegans in 1985[38]. There is iodine in vegetables and grains, and hence in animal foods, although amounts vary according to the iodine content of the soil and the fertilizers used. Much of the iodine in cow's milk comes from fortified animal feed, and from disinfectant dips used to clean cows' udders. Apart from seaweeds, vegetables and grains, other vegan sources of iodine include sea salt and *Vecon* yeast spread (which contains seaweed powder). According to a 1993 report, thirty-six of 38 British vegans said they included *Vecon* or seaweed in their diets[3].

MINERALS — SUMMARY

The Department of Health in the UK recommends that all breast-feeding women should increase their intakes of calcium, phosphorus, magnesium, zinc, copper and selenium.

Calcium consumption by vegans tends to be slightly below the recommended optimum, but a meat-free diet enhances calcium retention by the body. There have been no reports of calcium deficiency among adult vegans, and only three cases of bone fragility associated with calcium deficiency in vegan infants have been reported. Plenty of plant foods contain calcium, and should be included in the diets of women and their children, on a daily basis.

Phosphorus, zinc, magnesium and copper are present in vegan diets at, or in excess of, recommended amounts. One case of zinc deficiency in an infant has been reported in an atypical religious vegan community. Selenium may be slightly lower in vegan diets, but levels in the bloodstream of vegans were normal. Intakes of iodine by vegans may be lower than the recommended optimum, but only a single case of iodine deficiency in an infant has been reported.

With only exceedingly rare exceptions, vegan diets have been found to provide sufficient minerals to support good health during pregnancy, breast feeding and throughout infancy and childhood.

GENERAL HEALTH OF VEGAN MOTHERS AND CHILDREN

PREGNANCY, BIRTH WEIGHT AND BREAST FEEDING

The health and well-being of vegan women during pregnancy has been a topic of some interest among nutritionists. There is plenty of anecdotal evidence suggesting healthy pregnancies in vegan women, but few comprehensive reports have been published. A 1987 survey[7] of pregnant women at The Farm, a vegan community in Tennessee, USA, found that the incidence of pre-eclampsia was extremely low (one in 775). Pre-eclampsia is characterized by constriction of blood vessels, reduced blood flow to the placenta and premature delivery. The authors concluded that, far from being harmful during pregnancy, a well-planned and varied vegan diet could be beneficial in reducing the incidence of pre-eclampsia. Further studies of the health of pregnant vegan women would be welcome.

There has been a limited amount of research on birth weights of vegan infants. At The Farm, a vegan community in Tennessee, records showed that several hundred vegan infants had average birth weights[50]. The average birth weight of 19 British vegan children was, at 3.31kg, only fractionally lower than the 3.48kg averaged by babies of omnivore mothers in a 1992 study[43]. On the other hand, a report[9] of Dutch macrobiotic families showed that 4.3% of their babies weighed less than 2.5kg at birth, compared to 2% of babies in the general population. Among the macrobiotic families, babies of women who frequently ate dairy products or fish were heavier at birth than those of women who ate these foods less often. Although this may be of relevance to vegan families, it is important to realize that macrobiotic diets involve different nutritional restrictions.

Concern is growing about the possible health effects of chemical pollutants to adults and children. The organochlorines, such as polychlorobiphenyls (PCBs), DDT and dioxins, accumulate in body fat and are secreted into breast milk. These chemicals also reach the unborn child via umbilical cord blood, and may have detrimental effects on the developing immune and nervous systems[68]. More of these chemical pollutants are found in meat, fish and cow's milk than in plant foods, since animals are higher up the food chain and the chemicals lodge in fatty tissues. Proprietary infant formulas based on cow's milk may contain a certain amount of these chemicals.

There is little published information about organochlorine accumulation in vegans, but the umbilical cord blood of pregnant vegetarian women has been shown to contain markedly less of these chemicals than that of omnivores[69]. Additionally, an American study reported in 1981 revealed that of seven chemical contaminants, six were found at markedly lower levels in the breast milk of vegetarian women (who may have been vegans)[71]. Indeed, the *highest* vegetarian/vegan level was lower than the *lowest* omnivore level; and the average amounts of chemicals in the breast milk of the vegetarians/vegans were only 1%–2% of those found in omnivores.

STUDIES OF VEGAN CHILDREN

In a report published in 1980, of 28 American pre-school vegetarian children (2–8.4 years old), six were macrobiotic vegans and 22 were vegetarians, including Seventh Day Adventists and macrobiotics[8]. The above-average IQ for all subjects was 116, while the average for the vegan macrobiotic children was 119. The latter's average mental age was 16.5 months ahead of their chronological age, compared to 12.5 months for all the children together. The authors concluded that the above-average IQs and mental development of the macrobiotic vegan children were as likely to reflect the educational level of the parents as any nutritional factors, but showed that the vegan and vegetarian diets had obviously been able to support this advanced development. Anthropometric and clinical measurements were normal in all the children.

A more recent study of Dutch vegan and vegetarian macrobiotic children aged 4–5 years found their average IQ to be 126[19]. Some of the children were undernourished and had below-average growth, but it was concluded that this had not affected their mental development.

Although some results from studies of macrobiotic communities may be relevant to vegan families, there are many differences in the dietary practices of the two groups. More reliable information comes from studies of vegan children, and one such is the ongoing prospective survey of British vegan children conducted by Tom Sanders[24,44,63]. These children's energy intakes were similar to those of typical omnivore children, but their fibre consumption was very high. Their protein intake was normal and met the Department of Health's recommendations. Fat consumption, especially of saturated fats, was lower than in average children. Daily intakes of all essential nutrients were close to the British Dietary Reference Values, with the exceptions — for some children — of calcium and vitamin B_{12}.

Growth and development of these lifelong vegan children is normal, and their heights and weights are inside the accepted range. They are, however, markedly leaner than average children — especially in the first few years, and despite their generally normal energy intake. A possible explanation for this is that the large amounts of fibre in plant food slightly decreases digestibility, so that not all the energy contained in the food is available to the body.

A 1980 American study[26] reported on 48 pre-school children from a vegan community called The Farm, in Tennessee. Energy intakes by virtually all the children exceeded US RDAs, and they all ate at least as

---

KEY POINTS: THE HEALTH OF VEGAN CHILDREN

• The body tissues of vegan infants contain different proportions of fats compared with omnivore babies. Their health and development are normal but research is needed to discover if there are subtle differences in neural or visual functions.

• Some vegan children may grow more slowly in the first five years, possibly due to the lower energy supplied by bulky vegan diets when children's stomachs are small. Catch-up growth usually occurs by the age of ten years.

• Vegan children are of normal height and are usually leaner than average, although within the standard range.

• The energy intakes of older vegan children are similar to those of omnivore children.

• The only nutrients which are likely to be provided in less-than-average amounts by the diets of vegan children are calcium and vitamin B_{12}.

• Nutrients such as iron, carotene, thiamin, folate and vitamins C and E are more plentiful in vegan children's diets than in those of omnivore children.

---

much protein, including all the essential amino acids, as recommended. The children were nearly all within the normal ranges for height and weight.

A more extensive study of children on The Farm was published in 1989, so far the largest survey of vegan children yet conducted[50]. Information was collected on the growth of children, aged 4 months to 10 years, nearly three hundred of whom were vegan from birth. Much food eaten at The Farm was home-grown, and supplemented with vitamins A, B_{12} and D, as well as with some minerals. Birth weights were normal; most children's heights and weights for their ages, and their weights for their heights, were similar to the US reference population. The greatest differences from the reference population were at ages 1–3 years, but by the age of 10 years the children averaged within 0.7cm (less than one third of an inch) and

1.1kg (2.4lb) of the reference population. The authors speculate that the slight dip in weights and heights shown by the children at ages 1–3 years might have been due to seasonal variations in the energy density of weaning foods, many of which were plant foods grown at The Farm.

A different study found that, of nine American vegan children aged between 5 and 17 years, the weights and heights of eight were in the normal range (one girl being noticeably shorter and heavier than average)[62].

VEGAN CHILDREN VERSUS THE NORM

More detailed studies of the intellectual, neurological and physical development, and general health of vegan children (for example, the prevalence of allergies or dental decay) would be very useful. As the numbers of vegan children increase, it is hoped that such research will attract funding.

In the meantime, some general predictions about the health of vegan children can be made. It is known that atherosclerosis can begin in childhood and is influenced by diet. Vegan children are less likely to develop high levels of cholesterol in their bloodstream because of the smaller amounts of fat, especially saturated fat, in their diets[62]. In contrast, almost every study of omnivore children aged eight years and over, shows that most eat more than the recommended 35% of their calories as fat. Even in children as young as ten years, high fat intakes are associated with raised blood levels of cholesterol, while polyunsaturated fats, plentiful in vegan diets, are linked with healthier fat profiles in children's bloodstreams[65]. Thus the same relationships between diet and risk of heart disease appear to be present in young children.

The fact that vegan children tend to be slimmer than their omnivore counterparts may also be positive for their health. Overweight children experience social and emotional difficulties, and risk long-term health problems — half of all overweight adults were fat children, for example. Overweight children as young as five or six have been reported to have raised blood pressure[66].

Body weight and fatness are related to the age at which children mature sexually. Therefore it might be expected that vegan girls would be older than average when they begin to menstruate (the age of menarche). This has been reported in one study of vegetarian girls, and a slightly later age of menarche among British vegan girls was found by Tom Sanders[63]. A later age of menarche is associated with a lower risk of developing breast cancer.

Despite generally low infant mortality rates in Westernized societies, there is no evidence that the overall health of young children is improving and, in fact, some chronic conditions such as asthma and insulin-dependent diabetes are on the increase. Considering the possibility that early exposure of susceptible children to cow's milk is linked to insulin-dependent diabetes, we could speculate that there might be a lower prevalence of diabetes among young vegans.

In 1989 the UK Department of Health published a survey of food consumption by omnivore children[67]. This revealed that, measured by weight, the foods consumed most by British omnivore children aged 14 to 15 were: milk > soft drinks > chips and crisps > biscuits and cakes > meat and meat products > white bread > other potato > fruit > other vegetables (mainly baked beans). These findings are backed by a recent survey indicating that the fat and sucrose intakes of teenage children are much higher than recommended, while their consumption of starch and fibre is too low[60]. It is hard to imagine a less health-promoting kind of nutrition, and it is against this norm that the diets of vegan children should be compared. The foods most commonly eaten by British vegan children, in descending order by weight, are: pulses (including soya milk) > fruit juice and soft drinks > fresh fruit > potatoes > bread > vegetables[63].

Not only are they likely to benefit from the fresh whole foods, fruits and vegetables which most of them eat, but vegan children are also establishing healthy eating patterns which will have positive effects throughout their lives.

GENERAL HEALTH OF VEGAN MOTHERS AND CHILDREN — SUMMARY

Well-planned vegan diets which include a wide range of plant foods provide all the nutritional requirements of pregnant and nursing women, and their children, from infancy through adolescence. Some vegan children have slightly lower intakes of calcium and vitamin B_{12}, but using a wide variety of foods rather than a narrow range, together with fortified foods where appropriate, ensures good nutrition. The consumption by vegan children of all other nutrients is similar to or greater than that of omnivore children. Several studies have shown that vegan women have healthy pregnancies, and that their children thrive. Thousands of healthy children have now been reared on vegan diets, and can expect to look forward to a healthier-than-average adulthood.

From top to bottom: *Willow Arran (2 months),
Jamil Massiah (2 years), Sylvia Howard (17 years),
Louis & Billie Robinson (4 years and 21 months), Cai & Nerida Pearce (8 and 10 years).*

REFERENCES

1 Shearer, M.J. (1994). Vitamin K and childhood cancer. *BNF Nutr. Bull.* 19:5–8.

2 Department of Health and Social Security (1979). *Recommended Daily Amounts of Food Energy and Nutrients for Groups of People in the United Kingdom.* London: HMSO.

3 Draper, A., Lewis, J., Malhotra, N. & Wheeler, E. (1993). The energy and nutrient intakes of different types of vegetarian: a case for supplements? *Br. J. Nutr.* 69:3–19.

4 Millward, D.J., Newsholme, E.A., Pellett, P.L. & Uauy, R. (1992). *Amino acid scoring in health and disease.* In: Protein-Energy Interactions — Proceedings of a workshop held by the International Dietary Energy Consultancy Group. Switzerland: IDECG.

5 Zmora, E., Gorodischer, R. & Bar-Ziv, J. (1979). Multiple nutritional deficiencies in infants from a strict vegetarian community. *Am. J. Dis. Child.* 133:141–144.

6 Dagnelie, P.C., van Staveren, W.A., Vergote, F.J.V.R.A., Burema, J., van't Hof, M.A., van Klaveren, J.D. & Hautvast, J.G.A.J. (1989). Nutritional status of infants aged 4 to 18 months on macrobiotic diets and matched omnivorous control infants: a population-based mixed-longitudinal study. II. Growth and psychomotor development. *Eur. J. Clin. Nutr.* 43:325–338.

7 Carter, J.P., Furman, T. & Hutcheson, H.R. (1987). Preeclampsia and reproductive performance in a community of vegans. *Southern Med. J.* 80:692–697.

8 Dwyer, J.T., Miller, L.G., Arduino, N.L., Andrew, E.M., Dietz, W.H., Reed, J.C. & Reed, H.B.C. (1980). Mental age and IQ of predominantly vegetarian children. *J. Am. Diet. Assn.* 76:142–147.

9 Dagnelie, P.C., van Staveren, W.A., van Klaveren, J.D. & Burema, J. (1989). Do children on macrobiotic diets show catch-up growth? *Eur. J. Clin. Nutr.* 42:1007–1016.

10 Dagnelie, P.C., van Staveren, W.A., Verschuren, S.A.J.M. & Hautvast, J.G.A.J. (1989). Nutritional status of infants aged 4 to 18 months on macrobiotic diets and matched omnivorous control infants: a population-based mixed-longitudinal study. I. Weaning pattern, energy and nutrient intake. *Eur. J. Clin. Nutr.* 43:311–323.

11 Hughes, J. & Sanders, T.A.B. (1979). Riboflavin levels in the diet and breast milk of vegans and omnivores. *Proc. Nutr. Soc.* 38:95A.

12 Barker, D.J.P., Winter, P.D., Osmond, C., Margetts, B. & Simmons, S.J. (1989). Weight in infancy and death from ischaemic heart disease. *Lancet* ii:577–580.

13 Barker, D.J.P., Bull, A.R., Osmond, C. & Simmons, S.J. (1990). Fetal and placental size and risk of hypertension in adult life. *Br. Med. J.* 301:259–262.

14 Barker, D.J.P., Meade, T.W., Fall, C.H.D., Lee, A., Osmond, C., Phipps, K & Stirling, Y. (1992). The relation of fetal and infant growth to plasma fibrinogen and factor VII levels in adult life. *Br. Med. J.* 304:148–152.

15 Specker, B.L., Tsang, R.C. & Miller, D. (1987). Effect of vegetarian diet on serum 1,25-dihydroxyvitamin D concentrations during lactation. *Obstet. Gynec.* 70:870–874.

16 Hales, C.N., Barker, D.J.P., Clark, P.M.S., Cox, L.J., Fall, C., Osmond, C. & Winter, P.D. (1991). Fetal and infant growth and impaired glucose tolerance at age 64 years. *Br. Med. J.* 303:1019–1022.

17 Barker, D.J.P., Godfrey, K.M., Fall, C., Osmond, C., Winter, P.D. & Shaheen, S.O. (1991). The relation of birth weight and childhood respiratory infection to adult lung function and death from chronic obstructive airways disease. *Br. Med. J.* 303:671–675.

18 Dagnelie, P.C., van Staveren, W.A., Vergote, F.J.V.R.A., Dingjan, P.G., van den Berg, H. & Hautvast, J.G.A.J. (1989). Increased risk of vitamin B-12 and iron deficiency in infants on macrobiotic diets. *Am. J. Clin. Nutr.* 50:818–824.

19 Herens, M.C., Dagnelie, P.C., Kleber, R.J., Mol, M.C.J. & van Staveren, W.A. (1992). Nutrition and mental development of 4–5-year-old children on macrobiotic diets. *J. Hum. Nutr. Diet.* 5:1–9.

20 Abdulla, M., Andersson, I., Asp, N-G., Berthelsen, K., Birkhed, D., Dencker, I., Johansson, C-G., Jägerstad, M., Kolar, K., Nair, B.M., Nilsson-Ehle, P., Nordén, Å., Rassner, S., Åkesson, B. & Öckerman, P-A. (1981). Nutrient intake and health status of vegans. Chemical analyses of diets using the

duplicate portion sampling technique. *Am. J. Clin. Nutr.* 34:2464–2477.

21 Specker, B.L., Miller, D., Norman, E.J., Greene, H. & Hayes, K.C. (1988). Increased urinary methylmalonic acid excretion in breast-fed infants of vegetarian mothers and identification of an acceptable dietary source of vitamin B-12. *Am. J. Clin. Nutr.* 47:89–92.

22 Golden, M. (1982). Protein deficiency, energy deficiency, and the oedema of malnutrition. *Lancet* i:1261–1265.

23 Knapp, J., Barness, L.A., Hill, L.L., Kaye, R., Blattner, R.J. & Sloan, J.M. (1973). Growth and nitrogen balance in infants fed cereal proteins. *Am. J. Clin. Nutr.* 26:586–590.

24 Sanders, T.A.B. & Purves, R. (1981). An anthropometric and dietary assessment of the nutritional status of vegan pre-school children. *J. Hum. Nutr.* 35:349–357.

25 Wenlock, R.W., Disselsuff, M.M. & Skinner, R.K. (1986). *The Diets of British Schoolchildren. Preliminary Report of a Nutritional Analysis of a Nationwide Dietary Survey of British Schoolchildren.* Middlesex: DHSS Leaflets Unit.

26 Fulton, J.R., Hutton, C.W. & Stitt, K.R. (1980). Preschool vegetarian children. *J. Am. Diet. Assn.* 76:360–365.

27 Roberts, I.F., West, R.J., Ogilvie, D. & Dillon, M.J. (1979). Malnutrition in infants receiving cult diets: a form of child abuse. *Br. Med. J.* 1:296–298.

28 Lozoff, B. & Fanaroff, A.A. (1975). Kwashiorkor in Cleveland. *Am. J. Dis. Child.* 129:710–711.

29 Berkelhamer, J.E., Thorp, F.K. & Cobbs, S. (1975). Kwashiorkor in Chicago. *Am. J. Dis. Child.* 129:1240.

30 Shinwell, E.D. & Gorodischer, R. (1982). Totally vegetarian diets and infant nutrition. *Pediatrics* 70:582–586.

31 Truesdell, D.D. & Acosta, P.B. (1985). Feeding the vegan infant and child. *J. Am. Diet. Assn.* 85:837–840.

32 Wighton, M.C., Manson, J.I., Speed, I. Robertson, E. & Chapman, E. (1979). Brain damage in infancy and dietary vitamin B$_{12}$ deficiency. *Med. J. Australia* 2:1–3.

33 Sklar, R. (1986). Nutritional vitamin B$_{12}$ deficiency in a breast-fed infant of a vegan-diet mother. *Clin. Pediatr.* 25:219–221.

34 Higginbottom, M.C., Sweetman, L. & Nyhan, W.L. (1978). A syndrome of methylmalonic aciduria, homocystinuria, megaloblastic anemia and neurologic abnormalities in a vitamin B$_{12}$-deficient breast-fed infant of a strict vegetarian. *New Engl. J. Med.* 299:317–323.

35 Close, G.C. (1983). Rastafarianism and the vegans syndrome (letter). *Br. Med. J.* 286:473.

36 Abdulla, M., Aly, K-O., Andersson, I., Asp, N-G., Birkhed, D., Denker, I., Johansson, C-G., Jägerstad, M., Kolar, K., Nair, B.M., Nilsson-Ehle, P., Nordén, Å., Rassner, S., Svensson, S., Åkesson, B. & Öckerman, P-A. (1984). Nutrient intake and health status of lactovegetarians: chemical analyses of diets using the duplicate portion sampling technique. *Am. J. Clin. Nutr.* 40:325–338.

37 Åkesson, B. & Öckerman, P.A. (1985). Selenium status in vegans and lactovegetarians. *Br. J. Nutr.* 53:199–205.

38 Langley, G.R. & Wilcox, J. (1987). *Health profile and nutrient sources of vegan and vegetarian runners.* Unpublished.

39 Belton, N.R. (1986). Rickets — not only the "English disease". *Acta. Paediatr. Scand.,* Suppl. 323:68–75.

40 Anon. (1984). Rickets in a breast-fed infant. *Nutr. Rev.* 42:380–382.

41 Kanaka, C., Schütz, B. & Zuppinger, K.A. (1992). Risks of alternative nutrition in infancy: a case report of severe iodine and carnitine deficiency. *Eur. J. Pediatr.* 151:786–788.

42 Cocchi, M., Noble, R.C., Fallowfield, H., Speake, B. & Turchetto, E. (1993). The significance of n-3 fatty acids in fetal and neonatal development and some alternative sources. *Proc. Nutr. Soc.* 52:224A.

43 Sanders, T.A.B. & Reddy, S. (1992). The influence of a vegetarian diet on the fatty acid composition of human milk and the essential fatty acid status of the infant. *J. Pediatr.* 120:S71–77.

44 Sanders, T.A.B. & Manning, J. (1992). The growth and development of vegan children. *J. Hum. Nutr. Diet.* 5:11–21.

45 Acosta, P.H. (1988). Availability of essential amino acids and nitrogen in vegan diets. *Am. J. Clin. Nutr.* 48:868–874.

46 Jacobs, C. & Dwyer, J.T. (1988). Vegetarian children: appropriate and inap-

propriate diets. *Am. J. Clin. Nutr.* 48:811–818.

47 Department of Health (1991). *Dietary Reference Values for Food Energy and Nutrients for the United Kingdom.* Reports on Health & Social Subjects no. 41. London: HMSO.

48 Lombard, K.A. & Mock, D.M. (1989). Biotin nutritional status of vegans, lacto-ovovegetarians, and nonvegetarians. *Am. J. Clin. Nutr.* 50:486–490.

49 Department of Health (1992). *Folic Acid and the Prevention of Neural Tube Defects.* Manchester: Health Publications Unit.

50 O'Connell, J.M., Dibley, M.J., Sierra, J. Wallace, B., Marks, J.S. & Yip, R. (1989). Growth of vegetarian children: the Farm study. *Pediatrics* 84:475–481.

51 Stollhoff, K. & Schulte, F.J. (1987). Vitamin B_{12} and brain development. *Eur. J. Pediatr.* 146:201–205.

52 Kühne, T., Bubl, R. & Baumgartner, R. (1991). Maternal vegan diet causing a serious infantile neurological disorder due to vitamin B_{12} deficiency. *Eur. J. Pediatr.* 150:205–208.

53 Davis, J.R., Goldenring, J. & Lubin, B.H. (1981). Nutritional vitamin B_{12} deficiency in infants. *Am. J. Dis. Child.* 135:566–567.

54 Gambon, R.C., Lentze, M.J. & Rossi, E. (1986). Megaloblastic anaemia in one of monozygous twins breast fed by their vegetarian mother. *Eur. J. Pediatr.* 145:570–571.

55 Specker, B.L., Black, A., Allen, L. & Morrow, F. (1990). Vitamin B-12: low milk concentrations are related to low serum concentrations in vegetarian women and to methylmalonic aciduria in their infants. *Am. J. Clin. Nutr.* 52:1073–1076.

56 Michaud, J.L., Lemieux, B., Ogier, H. & Lambert, M.A. (1992). Nutritional vitamin B_{12} deficiency: two cases detected by routine newborn urinary screening. *Eur. J. Pediatr.* 151:218–220.

57 Frader, J., Reibman, B. & Turkewitz, D. (1978). Vitamin B12 deficiency in strict vegetarians. *New Engl. J. Med.* 299:1319.

58 Lacroix, J., Macher, M.A., Badoual, J. & Huault, G. (1981). Complications of a vegetarian diet in a breast-fed girl. *Arch. Fr. Pediatr.* 38:233–238.

59 Monfort-Gouraud, M., Bongiorno, A., Le Gall, M.A. & Badoual, J. (1993). Severe megaloblastic anemia in a breast-fed infant born to a vegetarian mother. *Ann. Pediatr. (Paris)* 40:28–31.

60 Crawley, H. (1993). The energy, nutrient and food intakes of teenagers aged 16–17 years in Britain. *Br. J. Nutr.* 70:15–26.

61 Department of Health (1989). *Dietary Sugars and Human Disease.* Reports on Health & Social Subjects no. 37. London: HMSO.

62 Resnicow, K., Barone, J., Engle, A., Miller, S., Haley, N.J., Fleming, D. & Wynder, E. (1991). Diet and serum lipids in vegan vegetarians: a model for risk reduction. *J. Am. Diet. Assn.* 91:447–453.

63 Sanders, T.A.B. & Reddy, S. (1994). Vegetarian diets and children. *Am. J. Clin. Nutr.* 59 (suppl.):1176S–1181S.

64 Payne, J.A. & Bolton, N.R. (1992). Nutrient intake and growth in preschool children. I. Comparison of energy intake and sources of energy with growth. *J. Hum. Nutr. Diet.* 5:287–298.

65 Berenson, G.S. (1980). *Cardiovascular Risk Factors in Children.* Oxford: Oxford University Press.

66 Gutin, B., Basch, C., Shea, S., Contento, I., DeLozier, M., Rips, J., Irigoyen, M. and Zybert, P. (1990). Blood pressure, fitness and fatness in 5- and 6-year-old children. *J. Am. Med. Assn.* 264:1123–1127.

67 Department of Health (1989). *The Diets of British Schoolchildren.* Reports on Health & Social Subjects no. 36. London: HMSO.

68 Hall, R.H. (1992). A new threat to public health: organochlorines and food. *Nutr. & Health* 8:33–43.

69 van Kaam, A.H., Koopman-Esseboom, C., Sulkers, E.J., Sauer, P.J., van der Paauw, C.G. & Tuinstra, L.G. (1991). Polychloro-biphenyls in human milk, adipose tissue, plasma and umbilical cord blood: levels and correlates. *Ned. Tijd. voor Geneeskunde* 135:1399–1403.

70 Klaper, M. (1987). *Pregnancy, Children and the Vegan Diet.* Florida: Gentle World Inc.

71 Hergenrather, J., Hlady, G., Wallace, B. & Savage, E. (1981). Pollutants in breast milk of vegetarians. *New Engl. J. Med.* 304:792.

MILK AND HEALTH

Cow milk has no valid claim as the perfect food. As nutrition, it produces allergies in infants, diarrhea and cramps in the older child and adult, and may be a factor in the development of heart attacks and strokes. Perhaps when the public is educated as to the hazards of milk only calves will be left to drink the real thing. Only calves should drink the real thing.

Dr Frank Oski, Professor of Paediatrics and past president of the US Society for Pediatric Research, 1983[31]

Although cow's milk contains useful amounts of protein and calcium, there are health problems associated with it: direct effects on the health of infants fed dairy milk, and longer-term problems of degenerative artery disease and immune function, to which milk can contribute.

CHILDHOOD ALLERGIES

Allergy to cow's milk protein is the most common food allergy in childhood, affecting between four and 75 babies in every 1,000, and causing diarrhoea, vomiting, persistent colic, eczema, urticaria, catarrh, bronchitis or asthma. Babies fed with cow's milk develop antibodies to it in their blood, which can cause problems later in life.

A group of eight infants (7–46 weeks old) was referred to a University Department of Pediatrics in Belgium because of **chronic sleeplessness**[1]. During an average night they slept about 4.5 hours and woke their parents five times. They were described as fussy and cried a lot during the day, and two had been given medication without effect. Standard medical and psychological tests found no cause for insomnia. Studies showed that the infants were allergic to cow's milk protein. When this was excluded from their diets the infants slept normally; when it was re-introduced, sleeplessness recurred. Rarer complications of milk allergy in children include **thrombocytopenia**, a disorder of the blood[2] and **lung disease** (pulmonary hemosiderosis)[3].

A five-centre study of the effects of feeding premature babies either with breast milk or with formula feed (based on cow's milk) was published in 1990[22]. The babies were monitored until 18 months after their expected delivery date, and assessed for eczema, allergic reactions to food or drugs, and asthma and wheezing. In general, no differences were found, but among infants with a family history of allergy, those given dairy-based formula milk were more likely to develop one or more allergies, notably eczema, compared with similar infants who were breast fed.

When pregnant women prone to allergies (ie. who were atopic) eliminated all dairy products from their diets for six weeks before delivery, their babies at the age of six months had dramatically lower levels of antibodies to non-human milk, as would be expected. In addition, **their infants suffered from significantly fewer allergic conditions** in the 12 months after birth, compared with the infants of atopic mothers who had not modified their diet[23]. Low-fat milk still contains all the proteins which cause allergies.

A meeting of the American Society of Microbiologists suggested that some of the thousands of cot deaths occurring in the USA each year may be attributable to cow's milk allergy, as babies who are breast fed are less likely to succumb to cot death[4]. **Infants with documented milk allergy need to be taken to the doctor more than twice as often** during the first year of life than do infants without milk allergy, and are **also hospitalized more often**[5].

IRON-DEFICIENCY ANAEMIA IN INFANTS

The consumption of whole cow's milk in the first year of life — a practice common fifteen years ago and still occurring today — is linked with iron-deficiency anaemia. Cow's milk contains about 0.5mg of iron per litre, of which only 5%–10% is actually available for use by the body (breast milk contains slightly more iron and it is better absorbed). If cow's milk is fed as the sole or major source of nutrition during the first year it cannot provide enough iron for the growing infant. In addition, **cow's milk appears to decrease the absorption of iron from other foods,** compounding the iron-deficiency problem[6,7].

A study of infants in a clinic reported that 60% (two out of three) fed whole cow's milk at an early age developed iron-deficiency anaemia, and 33% (one in three) developed iron deficiency without anaemia. This occurred despite the infants being fed iron-fortified cereal and while receiving personal pediatric care[8]. Another study found that the longer feeding with whole cow's milk was postponed, the less chance there was of infants aged 9–12 months developing iron deficiency. Of infants given cow's milk before six months of age, two-thirds had insufficient iron, and one-third had insufficient iron when cow's milk was introduced at 6–9 months of age[9]. Some studies suggest that children who have iron-deficiency anaemia in infancy are more likely to suffer long-lasting disadvantages in mental and muscular function[24].

In 1992 the American Academy of Pediatrics Committee on Nutrition reviewed the effects on cow's milk on infant health[25]. Citing its low content of iron with poor availability to the body, and the possibility of hidden blood loss caused by milk (*see below*), **the Committee concluded that whole cow's milk should be excluded from the diet in the first year of life**, in an effort to decrease iron-deficiency anaemia in infants. Despite this general agreement among expert committees that infants should not receive cow's milk before 12 months of age, a recent Scottish study of 128 infants found that 64% had been fed cow's milk before the age of nine months[28].

MILK-INDUCED BLEEDING IN INFANTS

In the 1970s a series of studies of infants led to the conclusion that feeding with whole cow's milk is associated with iron deficiency not only because it is a poor source of iron, but also because it causes iron loss due to hidden bleeding from the baby's stomach and intestine. In a 1971 study, 44 out of 100 infants receiving whole cow's milk had blood in their faeces[10]. In a 1974 report, 17 out of 34 infants (aged 6–25 months) with iron-deficiency anaemia had **gastrointestinal bleeding** caused by whole cow's milk. Bleeding stopped when a soya milk formula was substituted[11]

MILK AND JUVENILE DIABETES

Insulin-dependent or type-1 (juvenile-onset) diabetes is a disorder of the pancreas to which some young people have a hereditary susceptibility. However, although a quarter of the population carries some genetic susceptibility to diabetes, less than one in 100 actually develops the disease. Thus there must be one or more lifestyle factors that trigger the disorder, which is becoming increasingly common.

In the mid-1980s researchers began to find clues that something in cow's milk might be linked with juvenile diabetes. One of the first discoveries was that, at the population level, juvenile diabetes increases as milk consumption goes up. For example, the average annual consumption of cow's milk in Japan is about 38 litres per person, and fewer than two children per 100,000 of the population are newly diagnosed with juvenile diabetes each year. In contrast, in Finland, where the annual consumption of cow's milk averages about 229 litres per person, 29 children per 100,000 of the population are diagnosed with diabetes[26].

Other findings — such as the fact that breast-fed babies seem less likely to become diabetic — pointed to the same theory implicating cow's milk. More recent research by a team of Finnish and Canadian scientists has discovered a possible link[27]. Blood samples from several hundred newly diagnosed diabetic children contained antibodies to a fragment of milk protein. This fragment closely resembles another protein, known as p69, which is naturally produced by the pancreas.

The hypothesis is that babies with a genetic susceptibility to diabetes develop antibodies in their bloodstream to the milk-protein fragment, if they are given cow's milk before the age of five or six months. As a quite separate process, each time the babies suffer a viral infection the natural protein p69 comes to the surface of the pancreas cells to protect them from viral attack. The immune system, mistaking p69 for the cow's milk protein, pounces on it and destroys a little of the pancreas. Over a few years, with repeated infections, the pancreas may be damaged to the point that diabetes occurs.

The hypothesis is not yet proven, but the research is persuasive — although there is no evidence that early consumption of cow's milk would have the same effect on people without a genetic predisposition to diabetes. In 1993 a definitive study was launched, in which more than 3,000 newborn babies with a family history of diabetes were put on special diets for their first nine months. They will then be monitored for 5–10 years to see if fewer of them develop diabetes than would normally be expected.

LACTOSE INTOLERANCE

In the majority of the world's population, the ability to digest milk sugar (lactose) decreases after the age of five years, and drinking milk can lead to bloating, cramps, wind and diarrhoea. Four reports suggest that 20%–40% of patients aged 5–17 years who experienced repeated abdominal pains suffered from lactose intolerance, which can often be relieved by excluding dairy milk and its products from the diet[7].

MILK AND HEART DISEASE

A five-year survey of children in Bogalusa, USA, included a study of the relationship between diet and health in 185 ten-year-olds[13]. Fat accounted for 38% of their energy intake, and too much of this was in the form of saturated fats. Eighteen per cent of the children's total fat intake was contributed by dairy milk, as was 26% of their intake of saturated fats — more than twice the amount provided by any other food group. Levels of blood cholesterol were linked with milk intake: children with the highest levels of blood cholesterol had significantly higher intakes of total fat and saturated fats than children with low cholesterol levels. The 1994 COMA report[15] on diet and heart disease recommended that children aged five years or over, like adults, should eat no more than about 35% of their energy as fat, and that some of the necessary reduction could be achieved by partly substituting low-fat products for butter, margarine and whole dairy milk.

The process of heating milk in order to pasteurize it may cause proteins in cow's milk to denature. These denatured proteins are known to be **linked with atherosclerosis**, and hence with heart disease[16]. Milk and other dairy products account for more than a third of the saturated fats eaten in this country (meat contributes another quarter), and the UK has the highest level of heart disease in the world.

A high intake of **saturated fat is linked with heart disease**. In Switzerland, a falling death rate from heart disease was partly due to a drop of nearly a half in milk consumption between 1951 and 1976, and the story is similar in other countries[17]. Four studies have particularly implicated cow's milk in heart disease[18]. Milk and dairy products were the major source of saturated fat and cholesterol for 75 adult vegetarians living in the USA, and their blood levels of cholesterol were higher than those of vegans who ate no dairy products[19].

For a while in 1992 it seemed that the links between dairy products and heart disease were not what they had seemed. Results from the Caerphilly (in Wales) Prospective Heart Disease Study had shown that men who drank the *most* cow's milk were *least* likely to develop heart disease, and *vice versa*[29]. The popular press misinterpreted the finding by assuming that the consumption of milk offered protection against heart disease. In fact, the leading author of the report, Peter Elwood, later explained that the men who drank more milk also had higher energy intakes and took the most exercise, and the last two factors were likely to protect against heart disease[30]. So the association with milk was fortuitous, and not causative.

MILK AND OTHER HEALTH PROBLEMS

Antigen/Antibody complexes in the blood, formed as a result of feeding babies with whole or modified cow's milk, may be involved in the later development of **allergy and recurrent infections and with atherosclerosis**[20]. Immune complexes of this sort are also known to be capable of

damaging the joints and kidneys[20]. A report from London's Hammersmith Hospital described a patient with **rheumatoid arthritis and multiple drug allergies** who improved markedly when milk and cheese were excluded from the diet, and relapsed when they were re-introduced[21]. Many patients with rheumatoid arthritis take non-steroidal anti-inflammatory drugs, which make the gut leaky and can allow proteins, such as milk proteins, to enter the bloodstream. These may then cause immune reactions in the joints, further exacerbating inflammation.

An intriguing result has raised the possibility of a connection between dairy products and **disorders of the stomach and intestine**. A bacterium called *Helicobacter* is believed to be a cause of gastritis (inflammation of the stomach lining), stomach cancer and duodenal ulcer. Abattoir workers are more likely to have the bacterium, suggesting meat as a possible source of infection, so a study[12] was undertaken to compare the presence of *Helicobacter* in the stomachs of 18 omnivores, 18 vegetarians and 10 vegans. Surprisingly, the vegetarians had greater numbers of bacteria than either omnivores or vegans, the latter harbouring fewest of all three groups. An explanation of the finding, suggested by the authors of the study, is that dairy products may be a source of *Helicobacter* infection. As a consequence, they question the wisdom of recommending milk for people with duodenal ulcers.

MILK AND HEALTH — SUMMARY

Cow's milk is a common but sometimes still unrecognized cause of allergy in infants and children, and symptoms range from diarrhoea and vomiting to eczema, asthma and chronic sleeplessness. Infants under one year who are given cow's milk as the sole or major food may develop iron deficiency, not only because it is a relatively poor source of iron but also because it can cause iron loss through gastrointestinal bleeding. Lactose intolerance is a significant cause of repeated abdominal pain in children.

Milk and other dairy products account for about one-third of the saturated fat intake of omnivores in the UK, and a high intake of saturated fat is a risk factor for heart disease. Some studies have directly implicated cow's milk consumption in heart disease, and in insulin-dependent diabetes. Other health problems have also been associated with dairy milk.

REFERENCES

1 Kahn, A., Mozin, M.J., Casimir, G., Montauk, L. & Blum, D. (1985). Insomnia and cow's milk allergy in infants. *Pediatrics* 76:880–884.

2 Jones, R.H.T. (1977). Congenital thrombocytopenia and milk allergy. *Arch. Dis. Child.* 52:744–745.

3 Lee, S.K., Kniker, W.T., Cook, C.D. & Heiner, D.C. (1978). Cow's milk-induced pulmonary disease in children. *Adv. Pediatr.* 25:39–57.

4 Dunea, G. (1982). Beyond the Etheric. *Br. Med. J.* 285:428–429.

5 Gerrard, J.W., MacKenzie, J.W.A., Goluboff, N., Garson, J.Z. & Maningas, C.S. (1973). Cow's milk allergy: prevalence and manifestations in an unselected series of newborns. *Acta Paediatr. Scand.* Suppl. 234:1–21.

6 World Health Organization (1985). Control of nutritional anemia with special reference to iron deficiency. *Technical Report Series* 580. Geneva: WHO.

7 Oski, F.A. (1985). Is bovine milk a health hazard? *Pediatrics* 75:182–186.

8 Hunter, R. (1970). *Iron nutrition in infancy.* In: Report of the 62nd Ross Conference on Pediatric Research, p. 22. Columbus, Ohio.

9 Sadowitz, P.D. & Oski, F.A. (1983). Iron status and infant feeding practices in an urban ambulatory center. *Pediatrics* 72:33–36.

10 Anyon, C.P. & Clarkson, K.G. (1971). A cause of iron-deficiency anaemia in infants. *N.Z. Med. J.* 74:24–25.

11 Wilson, J.F., Lahey, M.E. & Heiner, D.C. (1974). Studies on iron metabolism. V. Further observations on cow's milk-induced gastrointestinal bleeding in infants with iron-deficiency anemia. *J. Pediatr.* 84:335–344.

12 Sundaresan, M., Hayllar, J.S. & Price, A.B. (1990). A comparison of colonization of gastric mucosa by *Helicobacter*-like organisms in omnivores, vegans and vegetarians. *J. Path.* 160:170A.

13 Berenson, G.S. (1980). *Dietary studies and the relationship of diet to cardiovascular disease risk-factor variables in children.* In: Cardiovascular risk factors in children: the early natural history of atherosclerosis and essential hypertension, pp289–307. Oxford: Oxford University Press.

14 National Advisory Committee on Nutrition Education (1983). *Proposals for Nutritional Guidelines for Health Education in Britain.* London: Health Education Council.

15 Committee on Medical Aspects of Food Policy (1994). *Nutritional Aspects of Cardiovascular Disease.* Reports on Health & Social Subjects no. 46. London: HMSO.

16 Annand, J.C. (1986). Denatured bovine immunoglobulin pathogenic in atherosclerosis. *Atherosclerosis* 59:34–351.

17 Segall, J. (1982). Communicable disease associated with milk and dairy products (letter). *Br. Med. J.* 285:575.

18 Davies, D.F., Rees, B.W.G. & Davies, P.T.G. (1980). Cow's milk antibodies and coronary heart disease (letter). *Lancet* i:1190.

19 Sacks, F.M., Ornish, D., Rosner, B., McLanahan, S., Castelli, W.P. & Kass, E.H. (1985). Plasma lipoprotein levels in vegetarians: the effect of ingestion of fats from dairy products. *J. Am. Med. Assn.* 254:1337–1341.

20 Delire, M., Cambiaso, C.L. & Masson, P.L. (1978). Circulating immune complexes in infants fed on cow's milk. *Nature* 272:632.

21 Woo, P. (1982). Anti-inflammatory drugs are the key. *Gen. Pract.* 17th September, 55.

22 Lucas, A., Brooke, O.G., Morley, R., Cole, T.J. & Bamford, M.F. (1990). Early

diet of preterm infants and development of allergic or atopic disease: randomised prospective study. *Br. Med. J.* 300:837–840.

23 Lovegrove, J.A., Hampton, S.M. & Morgan, J.B. (1993). Does a maternal milk-free diet prevent allergy in the 'at-risk' infant? *Proc. Nutr. Soc.* 52:217A.

24 Lozoff, B., Jimenez, E. & Wolf, A.W. (1991). Long-term developmental outcome of infants with iron deficiency. *New Engl. J. Med.* 325:687–694.

25 American Academy of Pediatrics, Committee on Nutrition (1992). The use of whole cow's milk in infancy. *Pediatrics* 89:1105–1109.

26 Rennie, J. (1992). Formula for diabetes? *Sci. American* 267:24–26.

27 Karjalainen, J., Martin, J.M., Knip, M., Ilonen, J., Robinson, B.H., Savilahti, E., Akerblom, H.K. & Dosch, H.-M. (1992). A bovine albumin peptide as a possible trigger of insulin-dependent diabetes mellitus. *New Engl. J. Med.* 327:302–307.

28 Savage, S.A.H., Reilly, J.J., Edwards, C.A. & Durnin, J.V.G.A. (1995). Weaning practice in Glasgow. *Br. J. Nutr.* In press.

29 Elwood, P.C. *et al* (1991). *Epidemiological Studies of Cardiovascular Disease.* Progress report VII. Cardiff: MRC Epidemiology Unit.

30 Elwood, P.C. (1991). Milk and heart disease. *BNF Nutr. Bull.* 16:6–7.

31 Oski, F.A. (1983). *Don't Drink Your Milk!* Syracuse: Mollica Press Ltd.

THE GENERAL
HEALTH OF
VEGANS

We can reduce cholesterol levels either by reducing animal protein intake or exchanging it for plant protein. Some of the plant proteins, particularly soy, have an impressive ability to reduce cholesterol.

Dr Colin Campbell MS, PhD, Professor of Nutritional Biochemistry at Cornell University, USA, and Senior Scientific Adviser to the American Institute for Cancer Research, 1994[29]

A number of studies have investigated the general health of vegans, although more detailed examinations would be welcome.

In 1970, Ellis and Montegriffo[1] examined 26 vegans of between 1–18.5 years' standing and compared various parameters of health with matched omnivore controls. They found no abnormal symptoms or signs of definite significance which could have been related to nutritional status. In the same year they also published a review of surveys of the health of British vegans compared to omnivores, and concluded that physical fitness and the incidence of disease were similar. Apart from the vegans being slightly lighter in weight, and having lower blood cholesterol and urea levels, there was little difference between the two groups[2].

The health status of 72 British vegans compared with 72 matched omnivores was assessed by the Cornell Medical Index questionnaire and the results were published in 1976[3]. These suggested that there was no difference between the men in the two groups, but that the **vegan women tended to be healthier than the omnivore women**, particularly with respect to cardiovascular disease, frequency of illness and number of days away from work due to illness. A review published in 1978[4] showed that vegans had lower serum cholesterol and triglyceride concentrations, normal blood formation, **but some differences in their electroencephalograms (brain waves) which did not, however, appear to affect health.** There were obvious differences in plasma lipid levels (*see* **Fats**, *for a fuller discussion of this*), and a **vegan diet may have protected against heart disease.**

A survey of the health of ten British vegans compared with vegetarians and omnivores published in 1985 found that there was no statistical difference between the groups in pulse rate, blood pressure, or incidence of allergies or other clinical parameters[6]. Haemoglobin levels, mean corpuscular haemoglobin, mean red blood cell volume, haematocrit and corpuscular haemoglobin concentration were similar in all groups. Four vegans and two omnivores had slightly low haemoglobin levels but all participants were in good health.

High intakes of fats, especially saturated fats, are risk factors for coronary heart disease, causing damaging changes in levels of cholesterols in the blood. Numerous studies show that vegans eat the least total fat, and particularly saturated fat, of all dietary groups, and have the lowest levels of LDL-cholesterol as well as the lowest LDL/HDL-cholesterol ratio in their bloodstream[15-20]. **The risk of coronary heart disease among vegans is likely to be lower than that of meat-eaters or even vegetarians.** The low levels of fat and plentiful supply of fibre in vegan diets are also likely to offer some protection against **gallstones.**

A number of illnesses are associated with being **overweight or obese.** Overweight is generally defined as a Body Mass Index of 25–29.9, where the BMI is weight in kilograms divided by height^2 in metres. Obesity is considered to be a BMI of 30 or more. Excess weight is associated with high blood pressure, raised blood levels of cholesterol and abnormally high levels of insulin in the blood — and all these are known risk factors for heart disease. It's estimated that cases of adult-onset diabetes could be halved if middle-aged people did not become overweight. People who are obese also have a greater risk of developing respiratory disease, gallstones, certain types of cancer and osteoarthritis.

A 1978 review indicated that vegans tended to be lighter in weight and less obese than omnivores[4], and were more likely to be closer to their ideal weight. More recent studies indicate that vegans are similar in weight or slightly lighter than the vegetarians and omnivores in the same studies, but considerably lighter than the general population where the average BMI is 25.6. For example, the Body Mass Index (BMI) of 10 vegans was reported in 1985 to be an average 23 for women and men, compared to 22 for lacto-ovo-vegetarians and wholefood omnivores, and 23 for average omnivores[12]. In a 1986 report[21], the vegans' average BMI was 21, compared to 23 and 21 for male and female omnivores. A study of male subjects showed the average BMI for 51 vegans was 22.2, and for omnivores was 23.2[13]. Vegan Seventh Day Adventists in the USA had an average BMI of 21.7, versus 22 in matched omnivores, but 24 in the general population[19]. In a 1993 report the mean weights of 38 British vegans were 55.4kg (women) and 64.4kg (men)[11]. Although not statistically significant, these average weights for vegans were lower than those of lacto-ovo-vegetarian (59kg and 69kg respectively) and fish-eating subjects (57.9kg and 74.7kg respectively).

Being overweight is a risk factor for several chronic illnesses. Studies suggest that the average Body Mass Index of vegans is considerably lower than the 25.6 for the general omnivore population in Britain — in which 41% of women and 53% of men are overweight or obese[24].

The opinion has been expressed that there may be a link between veganism/vegetarianism and **anorexia nervosa.** This was not supported by a study of 116 consecutive patients with anorexia nervosa who were seen by doctors at a hospital in New South Wales, Australia[9]. While 54% of the patients were found to be avoiding red meat, in only four cases did this precede the onset of anorexia nervosa. There were no vegans among these anorexic patients.

A link between the consumption of meat and various forms of dementia has been suggested by a preliminary study of Seventh Day Adventists in the USA[14]. **Subjects who ate meat, including poultry and fish, were twice as likely to suffer from dementia** as their lacto-ovo-vegetarian and vegan counterparts. The researchers speculate that there may be an infectious component to some dementias, and that the infectious agent, such as a virus, could be found in meat.

A study was undertaken to compare levels of a bacterium called *Helicobacter* in the stomachs of 18 omnivores, 18 vegetarians and 10 vegans[28]. *Helicobacter* is now known to be a cause of **gastritis, peptic ulcers and possibly stomach cancer too.** The researchers conducted the study to see if meat-eaters had higher numbers of bacteria in their stomachs, but the surprise finding was that, in fact, the vegetarians had the highest levels. The vegan subjects had the fewest numbers of *Helicobacter*. An explanation suggested by the researchers is that dairy products may be a source of the bacteria. Do vegans suffer less from gastritis and peptic ulcers than meat eaters? The research has yet to be done.

Vegetarians, including vegans, are **less at risk from non-insulin-dependent (adult-onset) diabetes**, and also **suffer less from obesity, coronary artery disease, hypertension and some types of cancer**[10]. While all the connections between diet and cancer are not yet understood, there is evidence from population studies that cancers of the **breast, womb, pancreas, prostate and colon are linked to a high fat intake and that breast**[25]**, womb**[23] **and colon cancers**[26,27] **are correlated specifically with the consumption of meat and animal fat and protein.**

It is now clear that changing the nation's diet could reduce the risk of cancer by between one-third and two-thirds. However, it is not yet known

TABLE 8.1
CURRENT THEORIES LINKING DIET AND CANCER

Higher consumption associated with lower cancer risks	Higher consumption associated with increased cancer risks
Fibre *(whole grains, vegetables)*	**Meat**
Antioxidants such as beta-carotene, and vitamins C, E *(vegetables, fruit)*	**Total fat consumption** *(meat, dairy fats etc.)*
Plant-derived oestrogens *(wheat, soya)*	**Saturated or animal fat**
Calcium *(tofu, green leafy vegetables)*	**Preserved foods**
Omega-3 fatty acids *(oily fish)*	**Alcohol**
Starch *(whole grains, vegetables)*	**Salt**

exactly how many or which cancers are affected by diet, or whether all the relevant dietary components and their effects have been identified.

Diet is a major influence on the risk of cancers of the bowel and stomach, and probably on cancers of the breast, prostate and womb too. The risk of other cancers — such as throat, lung and bladder — is also likely to be affected by diet, but there is not enough evidence yet to say for sure.

Table 8.1 (*above*) illustrates some of the current theories linking diet and cancer. Many of the protective factors are more prominent in vegan diets than in the average omnivore's diet, while the opposite is the case for the risk factors. The 10-year European Prospective Investigation of Cancer (EPIC) was launched in 1992 to test these theories. EPIC is the largest such study ever organized, recruiting more than 400,000 healthy men and women from seven European countries. 75,000 people from Britain will participate, involving detailed analyses of their nutritional status and their dietary and lifestyle characteristics.

These theories suggest that vegans would be less likely to suffer from some diet-related cancers, and this may well prove to be the case. The definitive research still remains to be done, but interesting preliminary results have come from the Oxford Vegetarian Study. A 1994 report analyzed the number of deaths from cancer among non-meat eaters (including vegetarians, vegans and fish-but-not-meat eaters) and among matched, 'health-conscious' meat eaters, over a period of 12 years[22]. There were fewer than expected cancer deaths in both groups of subjects, but premature cancer deaths among non-meat eaters were 40% fewer than among meat eaters — a result which could not be explained by differences in body weight, smoking habits or socio-economic status. Although there were too few vegan subjects to allow a separate analysis of their cancer deaths at this stage, in time this information may emerge.

The health of vegan women during pregnancy has been a topic of interest among nutritionists. Several studies have shown that babies born to vegan women and reared on vegan diets thrive (*see* **Vegan Mothers and Children** *for further details*). A 1987 report[7] of a survey of pregnant women at The Farm, a vegan community in Tennessee, USA, showed that the incidence of pre-eclampsia was extremely low (one in 775). Pre-eclampsia is characterized by increased vasoconstriction, reduced blood flow to the placenta and premature delivery. **The authors concluded that, far from being harmful during pregnancy, a well-planned and varied vegan diet could be beneficial by reducing the likelihood of pre-eclampsia.**

In a report published in 1980, of 28 American pre-school vegetarian children (2–8.4 years old), six were macrobiotic vegans and 22 were vegetarians, including Seventh Day Adventists and macrobiotics[8]. The above-average IQ for all subjects was 116, while the average for the vegan children was 119. The mental age of the vegan children was 16.5 months ahead of their chronological age, compared to 12.5 months for all the vegetarian children together. The authors believed that the above-average IQs and mental development of the children were as likely to reflect the educational level of the parents as any nutritional factors, but showed that **vegan and vegetarian macrobiotic diets had obviously been able to support advanced development**. Anthropometric and clinical measurements were normal in all the children.

Although the links between diet and health are attracting great interest among researchers, and the number of studies of vegetarians and vegans continues to increase, there is still a need for more detailed research. It is quite clear that most vegan diets support good health from infancy to the grave, but understanding the more subtle effects of various nutrients would provide additional guidance for vegans, as well as allowing better nutritional advice to be given to the general population.

REFERENCES

1 Ellis, F.R. & Montegriffo, V.M.E. (1970). Veganism, clinical findings and investigations. *Am. J. Clin. Nutr.* 23:249–255.

2 Ellis, F.R. & Montegriffo, V.M.E. (1971). The health of vegans. *Plant Fds. Hum. Nutr.* 2:93–103.

3 Ellis, F.R., West, E.D. & Sanders, T.A.B. (1976). The health of vegans compared with omnivores: assessment by health questionnaire. *Plant Fds. Man.* 2:43–52.

4 Sanders, T.A.B. (1978). The health and nutritional status of vegans. *Plant Fds. Man.* 2:181–193.

5 Sanders, T.A.B. (1983). Vegetarianism: dietetic and medical aspects. *J. Plant Foods.* 5:3–14.

6 Lockie, A.H., Carlson, E., Kipps, M. & Thomson, J. (1985). Comparison of four types of diet using clinical, laboratory and psychological studies. *J. Roy. Coll. Gen. Pract.* 35:333–336.

7 Carter, J.P., Furman, T. & Hutcheson, H.R. (1987). Preeclampsia and reproductive performance in a community of vegans. *Southern Med. J.* 80:692–697.

8 Dwyer, J.T., Miller, L.G., Arduino, N.L., Andrew, E.M., Dietz, W.H., Reed, J.C. & Reed, H.B.C. (1980). Mental age and IQ of predominantly vegetarian children. *J. Am. Diet. Assn.* 76:142–147.

9 O'Connor, M.A., Touyz, S.W., Dunn, S.M. & Beumont, P.J.V. (1987). Vegetarianism in anorexia nervosa? A review of 116 consecutive cases. *Med. J. Australia* 147:540–54.

10 Havala, S. & Dwyer, J. (1993). Position of the American Dietetic Association: vegetarian diets. *J. Am. Diet. Assn.* 93:1317–1319.

11 Draper, A., Lewis, J., Malhotra, N. & Wheeler, E. (1993). The energy and nutrient intakes of different types of vegetarian: a case for supplements? *Br. J. Nutr.* 69:3–19.

12 Carlson, E., Kipps, M., Lockie, A. & Thomson, J. (1985). A comparative evaluation of vegan, vegetarian and omnivore diets. *J. Plant Foods* 6:89–100.

13 Key, T.J.A., Roe, L., Thorogood, M., Moore, J.W., Clark, G.M.G. & Wang, D.Y. (1990). Testosterone, sex hormone-binding globulin, calculated free testosterone, and oestradiol in male vegans and omnivores. *Br. J. Nutr.* 64:111–119.

14 Giem, P., Beeson, W.L. & Fraser, G.E. (1993). The incidence of dementia and intake of animal products: preliminary findings from the Adventist health study. *Neuroepidemiology* 12:28–36.

15 Burslem, J., Schonfeld, G., Howald, M.A., Weidman, S.W. & Miller, J.P. (1978). Plasma apoprotein and lipoprotein lipid levels in vegetarians. *Metabolism* 27:711–719.

16 Sanders, T.A.B., Ellis, F.R. & Dickerson, J.W.T. (1978). Studies of vegans: the fatty acid composition of plasma choline phosphoglycerides, erythrocytes, adipose tissue, and breast milk, and some indicators of susceptibility to ischemic heart disease in vegans and omnivore controls. *Am. J. Clin. Nutr.* 31:805–813.

17 Melchert, H.-U., Limsathayourat, N., Mihajlovic, H. & Eichberg, J. (1987). Fatty acid patterns in triglycerides, diglycerides, free fatty acids, cholesteryl esters and phosphatidyl choline in serum from vegetarians and non-vegetarians. *Atherosclerosis* 65:159–166.

18 Thorogood, M., Carter, R., Benfield, L., McPherson, K. & Mann, J.I. (1987). Plasma lipids and lipoproteins in groups with different dietary practices within Britain. *Br. Med. J.* 295:351–353.

19 Resnicow, K., Barone, J., Engle, A., Miller, S., Haley, N.J., Fleming, D. & Wynder, E. (1991). Diet and serum lipids in vegan vegetarians: a model for risk reduction. *J. Am. Diet. Assn.* 91:447–453.

20 Thorogood, M., Roe, L., McPherson, K. & Mann, J. (1990). Dietary intake and plasma lipid levels: lessons from a study of the diet of health conscious groups. *Br. Med. J.* 300:1297–1301.

21 Rana, S.K. & Sanders, T.A.B. (1986). Taurine concentrations in the diet, plasma, urine and breast milk of vegans compared with omnivores. *Br. J. Nutr.* 56:17–27.

22 Thorogood, M., Mann, J., Appleby, P. & McPherson, K. (1994). Risk of death from cancer and ischaemic heart disease in meat and non-meat eaters. *Br. Med. J.* 308:1667–1670.

23 Xiao, O.S., Wei, Z., Potischman, N., Brinton, L.A., Hatch, M.C., Gao, Y.T. &

Fraumeni, J.F. (1993). A population-based case-control study of dietary factors and endometrial cancer in Shanghai, Peoples Republic of China. *Am. J. Epidemiol.* 137:155–165.

24 Office of Population Censuses and Surveys (1993). *Health Survey for England 1991.* London: HMSO.

25 Lee, H.P., Gourley, L., Duffy, S.W., Estève, J., Lee, J. & Day, N.E. (1991). Dietary effects on breast cancer risk in Singapore. *Lancet* 337:1197–1200.

26 Willett, W.C., Stampfer, M.J., Colditz, G.A., Rosner, B.A. & Speizer, F.E. (1990). Relation of meat, fat and fibre intake to the risk of colon cancer in a prospective study among women. *New Engl. J. Med.* 323:1664–1672.

27 Giovannucci, E., Meir, J., Colditz, G. A., Rimm, E.B. & Willett, W.C. (1990). Relation of diet to the risk of colorectal adenoma in men. *Am. J. Epidemiol.* 132:783.

28 Sundaresan, M., Hayllar, J.S. & Price, A.B. (1990). A comparison of colonization of gastric mucosa by *Helicobacter*-like organisms in omnivores, vegans and vegetarians. *J. Path.* 160:170A.

29 Barnard, N.D. (1994). The latest from the China Diet and Health Study. *Good Medicine* III (3):10–14.

VEGAN DIETS AS THERAPY

High blood pressure

Angina

Atherosclerosis

Kidney disease

Diabetic neuropathy

Rheumatoid arthritis

Asthma

Vegan diets as therapy — summary

References

Your food should be your medicine and your medicine food.

Hippocrates, 5th century BC

It is probable that vegan diets are beneficial in reducing the risks of some chronic illnesses, but once illness has struck can a vegan diet have a therapeutic effect? As research into possible health benefits of veganism increases, more studies of the role a vegan diet may play in the treatment of various diseases are likely to be conducted. So far, a number of such studies have been published.

HIGH BLOOD PRESSURE

In 1983 the results of a controlled trial of the blood pressure-lowering effect of a vegetarian diet were published[1]. In Australia, 59 healthy omnivore volunteers with normal blood pressure followed a vegetarian diet for six weeks. After adjusting results for variations in age, obesity, heart rate, weight change and blood pressure, it was found that systolic blood pressure fell by 5–6mm of mercury and diastolic pressure by 2–3mm while subjects were on a vegetarian diet, but not while on an omnivorous diet.

Following this, a randomized controlled trial was conducted in Australia on the effect of a vegetarian diet on patients with raised blood pressure[2]. Fifty-eight subjects with mild untreated hypertension were given a vegetarian diet for 6 weeks, during which time their systolic (but not diastolic) pressure fell by about 5mm of mercury. While on an omnivorous diet, the subjects experienced a fall of only 1–2mm. Greater changes would be expected with patients suffering higher blood pressure, and effects on diastolic pressure were also possible. A reduction of 5mm of mercury in systolic blood pressure might result in a 7% reduction in the number of major coronary illnesses in a middle-aged population.

A 1984 report from Sweden documented the effect of a vegan diet on 26 patients with long-established hypertension[3]. All the patients had been taking medication and while this had brought the pressure of most into the normal range, eight still had high blood pressure. The patients followed a strict vegan diet for one year, with the extra exclusion of coffee, tea, chocolate, and added sugar and salt. Vegetables were eaten mainly fresh and raw, and the volunteers were also given herbal preparations and encouraged to take physical exercise.

After one year, 22 subjects reported freedom from all adverse symptoms and the other four claimed that they had fewer symptoms, and 20 patients had been able to give up their medication completely. There was a general reduction in systolic (7–9mm of mercury) and diastolic (5–10mm) blood pressure and in pulse rate, and blood levels of triglycerides and cholesterol decreased. Although there were many factors involved in this study and no single one can be identified, the authors believe that a vegan diet can be beneficial for hypertensive patients.

An American study compared the effects of a 9-week out-patient programme, and a 25-day in-patient programme, of exercise and a wholefood, vegan diet[15]. Twenty-eight patients with essential hypertension followed the out-patient programme, and by the sixth week experienced an average decrease in blood pressure from 147/68 to 133/71. Most patients were able to decrease their reliance on drugs, and 17 of the 28 maintained a blood pressure of 140/90 without any medication. The results from the in-patient programme were even more dramatic. Fifty-six women and 46 men with hypertension participated. Average blood pressure readings fell from 152/79 (women) and 142/84 (men) at the start, to 134/74 and 123/74 respectively after three weeks. The majority of patients were able to cease their medication, and those who were obese lost an average 10lbs. Compliance with the diet and exercise regime was good: over half the patients remained on the programme for at least a year.

In general, recent research has suggested that the factors in a vegetarian or vegan diet which contribute to the blood pressure-lowering effect include a high ratio of polyunsaturated to saturated fats, high fibre and low protein intakes.

ANGINA

A report in 1977 reviewed the health of four patients with severe angina pectoris who had followed a vegan diet as treatment for their condition[4]. Although this condition is known to remit spontaneously, the authors thought it unlikely that this would occur in all four patients. One patient aged 65 years experienced complete remission of angina symptoms while on a vegan diet, which he followed for five years until death from pulmonary embolism. A second patient aged 48 years adhered to a vegan diet for several years during which time his condition improved markedly, but after giving up the diet his symptoms gradually recurred. The remaining two patients aged 44 and 46 years, who experienced severe angina on exertion, followed a vegan diet for several years and during that time were able to take fairly vigorous exercise without pain or shortage of breath. To the author's knowledge, there have been no controlled trials of the effect of a vegan diet on angina.

ATHEROSCLEROSIS

American scientists recruited patients suffering from atherosclerosis for a study to see if following a non-drug, dietary and behavioural programme could actually reverse the symptoms of their artery disease[8]. The programme, called the Lifestyle Heart Trial, was the first carefully controlled clinical trial to see if patients outside hospital could be motivated to make comprehensive lifestyle changes, and stick to them, in an effort to reverse their atherosclerosis.

The experimental group of 22 patients followed a low-fat vegetarian diet — not quite vegan — as well as a programme of moderate exercise, stress management, stopping smoking and group support. The control group of 19 patients were not asked to make lifestyle changes but were free to do so. The diet included fruits, vegetables, grains, legumes and soya bean products. No animal products were allowed except egg white and one cup a day of non-fat dairy milk or yoghurt.

After one year the blockage of the arteries of the lifestyle-programme patients had reduced by an average of 16.5%. Over the same period the control patients' arteries had become more blocked, by 15.5%. The improvement was more prominent in those whose atherosclerosis was most severe. The frequency, duration and severity of angina chest pains also reduced for the experimental patients over the year, but increased for the patients who did not make lifestyle changes.

The research showed that it is possible for patients to sustain a commitment to non-drug lifestyle changes, including a near-vegan diet, which can partially reverse their heart disease.

KIDNEY DISEASE

Some research has indicated advantages of vegan diets for patients with kidney disease (nephrotic syndrome), in which they lose protein in their urine, and have high levels of cholesterol in their bloodstream. In one study, thirty-four such patients were given a low-protein vegan diet, supplemented with essential amino acids, for an average of 4.5 months[9].

Various measurements of blood chemistry and kidney function were made before and after the diet was followed. Total cholesterol and LDL-cholesterol in the blood declined, while the so-called 'good' HDL-cholesterol increased. Protein in the urine and nitrogen excretion decreased, indicating an improvement in the patients' condition.

Some patients changed from an unrestricted protein, low-sodium diet to the special vegan diet and back again three times, and the improvements occurred each time the vegan diet was followed. It was concluded that the diet's low cholesterol content and high ratio of polyunsaturated to saturated fatty acids can be helpful for kidney patients.

Another report documented the effect of a supplemented vegan diet on patients with primary, steroid-resistant nephrotic syndrome[10]. Thirteen patients who followed the special diet for four months experienced reduced excretion of protein and nitrogen, lower rates of creatinine clearance, and a drop in blood levels of cholesterol. The researchers concluded that the special vegan diet had favourable effects on these patients.

A similar study with 20 patients used a low-fat (28% of energy), medium-protein (11%) vegan diet for eight weeks[13]. Animal proteins were replaced with soya products, and animal fats with polyunsaturated and monounsaturated vegetable oils. Again, total cholesterol and LDL-cholesterol levels dropped, and HDL-cholesterol declined by a smaller percentage. Protein loss in the urine and creatinine clearance also decreased.

The usual dietary approach to nephrotic syndrome is a low-saturated fat, low-cholesterol diet, sometimes supplemented with protein. These preliminary studies with vegan diets show that they beneficially affect blood fat levels, and possibly soya protein itself has a specific cholesterol-lowering effect. Whether vegan diets offer an advantage over the orthodox dietary therapy remains to be shown[11].

DIABETIC NEUROPATHY

Diabetic neuropathy is a neurological condition suffered by some diabetics, in which numbness as well as shooting or burning pains occur in the lower limbs. Twenty-one diabetics volunteered to follow a supervised programme comprising a vegan, wholefood diet and exercise, for 25 days[14]. Within four to sixteen days, 17 of the patients reported that the characteristic pain of neuropathy had been completely alleviated, and although the numbness persisted it decreased after 25 days. The other four patients experienced a partial improvement in their pain.

RHEUMATOID ARTHRITIS

Three studies have looked at the effects of fasting and/or a modified vegan diet on rheumatoid arthritis. Under medical supervision, 13 women with rheumatism followed a juice fast for one week and then a vegan diet for three weeks, with the additional exclusion of coffee, tea, chocolate, cereals, soya and wheat products, and added sugar and salt. Thirteen other female patients received conventional food[5]. Clinical and biochemical results after a month's dietary therapy showed significant and pronounced improvement in the vegan (but not in the control) group, in spite of the withdrawal of almost all pain-relieving medication.

A later report[6] concerned 20 patients with rheumatoid arthritis who followed a similar dietary regimen for three to four months. The 12 patients who reported an improvement felt less pain and experienced better function in the affected joints, although objective measurements of grip strength and joint tenderness showed no change. Five patients experienced no difference, and three felt worse. The authors concluded that many patients with mild or moderate rheumatism might benefit from adopting a vegan diet of this sort.

A report from Norway confirmed benefits from a vegan and vegetarian approach[12]. In a randomized, single-blind controlled trial, 27 arthritic patients started on a gluten-free vegan diet for 3.5 months, and then gradually introduced some vegetarian items. After only four weeks on the vegan diet, patients showed significant improvements in pain levels, number of tender and swollen joints, morning stiffness, grip strength and several blood-chemistry parameters. In the control group of patients, only pain scores improved.

ASTHMA

A special vegan diet has also been prescribed by Swedish doctors in an effort to treat bronchial asthma[7]. Twenty-four volunteers with long-established asthma were instructed how to follow a vegan diet which excluded tea, coffee, chocolate, added sugar and salt, and restricted certain fruits and vegetables, as well as cereals. With only a few lapses, the subjects followed the diet for a year and their health was assessed twice in that period. After one year, 92% of patients reported an improvement in or freedom from symptoms of asthma, with the number and severity of attacks having decreased. Clinical measurements confirmed the improvement. Some of the volunteers who had also suffered from rheumatism found a lessening of these symptoms.

195

VEGAN DIETS AS THERAPY — SUMMARY

A number of studies have indicated that vegan diets may have beneficial effects on several conditions, ranging from rheumatoid arthritis to atherosclerosis. It is not yet clear precisely which features of a vegan diet may be effective, but the generally encouraging results of these pilot investigations will, it is hoped, stimulate further research.

REFERENCES

1 Rouse, I.L., Beilin, L.J., Armstrong, B.K. & Vandongen, R. (1983). Blood pressure-lowering effect of a vegetarian diet: controlled trial in normotensive subjects. *Lancet* i:5–10.

2 Margetts, B.M., Beilin, L.J., Vandongen, R. & Armstrong, B.K. (1986). Vegetarian diet in mild hypertension: a randomised controlled trial. *Br. Med. J.* 293:1468–1471.

3 Lindahl, O., Lindwall, L., Spångberg, A., Stenram, Å. & Öckerman, P.A. (1984). A vegan regimen with reduced medication in the treatment of hypertension. *Br. J. Nutr.* 52:11–20.

4 Ellis, F.R. & Sanders, T.A.B. (1977). Angina and vegan diet. *Am. Ht. J.* 93:803–804.

5 Hamberg, V.J., Lindahl, O., Lindwall, L. & Öckerman, P.A. (1982). Fasting and vegetarian diet in the treatment of rheumatoid arthritis — a controlled study. *Rheuma* 4:9–14.

6 Sköldstam, L. (1986). Fasting and vegan diet in rheumatoid arthritis. *Scand. J. Rheum.* 15:219–233.

7 Lindahl, O., Lindwall, L., Spångberg, A., Stenram, Å. & Öckerman, P.A. (1985). Vegan regimen with reduced medication in the treatment of bronchial asthma. *J. Asthma* 22:45–55.

8 Ornish, D., Brown, S.E., Scherwitz, L.W., Billings, J.H., Armstrong, W.T., Ports, T.A., McLanahan, S.M., Kirkeeide, R.L., Brand, R.J. & Gould, K.L. (1990). Can lifestyle changes reverse coronary heart disease? *Lancet* 336:129–133.

9 Morelli, E., Cupisti, A., Pasquinucci, A., Guidi, A., Pino, C., Buoncristiani, E., Ciardella, F. & Barsotti, G. (1990). Effect of a special vegan diet on serum lipids in nephrotic patients. *Clin. Res.* 38:519A.

10 Barsotti, G., Cupisti, A., Morelli, E., Ciardella, F. & Giovannetti, S. (1991). Vegan supplemented diet in nephrotic syndrome. *Nephr., Dialysis, Transpl.* 5 (suppl. 1):75–77.

11 Dwyer, J. (1993). Vegetarian diets for treating nephrotic syndrome. *Nutr. Rev.* 51:44–46.

12 Kjeldsen-Kragh, J., Haugen, M., Borchgrevink, C.F., Laerum, E., Eek, M., Mowinkel, P., Hovi, K. & Førre, Ø. (1991). Controlled trial of fasting and one-year vegetarian diet in rheumatoid arthritis. *Lancet* 338:899–902.

13 D'Amico, G., Gentile, M.G., Manna, G., Fellin, G., Ciceri, R., Cofano, F., Petrini, C., Lavarda, F., Perolini, S. & Porrini, M. (1992). Effect of vegetarian soy diet on hyperlipidemia in nephrotic syndrome. *Lancet* 339:1131–1134.

14 Crane, M.G. & Sample, C.J. (1988). Regression of diabetic neuropathy with vegan diet. *Am. J. Clin. Nutr.* 48:926.

15 Crane, M.G., Diehl, H., Nixon, M.D. & Sturges, H.F. (1988). Effect of a vegan diet of unrefined foods on hypertension. *Am. J. Clin. Nutr.* 48:922.

THE LAST WORD

You have just dined, and however scrupulously the slaughterhouse is concealed in the graceful distance of miles, there is complicity.

Ralph Waldo Emerson, 1803–1882

Although veganism is now well recognized and increasingly widely practised, with ethical, economic, ecological and health benefits, scientifically it is still rather poorly understood. There is no evidence that vegans are more prone than omnivores to any dietary deficiency, with the occasional exception of vitamin B_{12}. Even so, for more than 30 years it has been a puzzle to doctors that so many long-term vegans remain well with no apparent dietary source of vitamin B_{12}. Do bacteria in the small intestine produce absorbable, active vitamin? The question of how much genuine B_{12} exists in various foods has become more, not less, complicated and badly needs to be clarified. Are elderly vegans less at risk of osteoporosis than omnivores? It now seems likely that vegan diets help protect against a number of diseases, including some cancers and probably heart disease. Are there other illnesses which could be avoided by following a vegan way of life? Do lifelong vegans suffer less from insulin-dependent diabetes, gastritis and duodenal ulcers?

In the light of discoveries that the weight of infants at birth is an indicator of their risk of certain diseases decades in the future, studies of vegan children are needed. What is the average birth weight of vegan infants? The breast milk of vegans contains less of the fatty acid docosahexaenoic acid than normal. Does this have a subtle effect on the development of brain and vision in vegan infants?

There is wide scope for further research, which would be welcomed by the Vegan Society and could be of potential benefit to the community as a whole. It will be important, however, to study vegans and vegetarians separately as distinct groups rather than lumping them together, because vegan diets are conspicuously different from other vegetarian diets, and may well have specific health consequences.

Many of the research reports discussed in this book have focused on possible risks of deficiency or the occasional problems which have arisen. It is natural for scientists to highlight variations from the norm, and for nutritionists to sound warning bells, but we should all remember that the norm itself may not be healthy; and that a case of deficiency reported in the medical press is the rare exception.

Despite the gaps in scientific knowledge, it is clear from the example of many thousands of vegans worldwide that a varied plant-based diet not only supports health and well-being but, additionally, can have positive health benefits.

RESOURCES

All the items appearing on these pages may be obtained by mail order from: The Vegan Society, Donald Watson House, 7 Battle Road, St Leonards-on-Sea, East Sussex TN37 7AA, United Kingdom. (Tel. 01424 427393). Please ring to check prices, postage and availability.

VEGAN NUTRITION: PURE & SIMPLE

MICHAEL KLAPER MD
GENTLE WORLD (US)
£7.95

An American physician demonstrates how sound vegan diets can satisfy all the body's needs and play a major role in the prevention and treatment of many degenerative diseases. Includes nutrient tables, meal plans and recipes. Large format.

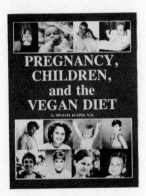

PREGNANCY, CHILDREN AND THE VEGAN DIET

MICHAEL KLAPER MD
GENTLE WORLD (US)
£7.95

A practical guide to ensuring health and balance throughout pregnancy and to raising healthy children on a 100% animal-free diet. Includes nutrient tables, meal plans and recipes. Large format.

A DIET FOR ALL REASONS

PAULETTE EISEN NUTRITIONAL SERVICES
VHS VIDEO (PAL), 60 MINS
£15.99

A video recording of an illustrated lecture given by
Dr Michael Klaper, author of *Vegan Nutrition: Pure
& Simple* and *Pregnancy, Children and the Vegan
Diet*.

TRUTH OR DAIRY — WHO, WHAT, WHERE, WHEN, HOW AND WHY VEGAN

VEGAN SOCIETY (UK)/WORD ‹› PICTURES
VHS VIDEO (PAL), 22 MINS
£9.00

An upbeat, informal introduction to the vegan diet
— the thinking behind it and the health and environmental benefits. Presented by vegan poet
Benjamin Zephaniah and featuring a host of vegan
athletes and celebrities.

THE ANIMAL-FREE SHOPPER
THE VEGAN SOCIETY (UK)
£4.95

Third edition of the popular shopping guide for those wishing to buy goods which are free of animal ingredients and involve no animal testing. Includes product listing sections — Food, Drink, Toiletries & Cosmetics, Remedies & Supplements, Baby & Infant Care, Footwear & Clothing, Home & Office, Animal Care, and Garden & Leisure; useful addresses; and information on animal substances and additives. New edition published every 18 months (approx).

THE CARING COOK: CRUELTY-FREE COOKING FOR BEGINNERS
JANET HUNT
THE VEGAN SOCIETY (UK)
£3.45

An easy-to-follow first vegan cookbook, written expressly for those new to cruelty-free living. Offers a comprehensive selection of everyday and special occasion recipes, plus a mass of hints and tips. Durable wipe-clean cover.

THE VEGAN COOKBOOK

ALAN WAKEMAN & GORDON
BASKERVILLE
FABER & FABER
£7.99

200 richly varied and carefully graded recipes, ranging from the quick and simple right through to the unashamedly gourmet. Complete with nutrition notes and checker.

THE VEGAN

THE VEGAN SOCIETY (UK)
£1.75 or £7pa

Quarterly journal of the Vegan Society. Contains news/features on nutrition, recipes, animal rights, new products, gardening etc.

INDEX